£ 20-00

THE MEDICAL PROFESSION
IN THE INDUSTRIAL REVOLUTION

Ivan Waddington

The
Medical Profession
in the Industrial
Revolution

GILL AND MACMILLAN
HUMANITIES PRESS

Published in Ireland by
Gill and Macmillan Ltd
Goldenbridge
Dublin 8
with associated companies in
Auckland, Dallas, Delhi, Hong Kong,
Johannesburg, Lagos, London, Manzini,
Melbourne, Nairobi, New York, Singapore,
Tokyo, Washington
©Ivan Waddington, 1984
7171 0983 6
Published in 1984 in USA and Canada by Humanities Press Inc.,
Atlantic Highlands, New Jersey 07716
ISBN 0-391-032534
Print origination in Ireland by
Galaxy Reproductions Ltd
Printed and bound in Great Britain by
Biddles Ltd, Guildford and King's Lynn

84 006651

For
Ilya Neustadt
Teacher, colleague and friend

Contents

Preface

IT may be useful, at the outset, to say a few words about the title of this book, in order to make clear to the reader what the book is about and, equally important, what it is not about.

Firstly, it should be made clear that the term 'industrial revolution' is *not* used in order to designate a particular period of time, but rather, it is used to refer to a social process or, perhaps more accurately, to refer to a number of inter-related social processes. Thus the title should not be taken as an indication that this book is concerned simply with the analysis of the medical profession in a clearly bounded period of time such as, for example, the period from 1780 to 1830 or 1840. Rather, the title of this book is meant to suggest that the central focus of the analysis is on the interrelationships between the development of the medical profession and a whole series of other processes – changes in the occupational structure and class structure, the development of a more prosperous society, increasing levels of centralisation of administration, and many other processes – all of which were associated both with the development of English society as an increasingly complex, modern, urban industrial society, and with the emergence of medicine as a modern profession. In a sense, therefore, a more precise title might have been something like 'The development of the medical profession and the development of England as a modern industrial society'. I trust, however, that the reader will understand my reasons for wishing to avoid such a cumbersome title.

Secondly, the reader, I am sure, will not have failed to notice the reference to England rather than to Britain in the above paragraph. Although there are occasional references to Scotland in this book, it should be pointed out that the analysis contained in the following chapters is concerned specifically with the development of the medical profession in England, and that much of this analysis is not directly applicable to the situation in Scotland. The major reason for this is that, as is well known, the development of Scottish society was in some important respects different from the development of English society and these differences were reflected in, amongst other things, a different structure of both medical practice and medical education in Scotland in the eighteenth and early nineteenth centuries. Thus, to cite but two examples, the apothecaries never developed as a distinct occupational group in Scotland, as they did in England, whilst at least some of the Scottish universities also instituted a regular and systematic programme of medical education long before such a programme was available in the English universities. The development of medical practice in Scotland raises, therefore, some rather different issues which merit separate treatment and, if only for the sake of simplicity, it has been decided to confine this work primarily to an analysis of the situation in England.

The book itself is divided into three major parts. The first part focuses on the rapidly changing structure of the medical profession in the early part of the nineteenth century, and with some of the intraprofessional conflicts which were associated with these changes. The second part consists of an examination of the lengthy campaign for medical reform which was associated with some extremely bitter disputes within the profession and which eventually led to the passage of the 1858 Medical Act and to the establishment of the General Medical Council which still remains the central governing body within the profession today. It was, of course, in the nineteenth century, and particularly in the latter half of the century, that the medical profession began to emerge in something like the form in which we know it today, and the third and final part of the book examines some of the major processes which were associated with the emergence of medicine as a modern profession.

In the course of writing this book and, indeed, for many

years before I began to write it, I have had the good fortune to enjoy the support and encouragement of many valued friends and colleagues. I received — and am still receiving — my education as a sociologist at the University of Leicester, and my thanks are due to all my colleagues, many of them my former teachers, at Leicester. In particular, I would like to express my thanks to Sydney Holloway, who first aroused my interest in the subject matter of this book, to Nick Jewson and David Field, whose constructive criticisms have always been most helpful, and to Eric Dunning and Geof Hurd for their unfailing support. In 1979 I was privileged to teach at the Sociologisch Instituut, University of Amsterdam, and it was there that I was able for the first time to teach a full course in what might, for want of a better term, be called the historical sociology of medicine. My thanks to all my former colleagues and students at Amsterdam, especially Abram de Swaan, Joop Jaspers and Henk Heijnen. The research for this book has necessitated my spending a good deal of time in specialist libraries in London, particularly in the Wellcome Institute Library which is always a delightful place to work in both because of the quality of the library and because of the efficiency of Eric Freeman and his expert staff. Thanks are also due to the Librarians of the Royal College of Surgeons, the Royal College of Physicians, and to the library staff of Leicester University. What must have seemed on occasions like the thankless task of typing the manuscript has been undertaken by Carmel James, June Lee, Judy Smith, Ann Brown, Doreen Butler, Charlotte Kitson, Val Pheby and Eve Burns, and I want them to know that their efforts are appreciated. My thanks also go to Hubert Mahony of Gill and Macmillan for his patience and indulgence.

Finally, my very special thanks to Ilya Neustadt, from whom I have learned so much, both of sociology and of many other things besides. I could not have asked for a better teacher or a more generous friend.

PART I

*The Medical Profession and
Medical Practice
in the Early Nineteenth Century*

1.

The Institutional Structure of the Medical Profession in Early Nineteenth Century England

'THE law recognises only three orders of the medical profession: physicians, surgeons and apothecaries.'[1] Thus wrote John Willcock in 1830, and the tripartite division of medical practitioners described by Willcock has generally been seen by modern historians as a major key to understanding the structure of the medical profession in the early nineteenth century. This is not perhaps very surprising, for this tripartite classification did indeed correspond not only to the three legally recognised groups of medical men, but also to the separation between the three major medical corporations in England, and to the type of education held to be appropriate for each of the three grades of practitioners. Although it will be argued later that this classification of practitioners also gives us what is, in certain other respects, a very misleading picture of the everyday structure of medical practice during this period, it is nevertheless the case that, without some understanding of this tripartite institutional structure, it is impossible to develop an adequate analysis of some of the major developments within the medical profession in the first half of the nineteenth century. Accordingly, therefore, our first task is to provide a brief outline of this tripartite structure; in the next chapter we will examine in some detail the extent to which this formal institutional structure actually corresponded to the routine day-to-day practice of medicine in the early nineteenth century.

In eighteenth and early nineteenth century England, there were three quite separate medical corporations — the Royal College of Physicians, the Company of Surgeons (from 1800 the Royal College of Surgeons) and the Worshipful Society of Apothecaries — each of which had its own charter and its own

bye-laws, and each of which granted licences to practise in
the particular branch of medicine or surgery for which it was responsible. The oldest and unquestionably the most prestigious
of these corporations was the Royal College of Physicians,
whose charter dated from 1518. With certain modifications
and extensions, the powers of the college were confirmed
by an act of 1522, which stated that it was 'expedient and
necessary to provide that no person . . . be suffered to exercise and practise physic but only those that be profound, sad
and discreet, groundedly learned, and deeply studied in
physic'.[2] It was therefore enacted that no person except a
graduate of Oxford or Cambridge should be allowed to practise
physic unless examined and approved by the College. Those
who had been examined and approved were divided into three
groups: fellows, licentiates and extra-licentiates. Whilst the
former two groups were licensed to practise medicine in
London and in an area seven miles around the capital, the
extra-licentiates held a licence which entitled them to practise
only outside of London. Neither the licentiates nor the extra-
licentiates, however, were allowed to take part in the formulation of College policy, nor were they allowed to vote in
College elections. All political offices and all decision-making
functions within the College were monopolised by the fellows,
almost all of whom were graduates of Oxford or Cambridge;
in the period from 1771 to 1833 only nineteen of the 149
practitioners admitted to the fellowship had not graduated at
one or the other of these universities.[3]

Throughout the eighteenth and early nineteenth centuries,
the College remained a small and exclusive body; in 1800, the
total number of fellows, licentiates and extra-licentiates was
just 179,[4] which probably represented about three per cent
of the qualified medical practitioners in England and Wales.[5]
However, as Peterson has pointed out, 'Size . . . was no measure of their strength. Their ancient collegiate foundation,
their tradition of classical learning, the absence of trade or
craft functions in the physician's work — all these contributed
to the position of the Royal College of Physicians as the most
prestigious of the medical corporations.'[6]

The image of the physician fostered by the College was
that of a gentleman, learned in the classics and educated

alongside the gentry at the English universities. Towards the end of the eighteenth century, Thomas Withers, physician to the York County Infirmary, wrote that 'The character of a physician ought to be that of a gentleman, which cannot be maintained with dignity by a man of literature.'[7] Classical, literary and philosophical studies were held to be at the very heart of a physician's education, for as the *Gentleman's Magazine* pointed out in 1834, the distinguishing characteristics of the English academic physician were 'large attainments as a scholar, . . . sound religious principles as a Christian, . . . practical worth and virtue as a good member of society, and . . . polished manners as a well-bred gentleman'.[8] Charles Newman has bluntly but accurately commented that 'the ideal aimed at was a cultured and highly educated gentleman, with, quite secondarily, an adequate knowledge of medicine'.[9]

It was in this context that the close relationship between the College and the universities of Oxford and Cambridge was of importance, for the real significance of these universities lay in the fact that they provided an education in classical languages and literature, and in morals and manners, which made the young physician fit to take his place in polite society; and, closely associated with this, in the fact that it was in these universities that the future leaders of the church and state were educated. Thus in 1834 William McMichael, physician to the king and a former registrar of the College, held that the high status enjoyed by physicians was primarily due to 'the circumstance of many physicians in this country being educated at the English Universities. There they have the same education as those who fill the highest stations in life; they are brought up with those persons, and afterwards become physicians. I think the distinguished post which they hold elevates the whole profession; that all physicians partake of the dignity which their education and their good conduct give.'[10] A similar point was made by Henry Holland, a fellow of the College, who pointed to the relationship which existed at Oxford and Cambridge 'between the College of Physicians, and the higher classes of the community', a relationship which he held largely accounted for the high status of the physician in the wider society.[11] The central importance of the close relationship between the College and the universities at Oxford and Cambridge thus lay in the way in which this relationship confirmed the dignity and the status of the physician as a gentleman; the fact that there was no regular teaching of medicine in these universities until the middle of the nineteenth century was, as far as the College was concerned, a consideration of quite secondary importance.[12]

In marked contrast to the physician, the surgeon had traditionally been regarded as a craftsman rather than a gentleman and, as befitted one who practised a craft, the surgeon received his training by apprenticeship. This training was practical rather than theoretical for, as Newman has noted, the surgeon 'was trained to be a skilful practitioner, not a learned one, and for that reason a university education was not held to be appropriate'.[13]

The craft origins of surgery were also clearly evident in the fact that, until the middle of the eighteenth century, the surgeons were united with the barbers in the Company of Barber-Surgeons. It was not until 1745 that the surgeons broke away to form a separate Company of Surgeons, but the history of this new company was a relatively short one, for after what Cope has called an 'uninspired existence'[14] of some fifty years, the Company was dissolved following a period of mismanagement of its affairs and shortly afterwards, in 1800, the surgeons were granted a new charter which established the Royal College of Surgeons of London. All practitioners who passed the examinations of the College were admitted as members, but the ordinary members were not allowed to participate in any way in the management of College affairs. The entire government of the College was in the hands of the twenty-one members of the Court of Assistants (renamed the Council in 1822), a body which was able to renew itself by co-option. This structure of government had, in fact, been laid down by the act of 1745 which established the Company of Surgeons, and was taken over without modification by the newly formed Royal College of Surgeons in 1800.[15]

The third of the medical corporations — and the lowest in status — was the Worshipful Society of Apothecaries. The Society had been formed in 1617 by the grant of a charter from James I, which separated the apothecaries from their former association with the grocers. The charter of the Society required seven years' apprenticeship to a member as an essential qualification for admission to the freedom of the company, and stated that at the end of seven years, 'every such apprentice ... shall be examined, proved and tried concerning the preparing, dispensing, handling, com-mixing and compounding of medicines'.[26] At this time the work of the apothecary — at least as far as medicine was concerned — was limited to the preparing and dispensing of medicines, but by the early part of the eighteenth century the apothecaries had successfully expanded the scope of their work to include medical as well as pharmaceutical practice, and had won legal recognition of their right not only to dispense, but also to prescribe medicines. Despite this change in the apothecaries' practice, however, the Society retained throughout the eighteenth and nineteenth centuries a con-stitution more typical of a city trading company than of a professional organisation, and in the 1820s, the *Lancet* disparagingly referred to the Society of Apothecaries — not entirely without justification — as 'these incorporated shop-keepers'.[17] As was the case with the other two medical corporations, those who held a licence to practise from the Society had no legal right to participate in the management of the affairs of the Society, for the government of the Society was vested entirely in the hands of the twenty-one members of the Court of Assistants, including a master and two wardens, a body which renewed itself by co-option.

From this brief discussion, it is evident that this tripartite structure of physicians, surgeons and apothecaries was clearly institutionalised in the separation between the three major medical corporations. Moreover, it is important to remember that these professional divisions were also clearly recognised in English law, for throughout the first half of the nine-teenth century each of the three grades of medical prac-titioners had certain privileges and certain limited spheres of practice which were legally defined. In this context, it is important to note that the general concept of the qualified or registered medical practitioner had no place in English law prior to the Medical Act of 1858; instead there were separate laws relating to physicians, to surgeons and to apothecaries.

The clearest contemporary statement of the laws relating to medical practice is probably that contained in J. W. Willcock's *The Laws Relating to the Medical Profession*, published in 1830. As we have already noted, Willcock pointed out that physicians, surgeons and apothecaries constituted the only legally recognised orders of the medical profession, and he went on to note that of these three groups physicians were 'the first class of medical practitioners in rank and legal pre-eminence'.[18] Under an Act of 1540, physicians had been given the right to practise physic in all its branches, amongst which surgery was included. However, the disdain which physicians, as a body of learned men, felt for manual work had led to a considerable contraction in their sphere of practice; and throughout the eighteenth and early nineteenth centuries the practice of the physician was 'universally understood, as well by their college as the public, to be properly confined to the prescribing of medicines to be compounded by the apothecaries; and in so far superintending the proceedings of the surgeon as to all his operations by prescribing what is necessary to the general health of the patient, and for the purpose of counteracting any internal disease'.[19] The legitimate sphere of practice of the physician thus revolved essentially around the twin tasks of diagnosing internal disease, and of prescribing an appropriate remedy; what was regarded as the manual work involved in surgical procedures and in the dispensing of medicines was to be left to the lower orders of the profession.

The laws defining the sphere of practice of the surgeon were a little more complicated. Willcock held that the 'peculiar practice' of the surgeon 'consists in the use of surgical instruments in all cases, and in the cure of all outward diseases, whether by external applications or by internal medicines'.[20] However, he went on to note that several diseases which were sometimes regarded as internal complaints had been recognised by the legislature, or by the charters granted to the surgeons, as falling within the scope of practice of the surgeon. Among these diseases Willcock listed 'the pestilence, syphilis, and such other contagious infirmities; letting of blood in all cases, and drawing of teeth, customable diseases, as women's breasts being sore, a pin and web in the eye, uncomes of hands, burnings, scaldings, sore mouths, the stone, strangury, sanceline and morphew, and such other diseases, apostemations, and agues; all wounds, ulcers, fractures, dislocations and tumours'.[21]

From this it is clear that the proper sphere of practice of the surgeon was by no means confined to the use of the knife in surgical operations. The legally defined sphere of practice of the surgeon was, nevertheless, a limited one. Thus, in general, the treatment of what were regarded as 'internal' as opposed to 'outward' disorders was held to fall within the legal province of the physician rather than that of the surgeon. This legal principle was upheld in 1828 when a member of the Royal College of Surgeons was non-suited in his claim for charges for medicines supplied to and attendance upon a patient who had contracted typhus fever, since it was ruled that typhus was a medical and not a surgical disease, and therefore not within the province of the surgeon. The trial judges emphasised the fact that there was a legally defined division of labour within the profession, and that each grade of practitioner was responsible for only a limited area of practice. Thus Chief Justice Best stated that 'I cannot admit that the legislature intended to give surgeons the privilege of practising in physic as well as surgery. . . . For some disorders relief is sought from medicine, for others from topical applications. A different education is necessary to prepare men to undertake the cure of either of these descriptions of complaints. . . . The first description belongs to the physician and the apothecary; the second to the surgeon.'[22]

As we have already indicated, the law relating to apothecaries had undergone an important change in the early years of the eighteenth century. However it is clear that although apothecaries had won the legal right to prescribe medicines in the celebrated Rose case of 1703,[23] the dispensing of medicines continued in law to represent an essential part of the apothecary's duties; indeed the dispensing of medicines became an even more central part of the apothecary's duties following the passage of the Apothecaries' Act of 1815, for clause 5 of the act made it an offence for an apothecary to refuse to make up, or deliberately to make up incorrectly, the prescription of a physician. The dispensing aspects of the apothecary's role were clearly brought out by Willcock, who wrote that their 'proper practice consists in preparing with exactness, and dispensing, such medicines as may be directed for the sick by any physician lawfully licensed to practise physic', although he also went on to point out that apothecaries were 'also at liberty to administer medicines of their own authority, and without the advice of a physician'.[24] The fact that apothecaries were under a clear legal obligation to dispense faithfully the prescriptions of physicians was of considerable importance within the context of the hierarchy of the medical orders, for this legal obligation served not only to emphasise the apothecary's close association with what were regarded as the trading or shopkeeping aspects of medicine, but more specifically, it also served to define in a quite unambiguous way the subordinate position of the apothecary in relation to the physician.

Thus throughout the first half of the nineteenth century, qualified medical practitioners in England were divided into three formally separated and legally distinct status groups, and the separation between these groups has sometimes been described in terms of the separation between the 'profession of physic', the 'craft of surgery' and the 'apothecary's trade'.[25] However, whilst it is in some respects useful to classify practitioners in this way — such a classification does, for example, serve to draw attention to a number of very important aspects of the institutional structure of the profession — it may nevertheless be argued that this tripartite classification of practitioners gives us what is, in many other respects, a very misleading picture of the everyday structure of medical practice in the rapidly changing social world of early nineteenth century England. This problem will be explored in more detail in the next chapter.

2.

The Changing Structure
of Medical Practice
in the Early Nineteenth Century

AS WE have seen, the formal structure of the medical profession in the first half of the nineteenth century constituted an hierarchical structure, with a clear and legally defined division of tasks and of status between physicians, surgeons and apothecaries. Given this situation, it is not perhaps surprising that medical historians have generally described the medical profession during this period in terms of this tripartite institutional structure. However, this tripartite classification of practitioners can be very misleading if it is assumed that these professional divisions corresponded to what practitioners actually did in the day-to-day practice of their profession, rather than simply to their formal or legal status. Indeed, it may be argued that the key to understanding many important aspects of the development of the medical profession in the early nineteenth century lies precisely in a recognition of the fact that this tripartite classification no longer bore any clear relationship to the everyday structure of medical practice. In order to understand this point more fully, it is necessary to direct our attention away from the sort of questions with which we have hitherto been concerned — questions relating largely to certain highly formal aspects of the structure of the medical profession — and to direct our attention towards an examination of what practitioners *actually did* in the routine day-to-day practice of their profession. If we do this then, as Holloway has noted,[1] we begin to get a rather different picture of the structure of the medical profession in the early nineteenth century.

According to the tripartite classification of practitioners, physicians were traditionally held to be scholars and gentlemen who possessed a university medical degree and confined their practice to internal medicine. According to Dr Newman, they 'used their heads not their hands', and they 'advised rather than did'.[2] Their fees were charged for advice only; they wrote prescriptions for the appropriate medicines, which were then dispensed by an apothecary.

There is, however, little evidence to suggest that many physicians were able to confine their practice to advising and prescribing in this way. Thus in 1834, John Sims, physician to the St Marylebone Infirmary, pointed out to the Select Committee on Medical Education that 'there are very few physicians who practise as such', and he added that 'the principal part of the practice is in the hands of the general practitioners'.[3] Thirteen years later, Professor Christison held that there were a great many physicians practising in England as general practitioners; the title of MD, he said, particularly in the provinces, did not exclude the practice of surgery by a member of the College of Physicians.[4]

There is, in fact, good reason to believe that, especially in the provinces, there were many physicians whose practice included surgery and midwifery, as well as pharmacy. In the north of England, in particular, there were numerous physicians holding Scottish degrees who were engaged in general practice.[5] In 1847 James Bird pointed out that 'Ever since the year of 1815, there has been a bone of contention between the Scotch and Irish graduates and the Society of Apothecaries',[6] because the Scottish and Irish graduates in general practice objected to the fact that under the terms of the 1815 Apothecaries' Act they were required to pass the examination of the Society of Apothecaries or risk prosecution for illegally practising as apothecaries. Readers of Trollope will recall that Dr Thorne, although a graduated physician, took over the practice of a 'humble-minded general practitioner' in Greshamsbury, and that the Doctor 'As was then the wont with many country practitioners . . . added the business of a dispensing apothecary to that of physician'.[7]

General practice amongst physicians was not, however, confined to country districts, or to the provinces, for in London, Scottish educated physicians were in general practice in sizeable numbers from the 1760s onwards.[8] There is little doubt that this practice became much more common in the first half of the nineteenth century. Thus by the early 1830s, even the most eminent physicians in London 'did not scruple to take fees in surgical cases'.[9] A few years later Professor Christison pointed out that 'it is very well known that at one time no physician would practise even the simplest operations in surgery, but I believe the whole profession has recovered from that delusion, and that even the purest physician in London will practise the minor operations of surgery when necessary'.[10] In 1834, Neil Arnott, a licentiate of the Royal College of Physicians, held that so many physicians were engaged in general practice that 'before long the body called physicians will wear out'.[11]

If we now consider the situation of those practitioners who were legally designated as surgeons it is clear that, as in the case of medicine, it was becoming increasingly difficult to preserve surgery as a pure branch of practice. When the Company of Surgeons was founded in 1745, the Company insisted on 'being now of no trade but of the profession of Surgery only',[12] and the emphasis on pure surgery was taken over by the Royal College of Surgeons on its foundation in 1800. Yet in 1834, Benjamin Brodie pointed out that of surgeons practising in England, 'only a limited number can confine their practice to surgery, even in London, and very few, if any, can do so in the country', and he went on to observe that over the previous fifty years the practice of the physician and the surgeon had become increasingly intermingled.[15] Sir Anthony Carlisle pointed out that the most eminent surgeons in London practised not only surgery, but medicine too, and he admitted that he saw as many patients 'in the character of a physician, as of a surgeon'. He held that the 'distinction between what ought to belong to a physician, and what belong to a surgeon, are quite undefinable'.[14]

Numerous witnesses who gave evidence to the 1834 Select Committee on Medical Education agreed that it was no longer possible to draw any clear distinction between medical and surgical practice. Thus John Scott, surgeon to the London Hospital, stated that the ancient boundaries of practice were entirely broken down;[15] while James Wardrop, a former surgeon to the king, held that it was highly desirable that physicians and surgeons no longer confined their practice to a single branch of the profession.[16] Certainly in the first half of the nineteenth century it was becoming increasingly rare, even amongst the leading surgeons in London, to find any who confined their practice to surgical cases. Thus George James Guthrie, who was on two occasions president of the Royal College of Surgeons, stated that when called in to consultation he did not usually ascertain beforehand whether it was a medical or surgical case. Asked if, when called into a case, he found it to be internal without any external appearances, he would decline to accept it, Guthrie stated, 'If I thought I was capable of curing the disease I should attempt it; if I thought I was not, I should desire them to send for some one else.'[17] Honoratus Leigh Thomas, who, like Guthrie, was president of the College of Surgeons on two occasions, was often called into consultation by J F Clarke for medical cases. Clarke wrote that Thomas was a poor surgeon, but that he was a 'shrewd practitioner in medical cases to which his practice was mainly limited'.[18] Perhaps the most celebrated of all nineteenth century surgeons was Sir Astley Cooper, yet not even he limited his practice to surgical cases. His biographer tells us that whilst Cooper was lecturer on surgery at St Thomas's Hospital, he encouraged poor patients to come to his home for gratuitous advice; in this way he was able to maintain a supply of interesting cases for the hospital. As an inducement to the poor to come to him, Cooper purchased a stock of common medicines, which he bestowed liberally 'on them whose means would not allow them to take his prescriptions to the chemist's shop in the usual way'.[19] There is, then, little reason to doubt the accuracy of James Bird's comment that 'it is difficult to define what pure surgery is. The fellows of the College of Surgeons, if they thought proper to practise as pure surgeons, might call themselves pure surgeons if they pleased; but I think very few of them practise it.'[20]

If the most eminent surgeons in London rarely confined their practice to pure surgery, this was even less common among rank and file surgeons. Thus in 1834, when there were some six thousand members of the College of Surgeons resident in England and Wales,[21] it was estimated that only two hundred of these confined their practice to surgery; the rest were general practitioners.[22] In the same year, James Wardrop pointed out that 'by far the greater number' of members of the College were in general practice;[23] whilst fourteen years later John Ridout, a fellow of the College of Surgeons, similarly estimated that 'by very far the largest proportion' of members of the College were general practitioners.[24] In 1848 James Bird, a member of the council of the National Institute of Medicine, Surgery and Midwifery, provided the Select Committee of that year with a breakdown of its membership: two thirds of the members of the Institute — an association of general practitioners — were members of the College of Surgeons.[25] That many surgeons dispensed medicines is clearly indicated by the fact that in his evidence before the same committee, Guthrie stated that when he was president of the College of Surgeons, he had offered to compile a register of surgeons who were general practitioners, but had been prevented from doing so because it was argued that he would 'show them up to the apothecaries to be prosecuted if they had not their license'.[26]

There is little doubt that, as Guthrie indicated, there were very many surgeons who acted as general practitioners without holding a licence from the Apothecaries' Society. Equally, there were very many apothecaries who similarly acted as general practitioners without holding a diploma from the College of Surgeons. In 1841, a correspondent of the *Lancet* told of a practitioner in Cornwall who had passed the examination of the Apothecaries' Society in 1828, but had never obtained the diploma of the College of Surgeons, 'nor ever attended a surgical lecture, or the surgical practice of an hospital; nor indeed, ever saw any surgical operation excepting those performed behind the counter of a drug shop — yet he calls himself a "surgeon", has "SURGEON" on his street door, and holds the appointment of a medical and surgical attendant on the poor in this district'.[27] The correspondent went on to enquire whether such practice was illegal, and the *Lancet* correctly replied that there were no laws to prevent apothecaries or anyone else practising surgery. There is little doubt that the vast majority of apothecaries availed themselves of this opportunity; such examples of general practice on the single qualification could be multiplied at great length.[28]

Although many general practitioners held only a single qualification, in most cases from either the College of Surgeons or the Society of Apothecaries, there is nevertheless clear evidence that, especially after the passing of the Apothecaries' Act in 1815, a growing number of practitioners did obtain a double qualification in both medicine and surgery. Thus by 1834, some 3,500 members of the College of Surgeons also held the licence of the Apothecaries' Society,[29] whilst in 1848 James Bird estimated that there were between 14,000 and 15,000 general practitioners in England and Wales, and that 'more than half of the 14,000 possessed the double qualification'.[30]

There can be little doubt that in the first half of the nineteenth century the overwhelming majority of the members of the College of Surgeons were practising as general practitioners. Similarly, the vast majority of apothecaries — and, indeed, very many physicians — were also acting as general practitioners. This conclusion, as well as the considerable confusion surrounding medical practice at this time, is aptly conveyed by the comment of James Bird that 'Scotch graduates and Irish graduates, and members of the College of Surgeons who are not also licentiates of the Society of Apothecaries, and licentiates of the Apothecaries' Society who are not members of the College of Surgeons, are all practising indiscriminately, as general practitioners in this country, in medicine, surgery and midwifery'.[31] The same point was made in the draft charter for a proposed Royal College of General Practitioners, drawn up in the 1840s, in which it was stated that 'there are now practising in England and Wales as Surgeon-Apothecaries, or General Practitioners, divers persons who have obtained the diploma of the College of Surgeons . . . but who have not obtained a certificate of qualification to practise as an apothecary from the . . . Society of Apothecaries . . . and divers other persons who have obtained such certificate of qualification as aforesaid . . . but who have not obtained the diploma of the College of Surgeons . . . and divers other persons who are not authorized by law to practise either as

Surgeons or Apothecaries in England and Wales, but who are legally authorized to practise either as Physicians, Surgeons or Apothecaries in some other part of the United Kingdom.'[32]

From what has been said, it is clear that by the early part of the nineteenth century, the traditional divisions between physicians, surgeons and apothecaries bore little relationship to what practitioners actually did in the day-to-day practice of their profession. This is not to say that these traditional labels ceased to be used as a way of describing medical practitioners, but that in this case, as in many others, changes in terminology lagged behind changes in the structure of the profession, and the traditional terminology was, therefore, misleading. If the terms 'physician', 'surgeon' and 'apothecary' remained common in the medical literature of this period, it was becoming increasingly difficult to identify more than a handful of 'pure' practitioners in any branch of practice.

During this period, as Holloway has pointed out,[33] the significance of these traditional professional divisions was increasingly being eroded as a new professional structure, based on the modern differentiation between general practitioners and consultants, began to emerge. Moreover, as practitioners increasingly came to identify with those who practised as they did, rather than with those who simply held a similar legal status, so the division between general practitioners and consultants increasingly became the major *de facto* line of division within the profession in the first half of the nineteenth century.

Perhaps the clearest contemporary analysis of these changes within the structure of the profession was contained in an essay published in *The London and Provincial Medical Directory for 1847*. The author began by describing what he called 'The Former Constitution of the Profession' in terms of the three traditional 'orders' of medical practitioners:

The Physician, the Surgeon, and the Apothecary mark its sub-divisions; and law and custom would seem distinctly to have defined the position and duties of each class. It is needless to observe, however, that practically this classification has become almost obsolete. The nomenclature alone remains in force, and its inapplicability to the existing state of things constitutes an admirable *argumentum ad absurdam* for the reorganization of the profession. In times past, these several practitioners, in their various grades, were no doubt equal to the sanatory requirements of the people; . . . in the present age, the public, advanced in knowledge and power, perceive that they are considerably benefitted by a departure from the economy of the profession as ordered of old. A change, accordingly, is now in progress, which, like all transitions, is marked by a confusion of position and character among individual members . . .

If we look around, indeed, it will be found that the Physician, the Surgeon, and the Apothecary, as distinct and separate practitioners, exist in but little more than their several designations. The many animadversions that appeared upon the publication of the case of a Surgeon, whose life was said to have been lost through the professional fastidiousness of a late president of the College of Physicians refusing to bleed, proclaimed the sense of the thinking public on such obsolete nonsense as the non-interference of physicians in other than medical cases; whilst Surgeons and Apothecaries are now daily and hourly called in to cases requiring prompt and unassisted action, in which, without a full knowledge of the practice of physic, they would be worse than useless . . .

The author then went on to examine 'The Present Constitution of the Profession', and he pointed out that with the breakdown of the tripartite structure, medical practitioners were being divided into what he called 'two fundamental orders'. Thus 'whilst Physicians, and Surgeons, and Apothecaries, appear to be so vitally interested in the continuance of useless titles, they really are, by the force of a public convenience they cannot withstand, being gradually classed into Consulting and General Practitioners . . .'[34]

Thus in the first half of the nineteenth century, the traditional professional divisions were increasingly being eroded and replaced by the modern division of the profession into consultants and general practitioners. The term 'general practitioner', which itself reflected the development of a new social role, appears to have come into use in the

early 1820s[35] — a considerable time, it should be noted, after
the role of the general practitioner first emerged[36] — and
from about 1830 onwards the title 'general practitioner' is
regularly encountered in the medical journals. As we have
already seen, numerous witnesses who gave evidence to both
the 1834 and 1847-8 Select Committees relating to the
medical profession pointed out that the vast majority of
medical practitioners were in fact engaged in general practice,
and by the mid-1830s, general practitioners probably
provided some ninety per cent of the qualified medical care
available in England. We have also seen that the general
practitioner may have been the holder of a university medical
degree, a diploma from the College of Surgeons, a licence
from the Society of Apothecaries, or any combination of
these. Whatever qualification he held, it was the general
practitioner who had emerged as the 'ordinary attendant in
private life'[37] or, as another contemporary observer put it,
it was the general practitioners who were employed 'on
ordinary occasions, and to whom the great majority of
society look in the first instance for assistance'.[38] In 1841, it
was held that 'Nine-tenths of the public must ever fall under
the charge of the general practitioner'.[39]

The number of consultants was, of course, very much
smaller than the number of general practitioners. The author
of the article in the *London and Provincial Medical Directory*
previously cited held that the consultant was a practitioner
of 'superior rank' who acted as 'the extra-ordinary adviser in
difficult cases',[40] whilst another author, writing in the
Quarterly Review in 1840, defined consultants as those
practitioners who were 'called into consultation in rare,
difficult, and dangerous cases, in all classes of society — at
the same time that their opinion is sought in cases of less
urgency among those who have the advantage of ease and
affluence'.[44] As we shall see, almost all consultants held
appointments at the major voluntary hospitals, and there
thus existed a clear institutional basis for the separation
between consultants and the rank-and-file general
practitioners; indeed the division between those practitioners who held hospital appointments, and those who
did not, was to emerge as an increasingly important line of

cleavage within the profession in the first half of the nine-teenth century as the traditional professional divisions increasingly broke down.

Although the very complex processes which gave rise to these changes in the structure of medical practice are by no means wholly understood, it is clear that these changes within the profession cannot be adequately understood without reference to other changes which were taking place in the wider structure of society, for the medical profession — like virtually all other institutions — was profoundly affected by those broader social changes which were associated with the process of industrialisation; in this respect, it may be said that, in the first half of the nineteenth century, the medical profession began to lose many of those features which were characteristic of occupations in pre-industrial England, and increasingly began to develop those features which we have come to recognise as the distinguishing characteristics of modern professions.

Perhaps the first point to note in this context is that, in order to understand the erosion of the traditional professional structure, it is necessary to appreciate that the three traditional 'orders' of the profession constituted not merely an occupational division of labour but that, as Peterson has noted, they also constituted a 'social division of medical practitioners into three status groups or estates'.[42] Estate systems of stratification are characterised not merely by a system of differential statuses — this is, of course, common to all stratification systems — but by the fact that the status and the rights and duties of each group are defined in law, and by claims to traditional and historical legitimacy of privileges on the part of the higher estates. As many writers have pointed out, estate systems of stratification of this kind are characteristic of pre-industrial rather than of industrial societies[43] and in this sense, the three 'orders' of the profession constituted what Peterson accurately describes as a 'pre-industrial form of social structure and stratification'.[44]

The pre-industrial character of this stratification system may perhaps best be illustrated by the fact that, as we noted in the previous chapter, the highest rank within the profession — the fellowship of the Royal College of Physicians — was virtually limited to graduates of Oxford and Cambridge, despite the fact that there was no regular teaching of medicine in these universities until the middle years of the nineteenth century. The poor quality of medical education in those universities was not, however, held to be a fact of any great importance as far as the Royal College was concerned, for the status of the physician had traditionally been based overwhelmingly on his claim to be a gentleman rather than a technical expert.

In this respect, the position of the eighteenth or early nineteenth century physician was quite different from the position of those involved in professional occupations in modern industrial societies, for modern professions base their claim to high status and to professional autonomy *primarily* on their claim to specialised occupational skills and knowledge. In the eighteenth century however — indeed, right through to the middle of the nineteenth century — the dominance of physicians within the medical profession, as well as their high status within the wider society, was rarely, if ever, justified in these terms. The usual line of defence was that taken by Burrows when, as late as 1847, he spoke of 'the great advantages which result to society from there being an order of men within the profession who have had an education with the members of other learned professions; from a certain class of the medical profession having been educated with the gentry of the country and having thereby acquired a tone of feeling which is very beneficial to the profession as a whole.'[45] It was this imprecisely defined but nevertheless crucially important 'tone of feeling', rather than the possession of occupational skills and knowledge, which was the hallmark of the gentleman physician. As Elliott has noted, the 'performance of the professional function appears to have been a less important aspect of the professional role than the ability to live a suitably leisured and cultured lifestyle'.[46] A similar point was made long ago by Carr-Saunders and Wilson who, in their classic study of the professions, drew attention to the fact that the leading eighteenth century physicians were 'remarkable for their literary tastes and their association with the world of wealth rather than for professional skill or scientific eminence', and they went on to note that the lifestyle expected from the physician involved participation 'in the ample life of the great houses where elegance and wit were pursued'.[47]

The physicians' dominant position within the profession was thus based on a very traditional claim to status which stressed their close association with the dominant groups — particularly landed groups — in pre-industrial England; it is precisely because of this fact that Elliott describes the position of the eighteenth and early nineteenth century physicians in terms of 'status professionalism' rather than in terms of the more modern form of 'occupational professionalism', for the specific nature of their occupational tasks or skills played little part in their claim to status or prestige.[48]

It is also important to appreciate that the traditional tripartite division between physicians, surgeons and apothecaries cannot be understood as a simple *technical* division of labour, for as Carr-Saunders and Wilson have again pointed out, this 'form of organisation was not dictated by the nature of medical technique';[49] indeed, in the early nineteenth century there was a growing realisation, which was frequently and forcefully expressed in the columns of the *Lancet*, that this tripartite division of labour actually militated against the full employment of the medical knowledge of the time. Rather, this professional division of labour must be understood as an aspect of what we have argued was a pre-industrial hierarchy of rank and status. In this context, it is important to bear in mind that, as we have already seen, the dominant groups within the profession — like the dominant groups within the wider society — did not derive their high status primarily from the work which they did, for work had not yet come to be the major determinant of social status which it subsequently became with the development of a more complex, industrial society.[50] Rather, it was the status claimed by particular groups of practitioners — for example, the physicians' claim to be gentlemen — which determined the sort of work they allowed themselves to do, and the sort of work which was to be left to the 'lower orders' of the profession.

This point may be illustrated by reference to the long-standing division between medicine and surgery, a division which has to be understood primarily in terms of the fact that for an extraordinarily long period, medicine remained under the influence of the aristocratic tradition which shunned work with one's hands as degrading. As Weber has noted, this prejudice against manual work is common amongst privileged status groups,[51] and the insistence of the College of Physicians on a clear separation between medicine and surgery must be understood in the context of the College's policy of maintaining the dignity and the status of the physician by avoiding anything which bore the stigma of manual work. Similar considerations of status underlay other aspects of the division of labour within the profession. Thus not only the Royal College of Physicians, but also the Royal College of Surgeons, refused to have anything to do with the practice of midwifery, which they regarded as a particularly undignified and low status form of manual work, whilst both Royal Colleges similarly set themselves clearly apart from the practice of the apothecaries, for the work of the apothecary carried a double stigma associated both with manual work and with 'trade'.

This tripartite division of labour did not, then, derive primarily from technical considerations relating to the nature of medical work, but rather it has to be understood as an aspect of the system of rank and status which had been institutionalised within the medical profession since the early sixteenth century. By the early years of the nineteenth century both this traditional hierarchy, dominated by the figure of the gentleman physician at its apex, and the division of labour which was an aspect of this hierarchy were increasingly being undermined; with the development of a more complex, industrial society, new sources of status and new patterns of stratification began to emerge in the wider society, and the dominance of traditional aristocratic attitudes towards work was increasingly being challenged by a rising and pragmatically oriented middle class. These changes within the wider society were closely associated with changes within the structure of the medical profession and, in particular, with what Elliott describes as the transition from 'status professionalism' to 'occupational professionalism'. Thus whereas, in the eighteenth century, 'the status professions were able to maintain a foothold among the ranks of the gentlemen by glossing over their work responsibilities and emphasising the leisured and honourable life-style which their members could adopt,'[52] in the nineteenth century the possession of occupational skills and knowledge came to be seen as an alternative and increasingly important source of social status.

This new form of occupational professionalism developed only slowly amongst the old established elite groups within the profession, who continued to emphasise their more traditional claims to status. Few rank and file practitioners, however, could lay claim to either a classical education or a cultured and leisured life style and it was amongst this section of the profession that greatest stress came to be placed on the possession of occupational skills as an alternative claim to status. This new emphasis on the performance of occupational tasks — on medical work *per se* — rather than on the more traditional 'non-work' aspects of the doctor's role, was of major importance, for it gave rise to a radical and particularly telling critique of the traditional tripartite division of labour within the profession. Increasingly, for example, a growing number of practitioners began to point out that this division of labour did not derive from the nature of medical work itself, but that it had its origins in what the *Westminster Review* called the 'spirit of caste and false notions of dignity'.[53] Perhaps more importantly, however, since this related directly to the efficient performance of medical work, there was also a growing realisation that this tripartite occupational division of labour actually inhibited the development of both medical science and medical practice. Thus the *Lancet* argued, in its own typically forceful style, that by maintaining what was increasingly seen as the outmoded status distinction between medicine and surgery, the Royal Colleges had 'actually cut the body of the science in two, and sent each half hopping off on one leg, telling us all the while, with infinite gravity, that medicine will get on much better that way, than if it remained a whole body and walked upon two legs'.[54] The *Westminster Review* similarly drew attention to the 'practical inseparableness' of the different branches of practice[55] and stated that the 'division of the profession into physicians, surgeons, and apothecaries, we cannot but regard . . . as inimical to the progress of medical science and the public welfare'.[56]

Within this context, those senior members of the profession who tried to maintain a clear separation between the different branches of practice were portrayed as men who were more concerned with the maintenance of traditional status divisions — the 'false notions of dignity' — than they were with meeting the health care needs of the population. The Royal College of Physicians, for example, which refused to allow its fellows to practise what it regarded as the manual art of midwifery, was lambasted in the following terms: 'notwithstanding the fact that women will persist in bringing children into the world, and that many of the gravest maladies which flesh is heir to consist of organic or functional diseases of the uterine organs, the College of Physicians was of opinion that the practice of midwifery and the collateral branches of that department of the profession is a degradation from which its fellows must be sacredly guarded'.[57]

The increased emphasis which came to be placed on the acquisition of occupational skills and on the performance of occupational tasks involved, at first implicitly but later quite explicitly, a radical re-evaluation of the status and significance of different kinds of medical work. Thus whereas certain branches of practice had traditionally been seen as ungentlemanly and therefore a bar to high status within the profession, by the early nineteenth century the growing number of practitioners who united all branches of practice saw the fact that they did so as something which both extended their sphere of competence and increased their usefulness as practitioners and, as such, this was increasingly seen not as a bar to status, but as a positive claim to status. As one contemporary put it, general practitioners united all the three branches of surgery, medicine and pharmacy, a circumstance which, he claimed, 'renders them, it must be allowed, the most efficient part of the profession', and he went on to argue that the 'General Practitioner seems to me to possess that sort of superiority, when compared to the exclusive Physician, which common sense always allows to the *practical* in preference to the theoretical part of any science whatever'.[58] In these terms, both the traditional status hierarchy within the profession and the division of medical labour associated with that hierarchy were increasingly challenged.

It is clear that these changes in the structure of the medical profession were closely associated with the relative decline of traditional sources of status and the emergence of a new form of professionalism in which the performance of occupational tasks and the possession of occupationally relevant skills and knowledge came to play an increasing part in the determination of status. There is, however, a further way in which these changes within the structure of the profession were related to changes in the stratification system of the wider society; for the development of general practice appears to have been, at least in part, a response to the growth of what was largely a middle class demand for family medical care. Early in the nineteenth century, Robert Masters Kerrison, writing on behalf of the apothecary as a general practitioner, drew attention to what he called 'the augmentation of the middle orders of the community', and he pointed to the importance of this development for medical men in the following terms:

> The state of the Society at the establishment of the Royal College of Physicians was widely different from what it is at present. The ancient nobility, and a few rich citizens, constituted one class; while the servants and dependents of the former, added to the workmen and labourers of the latter, formed another class. The noble and wealthy could afford to fee their Physicians; and it was not usual, in those days to legislate for the wants and convenience of others.
>
> The progress of commercial prosperity, since that time, has so greatly multiplied, that it may be almost said to have created a third, which is now the most numerous class of people — the middle order of society. . . . One effect of this augmentation of the middle orders of the community was a proportionate increase of sickness,

amongst people, who were unable to procure medical aid, by feeing Physicians as often as their situation required medical care, and the Members of the Royal College of Physicians, having made no diminution in their accustomed fee, to meet the actual wants of persons in this class of society, they were compelled to resort to others for advice.[59]

As Holloway has pointed out, this growth of the middle classes resulted in a significant change in the pattern of demand for health care, with a steadily increasing number of middle class families who required health care but were unable to engage consulting physicians and surgeons on the terms traditionally charged.[60] The middle class demand for health care was essentially for medical men who were able and willing to provide family medical care including midwifery and to charge for their services at modest rates; as Rachel Franklin has noted, the 'expansion of the industrial community . . . produced a greater demand less for the highly qualified physician than for the family doctor', a position which came to be filled by the general practitioner.[61]

One key to the rapid growth of general practice in the nineteenth century undoubtedly lay in the fact that general practitioners were catering for what was a rapidly expanding demand for relatively low cost family medical care; certainly it was the opinion of contemporary observers that the pattern of client choices was changing, and that general practitioners were effectively responding to this changing demand. In 1834, for example, George Birkbeck drew attention to 'a great tendency on the part of the public, of late years, to employ the general practitioners', a tendency which he attributed largely to the relatively modest cost of general practitioner care. Thus Birkbeck pointed to 'the change in the condition of society . . . which seeks for its assistance . . . in one individual, rather than in the more expensive form of three';[62] whilst James Wardrop made a similar point when he argued that the development of general practice was highly desirable 'for the public interests', because it meant that any medical attention which was required could be obtained from 'one competent medical man', rather than the patient having to be attended 'by a surgeon, a physician, and his apothecary; so that three advisers are paid, instead of one'.[63]

John Sims similarly pointed out that the fees of the general practitioner were relatively modest by comparison with those of the physician; and he also noted that where a medical man was unable to perform minor surgical operations, so that another practitioner had to be brought in, this generally entailed additional expense for the family. It was for this reason, argued Sims, that the general practitioner had a competitive advantage over those practitioners who confined their work to a single branch of practice. Not surprisingly, Sims agreed that 'Families in moderate circumstances will always prefer calling in a general practitioner', for such families preferred to call in a practitioner 'who embraces all, instead of him who can only act in one capacity'. It was this fact, suggested Sims, which had 'tended to limit the number' of physicians, and which largely explained the rapid increase in the number of general practitioners.[64]

Although relatively modest by comparison with the fees of the consultant physician and surgeon, general practitioners' fees were still sufficiently high to prevent most working class people from using the services of a general practitioner on a regular basis.[65] For the growing number of middle class families, however, general practitioners offered a form of qualified medical care which was both relatively inexpensive and relatively convenient, and there is little doubt that it was this growing middle class market which provided the basis for the rapid development of general practice. Thus whereas consultant physicians and surgeons, as we shall see, continued to orientate their private practices towards a relatively wealthy, but also relatively small, clientele, it was the general practitioners who were actively involved in exploiting the new and expanding market possibilities opened up by the growth in demand for relatively low cost family care.

The other major change within the structure of the profession during this period was, as we have already noted, the emergence of a class of consultants as a distinct group of practitioners and this process, as both McKeown and Peterson have pointed out, was closely associated with the development of hospitals in the eighteenth and nineteenth centuries. The growth of the hospital system from the middle years of the eighteenth century has been described by a number of writers,[66] and there is no need to repeat here the details of what is, to most historians, already a familiar story. It is, however, important to note that from the middle of the eighteenth century, hospitals came to play an increasingly important part in the provision of health care in the larger urban areas and that, from the early nineteenth century, the hospitals assumed a new significance within the profession as they increasingly emerged as the centres of medical education. As Peterson has noted, these developments — and in particular the emergence of the hospital as the major centre of medical education — opened up a new type of medical career structure in which hospital appointments came to be of increasing importance for those who aspired to reach the top of their profession.[67] The importance of hospital appointments in this context will be examined in more detail in the next chapter; for the moment we need simply note that consultants enjoyed considerable advantages over their colleagues in general practice deriving directly or indirectly from their hospital appointments. One important consequence of these changes in medical career structures was that a new line of differentiation began to appear within the medical profession for, as McKeown has noted, increasingly 'the important distinction was then between doctors who were appointed at the large voluntary hospitals, whether as physicians or surgeons, and those who were not'.[68] The increasing use of the term 'consultant' to refer to those who held hospital appointments thus 'reflected the development of a new distinction within the medical hierarchy' as 'consultants of the teaching hospitals — whether physicians or surgeons — became recognised as a separate group from the rank and file of medical men'.[69] In terms of the development of this new professional structure, the importance of the development of hospitals lay in the fact that they provided a clear insitutional basis for the emergence of a type of career structure which set consultants apart as a distinct group of practitioners within the profession.

Thus far we have examined some aspects of the changing structure of the medical profession in the first half of the nineteenth century, focussing particularly on the development of the modern structure of the profession, based on the differentiation between consultants and general practitioners. Our next task is to analyse in some detail the social — including the economic and political — situation of general practitioners and of consultants, and the relationship between these two groups of practitioners. This analysis, it is hoped, will throw some light on other aspects of the development of the medical profession, and in particular on the interrelated problems of intra-professional conflict and the development of the campaign for medical reform, both of which figure prominently in the history of the profession in the first half of the nineteenth century.

3.

Consultants and General Practitioners: the Structure of Intra-professional Conflict

WHICHEVER aspect of their situation we examine, it is clear that consultants enjoyed considerable advantages over their colleagues in general practice. As we have already noted, consultants normally held appointments on the staffs of the charitable hospitals of London and the major provincial cities, and since the advantages which they enjoyed derived, in large part, from their positions within these hospitals, it is necessary to examine the network of relationships which centred on these institutions.

In the older endowed hospitals in London, the physicians and surgeons had always received some form of payment for their services, although in the newer hospitals the doctors were generally unpaid. However, the older hospitals had failed to increase their salary rates to take account of the current value of the services they were receiving, and although small payments continued to be made in some hospitals, physicians and surgeons gradually acquired honorary status.

The direct rewards for medical attendance were thus, at best, very modest. However, as hospitals developed as major centres of medical education in the late eighteenth and early nineteenth centuries, the rewards from teaching came to be quite considerable. In 1844, Dr Carus noted that at St Bartholomew's, 'the physicians are not paid, as is the case so frequently in England, but several young men and surgeons attend their lectures, study their treatment of the patients, and pay for this privilege a considerable fee, so that in this way a few thousand pounds are easily made in the course of the year.'[1] During the early 1820s, the theatre of St Thomas's Hospital 'was crowded in every part by upwards of four hundred students of the most respectable description',[2] all of whom paid three guineas or more, the greater part of which went to the lecturer. In 1816, Benjamin Brodie's income from fees and lectures at St George's Hospital amounted to £1530.[3]

In addition to their lecture fees, surgeons in the larger voluntary hospitals in London often received large fees from apprentices. Sir James Paget recalled that in the 1830s the usual fee for the four or five years' pupilage was 500 guineas and for a resident pupil 1000 guineas.[4] In January 1826, Frederick Tyrrell, a surgeon at St Thomas's Hospital, received £1050 from or on behalf of William Tice James, and four years later Tyrrell received the same sum again when he accepted James Dixon as an apprentice. In December 1825, John Alexander Harper's premium to Aston Key, a surgeon at Guy's, was £1000. In 1822, Edward Stanley, surgeon at St Bartholomew's Hospital, received £700 as a premium on behalf of William Pennington, whilst in the same year William Money received £800 when he accepted Thomas Egerton as an apprentice. When Samuel Solly was apprenticed to Benjamin Travers the fee was 500 guineas, but in 1834 Solly himself required 600 guineas as a premium. The standard fee for an apprenticeship to a leading hospital surgeon in London appears to have been in the order of 500 to 600 guineas; sums in this range were repeatedly paid to Green, Abernethy, Earle and Stanley.[5] Fees in provincial hospitals were lower, but still considerable. In 1815 when Thomas Ash was apprenticed to Samuel Dickenson, surgeon to the Birmingham General Hospital, the premium was £210,[6] whilst the fee for an apprenticeship to one of the surgeons at the Bristol Infirmary in 1813 was 150 guineas.[7]

The direct income from teaching could thus be very considerable. Nevertheless, the greater part of consultants' incomes was derived not from teaching, but from private practice. Here again, an appointment at one of the larger teaching hospitals was a major asset, for many consultants were able to build up lucrative private practices based largely on their success in the hospital. Thus, in the first place, teaching enabled consultants to establish contacts with large numbers of students who in later years sent their own private patients for remunerative consultations. The value of hospital connections in this context was, for example, clearly recognised by Sir James Paget, who had one of the most profitable practices in London, and who, in his memoirs, drew attention to the 'regularly increasing number of cases to which I was called into consultation . . . especially by old Hospital-pupils who were in large practice'.[8] Secondly, the lay governors of the charitable hospitals were both wealthy and influential; holding an appointment at one of these hospitals meant that there was a good chance of becoming the private medical adviser to the lay members of the board. Thirdly, a hospital appointment was an excellent advertisement in attracting wealthier clients for, as Abel-Smith has noted, it 'became known by private patients that the hospital staffs possessed the most advanced knowledge. Charitable work became the key to fame and fortune.'[9]

Rather than confining their work to consulting practice, most consultants also acted as general practitioners to the nobility and wealthy merchants. In this capacity consultants, whether physicians or surgeons, practised both medicine and surgery, but rarely pharmacy or midwifery. General practice was frequently financially rewarding; as a writer in the *Quarterly Review* pointed out in 1840, consultants were the regular attendants 'among those who have the advantage of ease and affluence'.[10] Consulting practice was also lucrative. In 1813, Sir Astley Cooper performed the operation for stone upon Mr Hyatt, a wealthy merchant, for which he received 1000 guineas. The two physicians who attended with him each received £300.[11]

The combined income from teaching, consulting and general practice was often very high. Sir Astley Cooper's annual income was in excess of £15,000, and in 1815 he earned £21,000.[12] Like other consultants, Cooper treated a wealthy rather than a numerous clientele; his biographer recalled that it was not unusual for Cooper to receive only five fees in the course of a morning's work, 'and yet the sum he received might be large, for they almost all paid in cheques'.[13] Although Cooper's income in 1815 was quite exceptional, other consultants earned very large incomes. Between 1824 and 1846, for example, Sir Benjamin Brodie's earnings varied between eight and ten thousand pounds a year, an income which was more than sufficient to support Brodie in the lavish lifestyle which he favoured; in his later years he invested in a country estate with 450 acres of land.[14] Sir James Paget's earnings at the peak of his career were in excess of £10,000 a year,[15] whilst on occasions John Abernethy also earned £10,000, and Robert Liston nearly £7000 a year.[16] Among the consulting physicians, Matthew Baillie, who was for twelve years physician to St George's Hospital, earned £10,000 a year for many successive years early in the century,[17] whilst in the 1820s and 1830s Sir Henry Halford, for many years the president of the Royal College of Physicians 'made his £10,000 a year regularly'.[18] William Chambers, physician to St George's Hospital, also had a very lucrative practice in London; between 1836 and 1851, his income is known to have ranged between seven and nine thousand guineas a year.[19]

Many consultants thus enjoyed a market situation which was extremely lucrative; as Peterson has noted, with incomes such as these 'medical men in the upper ranks lived comfortably, when not truly lavishly'.[20] In addition to their favourable market situation, however, consultants also held a virtual monopoly of the major political offices within the profession. As we shall see below, general practitioners were effectively excluded from the governing councils of the Royal College of Physicians and the Royal College of Surgeons, and the offices which the consultants held within the Royal Colleges enabled them to perpetuate the advantages which they enjoyed, sometimes at the expense of other members of the profession. Thus in December 1822, the Court of Examiners of the College of Surgeons resolved that only those lectures on anatomy which had been delivered in the winter session would be recognised by the College.[21] The effect of this new regulation was to withdraw official recognition from the courses given during the summer session by excellent teachers in the private schools not attached to the hospitals. At a protest meeting of members of the College of Surgeons, held at the Freemasons Tavern in February 1826, two speakers expressed concern at the effect this regulation was having on Joshua Brookes' famous school in

Great Marlborough Street.[22] Their fears were not unjustified, for as Cope has noted, by this regulation 'the well-known and popular courses of Joshua Brookes were banned and that celebrated teacher was ruined'.[23]

Two years later, the Court of Examiners of the College of Surgeons passed a second regulation which, like that of 1822, had the effect of restricting competition from other teachers, and thus of preserving the very lucrative teaching monopoly of the consultants in the larger hospitals. The regulation of 1824 stated that in future the only schools of surgery to be recognised by the College would be those of London, Dublin, Edinburgh, Glasgow and Aberdeen, and that certificates of attendance at lectures and of attendance upon the surgical practice of an hospital would only be accepted if the teachers and hospitals were in one of the above recognised schools.[24] The *Lancet* was not slow to draw attention to the way in which these regulations worked to the advantage of surgeons holding appointments at the larger voluntary hospitals. 'The hospital surgeon,' it wrote, 'is the pupil's master, and pockets the money for his "walking" through the wards, and the same surgeon is the pupil's lecturer, and pockets the fees for the regular courses. Thus far he filches the fees as surgeon to the hospital, as lecturer on anatomy, as lecturer on surgery, and as demonstrator. . . . Mark further! This surgeon, lecturer and sinecure demonstrator, takes his station amongst the Council of the College of Surgeons, where he manufactures the "regulations" which are to enforce attendance upon his lectures and hospital practice.'[25] The *Lancet* wrote of these regulations that 'we never beheld any resolutions more hostile to science, or more decidedly avaricious'[26] and, addressing its words specifically to the Examiners of the College, it pointed out that 'gentlemen, you have been, or are still, hospital surgeons yourselves, and therefore you have passed this measure for your own advantage, and that alone'.[27]

Thus consultants not only found that the economic rewards of their profession were frequently very high, but they also held a virtual monopoly of the key political offices within the profession. These were, however, not the only advantages enjoyed by consultants for, in addition to the high prestige associated with hospital appointments, consultants also had access within the hospitals to research facilities which were normally unavailable to general practitioners and which, with the development of modern medicine in the nineteenth century, came to be of steadily increasing importance.

If we now examine the situation of general practitioners, it is clear that most rank and file members of the profession had few of the benefits enjoyed by consultants. Unfortunately it is not easy to generalise about the economic situation of general practitioners, since the available evidence on incomes in general practice is very fragmentary. Nevertheless, two points are clear. The first is that the incomes of general practitioners varied considerably, depending on the type of practice. Thus a small practice in a fashionable seaside town or an inland spa town would be worth considerably more than a larger practice in a predominantly working class industrial area. Similarly, a practice situated in a sparsely populated rural area often involved a great deal of work for a comparatively small income. That seaside and spa towns, together with some of the older cathedral cities, offered a better livelihood to medical men is indicated by the fact that throughout the nineteenth century these towns attracted more practitioners in relation to population than did the newer industrial areas or thinly populated rural districts.[28] Medical men tended to go where the returns from practice were greatest.

The second point is that those practitioners with less fashionable practices frequently earned only small incomes. Readers of Thackeray will recall that John Pendennis was a surgeon-apothecary in the west of England and that he had a 'very humble little shop'. He had 'for some time a hard struggle with poverty; and it was all he could do to keep the shop and its gilt ornaments in decent repair, and his bed-ridden mother in comfort'. It was not until, by accident, he received the patronage of Lady Ribstone, who introduced him into 'the good company of Bath', that he began to prosper.[29] Many practitioners kept open shop in order to supplement their meagre incomes. Thus Pendennis 'not only attended gentlemen in their sick-rooms, and ladies at the most interesting periods of their lives, but would condescend to sell a brown-paper plaster to a farmer's wife across the counter — or to vend toothbrushes, hair powder and London perfumery'.[30] In 1840, a correspondent of the *Lancet* suggested that practitioners should 'abandon the sale of patent pills, pastilles, perfumery, soap, etc',[31] a view which derived from the fact that retailing was frequently held to be degrading to members of a profession. Since, however, retailing provided an important source of income for many poorer practitioners, it was a practice which could not be given up without serious financial loss.

Those medical men whose practices were situated in poorer neighbourhoods found it especially difficult to obtain more than a very modest income from medical practice. In 1900 H N Hardy recalled that 'in the early part of the century, medical men were content to accept rates of payment which, though known to be inadequate, were often as much as could possibly be spared from too scanty wages.'[32] This situation persisted, of course, well beyond the early part of the century; in 1875 it was pointed out that a 'medical man, living in a poor part of town, has to find his account amongst a population ill able to bear *any* charge for medicines and attendance in sickness'.[33] In such neighbourhoods, the problem for medical men, in terms of securing an adequate income, was not simply one of attracting patients from amongst a population which could ill-afford medical care for — difficult though this was — there was still another problem to be overcome: as one practitioner put it, 'to get a patient is one thing; but to obtain the fee quite another.'[34] Non-payment of fees was a major problem for medical practitioners, particularly for those working in poorer districts; in the 1830s, doctors in the poorer parts of Manchester and London could expect to receive only about one-third of their fees.[35]

Whilst those at the top of the profession could accumulate considerable fortunes, the economic situation of the great majority of general practitioners was very much more modest. Some very rough idea of the variation in earning power between those at the top and those at the bottom of the profession may, perhaps, be gauged by the fact that of the three hundred members of the profession who died in 1858, three left sums in excess of £50,000 and an additional seventeen left sums ranging between £10,000 and £50,000; whilst, at the other end of the scale, more than one practitioner in nine died leaving less than £100.[36] Not surprisingly, perhaps, many poorer practitioners found their incomes insufficient to enable them to make adequate provision, upon their deaths, for their families. The Society for the Relief of Widows and Orphans of Medical Men, which was formed to provide for the families of deceased practitioners who found themselves in straightened circumstances, reported in the early 1840s that 'one in four of the members of the society has left a widow or orphans claimants on its funds'.[37] Although, as we shall see later, there is good reason to believe that the economic situation of most medical men began to improve quite substantially towards the end of the century, Hardy indicates that financial hardship persisted amongst certain sections of the profession throughout the nineteenth century. Thus at the end of the century there were still three charitable societies in London alone which aimed at 'relieving cases of pecuniary distress among medical men, their widows and orphans', a fact which Hardy claimed indicated that 'in the battle of life but too many practitioners and their families come to grief'.[38]

If the market situation of many general practitioners was not financially very rewarding, this was not however their major complaint. Although comment on their modest financial situation was not infrequent, the major grievance of the general practitioners centred on the relationship between themselves and the medical corporations — in particular, the Royal Colleges. In order to understand the causes of these complaints, we have to relate the policies of the Royal Colleges to the changing structure of the profession outlined in the previous chapter.

The traditional structure of the medical profession had involved the differentiation between three groups of practitioners, namely physicians, surgeons and apothecaries. Corresponding to this tripartite structure, there were three major medical corporations, each with its own charter or Act of Parliament and its own bye-laws, and each granting

licences to practise in the particular branch of the profession for which it was responsible. Moreover, not only were
physicians, surgeons and apothecaries organised in quite
separate medical corporations, but the policies of the
medical corporations had long been designed to maintain
the barriers separating the different types of practitioner and
the different branches of practice. Thus throughout the
eighteenth century, no apothecary could obtain the licence
of the Surgeons' Company without ceasing to be a member
of the Society of Apothecaries.[39] Similarly, no apothecary
or surgeon could take out a licence from the College of
Physicians without relinquishing his membership of the
Apothecaries' Society or the Company of Surgeons. Thus in
1756, William Hunter had to pay forty guineas to withdraw
from the Company of Surgeons because he wished to take
out a licence to practise as a physician;[40] whilst in 1795 the
College of Physicians approved the refusal of its president,
Sir George Baker, to examine an apothecary who applied
for a licence to practise physic, and instructed the officers
of the College to prepare a statute authorising the similar
rejection of any person employed as an apothecary or
surgeon.[41] In the early years of the nineteenth century,
Charles Locock was required to disfranchise himself from the
College of Surgeons on becoming a licenciate of the College
of Physicians[42], whilst George Mann Burrows had to withdraw from both the College of Surgeons and the Society of
Apothecaries before taking out a licence to practise as
a physician.[43] In 1834, the College of Physicians had still
not modified this regulation, the purpose of which was
made quite explicit by the president of the College, Sir
Henry Halford. In his evidence to the 1834 Select Committee on Medical Education, Sir Henry said the regulation
was maintained because, if applicants for a licence from the
College were not required to disfranchise themselves from the
other corporations, 'it would diminish somewhat the high
respectability of men of education, who stand on the same
ground as members of the English Universities.'[44] The object
of the regulation was thus quite clear; as Sir Henry put it,
'we wish to keep the practice [of physic] as respectable as
possible, and as distinct.'[45]

Throughout the first half of the nineteenth century, both Royal Colleges persisted in this traditional policy of trying to maintain the separation of medicine and surgery and, in particular, of rigidly separating both these branches of practice from what the Colleges regarded as purely manual or trading activities. To further this policy of maintaining the purity of medicine and surgery both Royal Colleges excluded from their governing councils those who practised as apothecaries or who practised midwifery. In the College of Physicians, this had traditionally been effected by restricting the fellowship of the College to graduates of Oxford and Cambridge: that is, to gentlemen by whom the manual work involved in pharmacy and midwifery was seen as degrading. In 1771, however, the bye-laws of the College were revised, and the ban on the practice of midwifery and pharmacy was made explicit. The new bye-laws stated that no person practising midwifery was to be admitted to the fellowship, that physicians practising as apothecaries were not to be admitted, and that fellows who entered on practice as apothecaries were to be expelled.[46]

In the Company of Surgeons, it had been stipulated by a bye-law of 1748, that 'no person practising as an apothecary or following any other trade or occupation besides the profession . . . of a surgeon, shall be capable of being chosen into the Court of Assistants (Council)'.[47] This emphasis on the practice of pure surgery was retained by the Royal College of Surgeons on its foundation in 1800. Thus, in his evidence before the 1847 Select Committee on Medical Registration, John Ridout pointed out that the College of Surgeons had persistently shown itself unwilling to undertake an efficient examination with regard to general practitioners as well as surgeons: 'it was proposed in 1812, 1813 and 1814, that they should then undertake the superintendence of the medical as well as the surgical education of the surgeon or surgeon-apothecary; but the opinion of the council at that time was, that they wished to confine their attention to surgery exclusively, and they have continued to express a similar opinion down to the present time.'[48]

Moreover, like the Royal College of Physicians, the Royal College of Surgeons continued to exclude from its Council those who practised as apothecaries and those who practised midwifery. Thus in 1834, the president of the College, George James Guthrie, pointed out that 'The Council is selected from those surgeons who practise surgery only. A gentleman is not admissible who practises as an apothecary; and this has been so for a long time, certainly ever since the Act of Parliament separating the surgeons from the barbers. It is contrary to the bye-laws to elect into the Council a gentleman who practises as a midwife; nor is any one eligible unless he practises surgery only. It is open to all persons of that description.'[49] However, as Guthrie himself acknowledged, there were only about two hundred persons 'of that description' in the whole of the membership of the College; the remaining six thousand or so members of the College resident in England and Wales were excluded from membership of the Council on the ground that they were 'persons who practise as surgeon-apothecaries'[50] or, as they were increasingly coming to be called, general practitioners. Thirteen years later, Benjamin Travers, who had by that time taken over as president of the College, indicated that the College had not changed its attitude towards those who practised as surgeon-apothecaries. There was, said Travers, 'not perfect eligibility to the Council; a man, for example, must have nothing to do with the practice of pharmacy to take a seat in the council'.[51]

Nor did the Royal Colleges change their attitude towards the practice of midwifery which, like the dispensing of medicines, necessarily formed an important part of the practice of very many general practitioners. Thus in the 1820s, after a suggestion that the Royal College of Physicians should examine in midwifery, a committee reported to the College, giving a plethora of historical information tending to show that 'the object of the College has been to confine the fellows to the pure practice of physic'.[52] In 1834, the attitude of the president, Sir Henry Halford, was equally uncompromising. Thus he said of midwifery that

I think it is considered rather as a manual operation and that we should be very sorry to throw anything like a discredit upon the men who have been educated at the

Universities, who have taken time to acquire their improvement of their minds in literary and scientific acquirements, by mixing it up with this manual labour. I think it would rather disparage the highest grade of the profession, to let them engage in that particular branch, which is a manual operation very much.[53]

The admission to the fellowship of those who practised midwifery was, said Halford, something which 'has never been done; it has always been objected to; there is a mixture of manual operation, with the practice of physic, which we think does not quite accord'.[54] Halford's sentiments were echoed by James Wilson, a fellow of the College of Physicians, who was equally adamant that midwifery could not be accepted as a legitimate part of the practice of the physician. 'With no disparagement at all to that branch of the profession,' said Wilson, '. . . I would not admit a physician actually practising midwifery to the fellowship.' If such people were admitted, he said, 'the effect would not be at all conducive to the dignity of the College', with the result that the College 'would rather lose consequence in public estimation'.[55]

The College of Surgeons similarly maintained a hostile attitude towards the practice of midwifery. Thus Guthrie concluded his observations on those who practised midwifery with the comment that 'with all possible respect for this class of gentleman, I must say, that I should be exceedingly sorry to see the first *accoucheur* in this town president'.[56] There was, of course, no possibility of such a situation arising since, under the bye-laws of the College, those who practised midwifery were not even eligible for membership of the Council.

In the College of Surgeons, the official reason for the exclusion from the Council of those who acted as apothecaries and those who practised midwifery was that such practitioners had no time to devote to specialising in the study of surgery.[57] Underlying this policy, however, both in the Company of Surgeons and later in the Royal College of Surgeons, was a concern to improve and later to maintain the status of surgery by insisting on a clear separation between surgical

work and what were considered to be lower status branches
of practice; as one observer bluntly put it, both the College
of Surgeons and the College of Physicians had adopted an
'exclusive system . . . in order to gratify the spirit of caste, by
keeping their respective departments "respectable and
distinct".'[58] Moreover, the leading surgeons became increasingly concerned to maintain the practice of surgery as a
'respectable and distinct' branch of practice as the status of
surgery itself began to improve markedly from the latter part
of the eighteenth century, a process which was both recognised and further enhanced by the grant of a royal charter to
form the Royal College of Surgeons in 1800. This rise in the
status of surgery may, in part, have been associated with
certain improvements in surgical technique, but it was
probably more closely related to the fact that many leading
surgeons acquired a new status by virtue of their association
with the increasingly important hospital sector. Thus, as the
major division within the profession increasingly came to be
that between practitioners who held hospital appointments
and those who did not, so all hospital practitioners, whether
physicians or surgeons, increasingly came to enjoy a common
status and common privileges by virtue of their hospital
appointments. Whatever the precise reasons for this process,
however, it is clear that from the latter part of the eighteenth
century, the status of the surgeon began to improve quite
markedly, and that by the early part of the nineteenth
century, the status of the leading hospital surgeons was not
very different from that of the leading physicians. Thus in
the early 1740s the status of surgery had been very much
lower than that of medicine, the surgeons at that time still
being associated with the barbers in the Company of Barber-
Surgeons. Less than a century later, however, the status of
surgery had risen so considerably that Paget was able to recall
that when he entered St Bartholomew's in 1834, 'the main
interest and power of the Hospital were surgical . . . the
teaching and importance of medicine were made to seem very
inferior to those of anatomy and surgery; and the contrast
was sustained in many things outside the hospital.'[59]
In the College of Physicians, the problem had been not so
much to raise the status of physicians, as to maintain the high

status which they had for long enjoyed. As we have seen, the physician had traditionally enjoyed the status of a learned and cultured gentleman; and the ban on the practice of midwifery and pharmacy for those who aspired to the rank of fellow was aimed at preserving this status by obliging fellows to abstain from those tasks which were considered to involve manual work. As the president of the College indicated, the College had no intention of allowing the status of the physician's practice to be threatened by, as he put it, 'mixing it up with this manual labour'.

Thus throughout the first half of the nineteenth century, both Royal Colleges persisted in their traditional policies of trying to maintain the purity of their respective branches of practice. This point is of major importance, for what the Royal Colleges were, in effect, trying to do was to maintain the traditional structure of the profession based on the distinctions between physicians, surgeons and apothecaries, at the very time that changes within the wider structure of society were bringing about changes within the structure of the profession itself. As we have seen the tripartite structure of the profession was increasingly breaking down and being replaced by a new structure, in which the two major groups were general practitioners and consultants. Of these two groups, the general practitioners were by far the larger, and by the 1830s general practitioners probably provided some ninety per cent of the qualified medical care in England. But the role of the general practitioner necessarily involved not only medicine and surgery but, in a period in which the birth rate had not yet begun to decline, a good deal of midwifery, and generally pharmacy too. Thus the development of the general practitioner was a process which necessarily undermined the tripartite structure since the development of general practice involved a breaking down of the barriers separating what the Royal Colleges saw as distinct areas of practice, some of which they considered to be of much higher status than others. The Royal Colleges, dominated by the consultants, bitterly resisted this development, however, for they feared that the incorporation of what they regarded as manual and trading elements into the doctor's role threatened the high status which physicians had long enjoyed, and which surgeons had recently attained. Thus the attempt on the part of the Royal Colleges to maintain the traditional tripartite structure was simultaneously an attempt to stem the rise of the general practitioner: a policy which not surprisingly gave rise not only to a good deal of resentment amongst a large section of the profession, but also to a very long and very bitter campaign for medical reform on the part of the general practitioners.

The effect of the policies of the Royal Colleges was, of course, to deny general practitioners any participation in the decision-making processes within the two most prestigious medical corporations; general practitioners were thus effectively excluded from the major institutions of professional power. As one practitioner put it, the great majority of the profession was 'excluded from all power and influence in the corporations; the Colleges and Companies being closed in their face; and they having not the slightest chance of attaining places in the Council of the College of Surgeons'.[60] Thus while the consulting surgeon — who held a qualification in surgery only — was eligible for election to the Council of the College of Surgeons, the general practitioner — who frequently held, in addition to his surgical diploma, a qualification in medicine from the Society of Apothecaries — was excluded. Commenting on this situation, the *Lancet* held that the Royal Colleges

> have discovered the most extraordinary ground for creating professional distinction that ever entered into the mind of man. With them the chief qualification for eminence in the healing art is ignorance of one or the other half of it. A physician need not know much of physic; an entire ignorance of surgery will be sufficient to give him a respectable standing; a surgeon need not possess any real knowledge of surgery, but if he be sufficiently ignorant of physic — if he do not know the gout from the measles — that will render him 'pure', and make him eligible to receive the highest appointments; but a 'general practitioner' — a man who is so preposterous as to understand both physic and surgery — is fit only to become a subordinate.[61]

In addition to the Royal Colleges there was, of course, the Society of Apothecaries. Few general practitioners, however, looked to the Society to represent their interests; for not only had the Society retained a constitution more typical of a city trading company than of a professional organisation, but it also had a long association with the apothecary as the inferior member of the medical profession and as recently as 1815 had been a party to the Apothecaries' Act, which defined more clearly than ever the inferior status of the apothecary.[62] As James Bird explained in 1848, many rank-and-file members of the profession preferred the title 'general practitioner' to the more traditional one of 'surgeon-apothecary', since the term 'apothecary' 'was intended to denote an inferior grade'.[63] The long association with 'Rhu-barb Hall', as the *Lancet* called it, was more a hindrance than a help to the general practitioners in their fight for professional advancement.

In the first half of the nineteenth century, there was thus no medical corporation to represent the interests of general practitioners. As James Bird pointed out, 'neither the College of Surgeons nor the College of Physicians has any sympathy with the general practitioners; the interests of that body have at all times been placed in abeyance, and for want of a recognised position they have hitherto been disregarded in all communications with the Government.' He added that 'whenever any medical question, or any question affecting the public health, is brought before the Legislature, there is no body, no head, to represent the interests of nine-tenths of the profession.'[64] The same point was made by a correspondent of the *Lancet*, who pointed out that general practitioners 'have no colleges at which to confer; nor have they any other means by which, as a body, to make known their wants, to protect their rights, or to redress their grievances'. He went on to note that general practitioners had not even been represented amongst those bodies which gave evidence to the 1834 Parliamentary Select Committee on Medical Education: 'the colleges of physicians and surgeons have been there represented; the members of both have given their evidence; whilst the most numerous body of the profession (without a head) have silently looked on.'[65] The situation of general practitioners within the profession, as well as the increasing anger and frustration felt by many general practitioners, was perhaps most clearly pointed out by the *Lancet* when it asked, 'where have the surgeons in general practice their headquarters? What body presides over their interests? Alas! they have no local habitation, and no presiding body. Positively, the only set of men who have a right to be considered as forming the medical profession in this country have neither representatives nor protection.'[66]

In addition to excluding the general practitioners from their governing Councils, both Royal Colleges persistently refused to make provision for the type of education required for general practice. Thus the general practitioner required an education and examination in medicine, surgery, midwifery and pharmacy, but no medical corporation would agree to provide or examine an integrated syllabus embracing all branches of practice. As we have seen, the College of Surgeons consistently refused to make provision for the medical as well as the surgical education of the general practitioner, preferring to confine its interest to pure surgery, while the College of Physicians similarly refused to alter its traditional policy of examining in physic only. Thus the general practitioner was compelled to go to the Society of Apothecaries for his examination in medicine and pharmacy, and to the College of Surgeons for a separate examination in surgery. Moreover, for the first quarter of the nineteenth century, neither the Royal Colleges nor the Society of Apothecaries would have anything to do with the practice of midwifery. From 1827, the Apothecaries' Society required candidates for its diploma to provide evidence that they had received training in midwifery, but the Royal Colleges continued to maintain their traditional examinations in physic and surgery only. Educationally, politically and socially, the general practitioner was rejected.

Given this situation, it is hardly surprising that consultants and general practitioners should have viewed the tripartite institutional structure of the profession in radically divergent ways. Although the nineteenth century consulting practitioner no longer corresponded in all respects to the traditional 'pure' physician or surgeon, there were, nevertheless, a number of similarities between the consultants and the pure physicians and surgeons which meant that consultants, unlike general practitioners, could be assimilated into the traditional professional structure without any great difficulty. Consultants normally held a qualification in either medicine or surgery, but rarely both; they could thus continue to designate themselves as physicians or surgeons, to enjoy the legally defined privileges of those groups and, indeed, to maintain the fiction that medicine and surgery were quite separate branches of practice which were best left to separate groups of practitioners. Moreover, like the pure physician and surgeon, consultants rarely practised pharmacy or midwifery; hence they were not excluded from the Councils of the Royal Colleges and indeed the consultants effectively monopolised membership of these Councils throughout the first half of the nineteenth century. Moreover, if consultants could easily be assimilated into the traditional institutional structure of the profession, there was also no reason why they should desire to change it. Not only did the hierarchical tripartite structure legally confirm their superior status over the general practitioners, but within this structure the consultants continued to enjoy a disproportionate share of the financial, social and political rewards within the profession. In short, a radical change in the institutional structure of the profession offered little prospect to the consultants of improving their already favourable situation, whilst there was every possibility that such a change might involve a radical change in the balance of power within the profession, and that general practitioners might benefit at the expense of consultants.

The situation of general practitioners, on the other hand, was quite different. As we have seen, general practitioners were a new group, who had developed in the late eighteenth and early nineteenth centuries alongside a much older professional structure. The general practitioner was not a physician, a surgeon, nor an apothecary. Nor was his situation within the medical profession adequately conveyed by the term surgeon-apothecary, in spite of the fact that by the middle of the nineteenth century most general practitioners held a double qualification from the College of

Surgeons and from the Society of Apothecaries. For the title of surgeon-apothecary implies that the role of the general practitioner could be defined in terms of the traditional categories within the profession; this, however, is quite wrong, for in combining the roles of surgeon and apothecary a quite new type of practitioner had emerged. As one observer put it, general practitioners were 'a new class . . . different from any hitherto known, formed by a combination of the three already in existence, but having no exact resemblance to any of them'.[67]

For this reason, it is suggested that the term general practitioner was more accurate than surgeon-apothecary; the new terminology reflected the emergence of a new role, one that could not be fitted into the traditional professional structure. While there was a place within the traditional structure for the surgeon and for the apothecary, there was no place for the practitioner who combined both roles. The position of general practitioners, as Peterson has noted, was anomalous; they were a 'hybrid class . . . relegated to inferior positions within the corporations and neglected by their leadership'.[68] A correspondent of the *Lancet*, writing on behalf of the general practitioners, summed the situation up in the following manner. General practitioners, he said,

> form the principal body of medical practitioners, and yet, strange to say, we are the outcasts of every medical corporation. The College of Physicians spurn us; no merit, however exalted, could ever qualify one of our body for admission to the sanctum sanctorum of Pall Mall East. The College of Surgeons, although it accepts our guineas, and permits us to be called 'Members', excludes us from ever having a voice in its proceedings. Even the Worshipful Company of Apothecaries turn up their noses at us. But is this as it ought to be? Assuredly not; and it only remains for ourselves, calmly and deliberately, but firmly and in unison, to bring the matter forward, and the system must be altered.[69]

The structure of the medical profession involved a basic contradiction. On the one hand, the institutional framework of the profession continued to be organised around a rigid separation of the roles of the physician, the surgeon and the apothecary. On the other hand, in practice these traditional divisions were rapidly breaking down as a new professional structure emerged in response to changes in the wider network of relationships in which practitioners were involved: hence the contradiction between a newly emerging professional structure and traditional professional institutions organised on quite different principles. It was this structural tension within the medical profession which gave rise to a movement for medical reform amongst general practitioners, for since the general practitioner corresponded to none of the traditional types of practitioner, there was no place for him within the traditional institutional structure. Unwanted by all the medical corporations, the general practitioner was at best tolerated, never welcomed as a full member of the professional community.

For much of the first half of the nineteenth century — and in particular, from the mid 1820s — the relationship between the general practitioners and the consultants who controlled the Royal Colleges was more or less openly hostile, as the general practitioners began a long struggle for medical reform aimed at achieving recognition of what they held to be their rightful place within the profession. Amongst other things, they put forward demands for the democratic reform of the medical corporations, for the reform of medical education and licensing, and for the abolition of the tripartite structure based on the differentiation between physicians, surgeons and apothecaries. This latter point was of major importance, for it was only by breaking down the traditional separation between the different branches of practice, and by developing institutions which more adequately represented their interests, that general practitioners could hope to achieve recognition of general practice as a legitimate and honourable form of medical activity.

Inevitably, one consequence of the development of this reform movement within the profession was the polarisation of general practitioners and consultants into opposite camps; for, as we have seen, the consultants had a strong vested interest in maintaining the established institutional structure of the profession. Moreover, the fact that the consultants

monopolised the key political offices within the most powerful institutions within the profession enabled them to block,
for very many years, the general practitioners' demands for
reform. The result was that the struggle for reform was very
lengthy, frequently very bitter, and even violent on occasions.
Some of the major aspects of this reform movement will be
examined in the next three chapters.

PART II

The Campaign for Medical Reform

4.

The Campaign for Medical Reform:
the Early Stages

BY THE 1820s, the major line of division within the profession was becoming increasingly sharply drawn, and it is hardly an exaggeration to say that from then until the passing of the Medical Act in 1858 the medical profession was characterised by more or less permanent conflict as the general practitioners and the Royal Colleges engaged in a protracted and sometimes bitter struggle.

The general practitioners' campaign for reform was not only very long but also very complex; for although many of the general practitioners' demands for reform were closely interrelated, slightly different issues tended to come to the fore at different times. Moreover, the general practitioners' movement was anything but monolithic for, especially during the 1830s and 1840s, a multiplicity of medical reform associations was founded, some of which had only a very brief existence; whilst the leadership of the general practitioners' movement tended to pass rapidly from one organisation to another. The picture is further complicated by the fact that, although the general practitioners were generally united in their opposition to the policies of the Royal Colleges, they were on occasions deeply divided amongst themselves as to the precise nature of the reforms which they wished to bring about. Finally, the situation in relation to the medical reform movement within Parliament also became very confused at times, for between 1840 and 1858 there were no less than seventeen different medical reform Bills introduced into the House of Commons and, on one occasion, there were three separate Bills before the House at the same time.

In view of both the length and the complexity of the general practitioners' campaign for reform, the present work does not claim to offer a comprehensive analysis of the development of the medical reform movement; rather, we must be content simply to concentrate on some of the major aspects of this development. This will, however, serve to indicate something of the multi-faceted character of the general practitioners' campaign, as well as giving some indication of the intensity of the conflict, and even the bitterness which sometimes characterised relationships in what was (especially in the 1830s and 1840s) a deeply divided profession. This examination of some of the major aspects of the reform movement will also be useful in illustrating the degree to which the Royal Colleges set themselves firmly — and with considerable success — against any reforms which threatened the basic institutional structure of the profession and their dominant position within it. Later in the book, we will examine in some detail what is generally seen as the culmination of the efforts of the medical reformers, namely the 1858 Medical Act.

Lancet's role

A major part in the general practitioners' campaign for reform was taken by the *Lancet*, which was founded in 1823 by Thomas Wakley who, in addition to being a member of the College of Surgeons, subsequently became the radical Member of Parliament for Finsbury. From the beginning, the *Lancet* unambiguiously identified itself not with the hospital physicians and surgeons, but with the rank and file members of the profession; and the new journal ceaselessly complained of what it, together with a growing section of the profession, regarded as the abuses and the undemocratic practices within the Royal Colleges. Moreover, the *Lancet* quickly established for itself a large readership amongst members of the profession. Wakley's biographer estimates that by 1825, the *Lancet* had a regular circulation of upwards of four thousand,[1] which probably made it the most widely read medical journal of the period. From 1823, therefore, the general practitioners had an important ally amongst the national medical press.

Two or three years after the *Lancet* began publication, the struggle for reform began in earnest. The immediate target for the reformers was the Royal College of Surgeons, and the struggle within the College was particularly intense during the

period from 1826 to 1831. This particular campaign is of
some interest, not least because it raised an issue which, to
some extent, proved to be a source of division amongst the
reformers themselves, at least until the 1840s. This issue
related to whether the members of the College of Surgeons —
the 'surgeons in general practice', as the *Lancet* called them —
should seek to democratise the structure of the College of
Surgeons and to extend their rights as members within the
College, or whether, instead, they should seek to make
common cause with other general practitioners, including
those who were not members of the College of Surgeons,
in establishing a new institution which would more adequately
represent their interests. In the years 1826-7, the reformers
sought to claim what they felt to be their rights as members
of the College; in 1831, however, the experience of five years
of unsuccessful struggle had given rise to the first plan for
what would have been, in effect, a separate college of general
practitioners.

The immediate cause of discontent within the College of
Surgeons was the new regulation relating to surgical education
issued by the Court of Examiners of the College in 1824.
In 1822 the Court of Examiners had issued a regulation
which stated that the College would only recognise those
courses on anatomy which had been delivered in the winter
session, and this was followed, two years later, by a second
regulation which severely restricted the number of hospitals
which the College would recognise for teaching purposes.
The *Lancet* immediately responded to the new regulation by
pointing out that most members of the Court of Examiners
were themselves teachers at the large London hospitals, and
it accused them of passing the regulation purely out of self-
interest.[2] Certainly it is clear that both regulations had the
effect of restricting competition from other teachers, the
former by withdrawing recognition from the courses given
by the private schools, and the latter by compelling many
students in the provinces to come to the London hospitals
for their professional education. Shortly afterwards, further
criticism of the regulation came in the form of a pamphlet
by Dr. John Armstrong, a lecturer at the Grainger Brothers'
Webb Street School, in which he drew attention to the

'injurious conduct, and defective state' of the College, and in which he pointed to the damaging consequences of the new regulation for some of the excellent private schools.[3]

Criticism of the College was not long confined to criticism of the new regulations, for many practitioners saw the new regulations as simply one more symptom of the unrepresentative constitution of the College, a constitution which centralised all decision-making powers within the College in the hands of a small self-appointed group of hospital surgeons. Consequently the attack on the College broadened. In 1825-26, the *Lancet* published a series of letters from James Wardrop, under the pen name 'Brutus', attacking not merely the new regulations but the whole structure of the College.[4] On February 18, 1826, a protest meeting of members of the College was held at the Freemasons' Tavern.

As Sprigge has noted[5], this was an important development, for it represented the first organised step taken by the members against the College Council. At the meeting, resolutions were passed criticising the new regulations, the examinations of the College, the mismanagement of the museum and library, and complaining of the fact that the members were required to enter and leave the College by the back-door entrance, the front door being reserved for Council members.[6] Most importantly, however, the members passed a resolution which demanded a fundamental change in the structure of the College. It was agreed that a petition be 'immediately prepared and presented to the House of Commons, praying for the appointment of a Committee to inquire into the abuses of the said College, with a view to ultimately obtaining from His Majesty a New Charter, which shall provide that the officers of the College be annually chosen by the members, so that EACH MEMBER may have a voice in the election of those persons who are to regulate the proceedings of that College.'[7]

The members of the College re-assembled on 4 March 1826 to receive a report from the petition committee appointed at the previous meeting. The committee had approached the Council of the College asking them to join in the application to Parliament; the Council, however, had 'contemptuously refused',[8] and on 26 April 1826 the Council of the College issued a long statement replying to the members' demands. The Council denied that the constitution of the College was the cause of the 'alleged injuries and grievances', and it went on to argue that the 'evident object of this representation is the subversion of the present government of the College, and the substitution of elections to offices of control and responsibility, by members, who for the most part exercise the professions of apothecaries and accoucheurs. There can be little doubt, that in the event of such an innovation, the Institution would soon cease to be a College of Surgeons or of Surgery.'[9] It is clear from this statement that the Council recognised that by this time most members of the College were, in effect, general practitioners, and that any constitutional change along the lines demanded would open the way to control of the College by surgeons in general practice, with a consequent shift away from the College's traditional policy of emphasising the practice of pure surgery. The Council saw itself as, in effect, the last bulwark against the 'degradation' of the College into a college of surgeon-apothecaries or general practitioners.

The petition to the House of Commons for the abrogation of the Charter of the College was drawn up in 1826 and, early in 1827, preparations were made to present the petition to Parliament. It was at this stage that the College was to use its considerable influence to undermine the movement for reform. Edwin Lankester, who was a prominent figure in the early history of the British Medical Association, was later to refer to the influence which the Royal Colleges were able to exert through both formal and informal channels, and the difficulty of implementing any plan for reform to which they were opposed. 'Few persons, unless they have lived in London, could form any idea of the power of the ruling body of these Colleges, not so much in their corporate capacity, as in that of individuals. They were the medical attendants of nearly every member of both Houses of Parliament, and they were frequently consulted by these members with regard to particular bills which came before them.'[10] The campaign of 1826-7 provides a clear illustration of the problem to which Lankester referred.

In March 1827, the members of the College approached

Robert Peel to ask him to present their petition. As Home Secretary, Peel would have been an important ally had the members been able to persuade him to support their cause. Peel, however, was a personal friend of John Abernethy, president of the College in 1826, and of Sir Astley Cooper, president in 1827; not surprisingly, he declined to present the petition. The petition was ultimately presented to Parliament by Henry Warburton, MP for Bridport, on 20 June. By the time Warburton presented the petition, Peel, together with a number of other MPs, had been well briefed by the College. Warburton's fellow MP, Joseph Hume, recalled in 1831 that Warburton had been anxious to introduce into the House a motion founded on the members' petition; however, Warburton 'found the influence in the house so great against it, that so many hon-members had been sent to upon it, consulted upon it, and had been so much prejudiced and influenced against it, that Mr Warburton, after consulting with me, abandoned the attempt to bring forward a motion founded upon that petition, for the appointment of a committee to inquire into the abuses of the college. He felt that it would be better (and I advised him to the same course) to let it drop than bring forward a motion which was sure to fail.'[11]

Warburton accordingly proposed a much more modest motion. In his speech to the House, he listed the members' grievances, including the fact that the College Council considered that those who practised as surgeon-apothecaries and those who practised midwifery 'were less qualified than others for the honours and advantages of that institution'.[12] He then moved a relatively uncontroversial motion, which simply required the College to provide the House with certain information. In particular, the motion called for a return from the College of all public money lent or granted to the College from 1799, and an account of all monies received by the College from its members in 1825 and 1826. Warburton's motion also required the College to supply information concerning the regulations under which members and students were admitted to the museum and library and a statement of the number of persons examined by the College since 1800. Peel defended the College, saying that the actions of its Council had met with the approval of a number of eminent surgeons, and that he had found the Council 'very willing to remove every evil of which the petition complained'.[13] He did not, however, oppose Warburton's modest request for information, to which the House agreed.

Following this debate in Parliament, the Council made two minor concessions: the library was finally opened for the use of members and the back-door entrance was abolished, apparently on the suggestion of Peel[14] — only to be replaced by a new side entrance for members, who were still forbidden to use the front door in Lincoln's Inn Fields. These were, however, the only concessions. Warburton had been unable to raise the fundamental issue — the constitution of the College — and the Council was determined that the constitution would remain unchanged. The College duly supplied the returns required by the House of Commons, but no member apparently felt sufficiently interested or well-informed to carry the matter further, especially in the light of the support which the College had been able to organise in its defence.[15] The returns were simply laid upon the table of the House and no debate ensued. Apart from a little publicity for their cause[16], the members had gained virtually nothing.

For the next three or four years, relations between the Council and the members of the College remained strained. The *Lancet* continued to condemn almost weekly the conduct of the Council; in January 1831, it raised the possibility of establishing a new college which would represent not merely the surgeons in general practice, but all general practitioners, whether or not they were members of the College of Surgeons. The *Lancet* argued that 'However much the timid may dread the word, we hesitate not to say, that in our profession a *revolution* is much wanted — a complete breaking up of the restrictions and monopolies by which the members of the different colleges have been plundered of their rights ... The members of the profession should duly investigate such facts as these, when they will soon be taught that evils of such vast magnitude can only be effectually, radically, removed by the establishment of a NEW MEDICAL COLLEGE.'[17] This plan for a new college, elaborated in the

course of a particularly bitter dispute within the College of
Surgeons in 1831, was to be the first of a number of plans
to establish a college which would represent all general
practitioners and would, therefore, cut across the traditional
institutional affiliations to one or other of the medical
corporations.

The incident which sparked off the new conflict within
the College of Surgeons in 1831 was a relatively trivial one,
but within a context of mutual suspicion and hostility much
broader issues were soon to be raised. On 5 February 1831,
the *Lancet* reported that a circular had been sent to surgeons
serving in His Majesty's Navy, to the effect that they were
not to attend the King's levees. The circular was, said the
Lancet, 'a deliberate, cold-blooded insult'[18] to naval surgeons,
and the following week it called on members of the College
to assemble at the College on the occasion of the Hunterian
Ovation in order to discuss the matter. This call to the members was, in effect, an assertion that the members and not
the Council had a right to decide on the business of the day;
as the *Lancet* put it, the theatre 'belongs to the MEMBERS,
and surely they could not employ it for a better purpose
than in making an attempt to rescue from insult a most
important branch of the profession'.[19] On the appointed day,
the members assembled in the lecture theatre, which was
'crowded to excess', and prior to the Hunterian Oration two
resolutions were passed, one of which requested the president
and Council to memorialise the Lords of the Admiralty with
a view to having the offending circular withdrawn. After the
oration, the acting-president, Robert Keate, met the members
and agreed to lay the members' request before the Council.[20]

The members' resolution was presented to the Council at
its meeting on 22 February, when it was resolved 'that such
documents cannot be received on account of the irregularity
of the proceedings'.[21] The *Lancet* responded by saying that
'the members, doubtless, gave offence to the worthy and
liberal-minded Council, because they presumed to disturb the
awful silence, which has so many years prevailed within the
walls of the College, by discussing a professional grievance *in
their own theatre*.' It called on the members to 'assert their
rights in a place where they never ought to have remained

dormant' and to demonstrate that they were 'no longer the miserable tools of a despicable, dark-minded oligarchy'. Finally, the *Lancet* suggested that the members should meet again in the theatre of the College on the following Tuesday. A lecture was due to commence at 4 pm; the doors were to be opened at 3 pm, and the meeting should commence as soon after 3 pm as possible. Once again it claimed that the theatre belonged to the members, and that they therefore had the right to decide the purposes for which it was to be used: 'Let us prove that we are not to be checked; that we are not to be defeated in our efforts, by this miserable, self-conceited, self-perpetuating oligarchy; but let us meet like men of rank and character, and of education and of knowledge, *in our own theatre*, and there discuss in the presence of our charter-protected tyrants, those measures which we may deem best calculated to uphold the honour, and maintain inviolable the rights and privileges, of our profession.'[22]

On Tuesday 8 March, the day of the lecture, the Council placed an advertisement in *The Times* and other morning papers, to the effect that the door of the College would not be opened until shortly before the start of the lecture. The Council also stated that 'the theatre is opened for the sole purpose of the lectures', and gave notice of their determination 'henceforth to prevent discussions on any subject from taking place in the theatre of the College'.

That afternoon, some three to four hundred members assembled at the College and occupied the theatre, thus preventing the lecture from taking place. When the president and Council entered, they tried without success to have Thomas Wakley, editor of the *Lancet*, removed by a Bow Street officer. Deciding that it was impossible to go ahead with the lecture, the Council finally withdrew amidst loud cheering. The members then went ahead with their own meeting, in the course of which it was pointed out that the issues involved had now become much broader than the one which had originally sparked off the dispute. As Wakley put it, 'when this subject — the exclusion of naval surgeons from attending his Majesty's levees — was brought before the attention of the College . . . it stood as a detached subject —

one which was entirely unconnected with our rights as members of this College. Unfortunately from the very untoward circumstances, the question has now become involved with many others which seriously, most seriously affect our rights.' Thus more fundamental questions had once again been raised concerning the structure of the College as a whole, a fact which was clearly recognised in a motion carried with only two votes against to the effect that the members regretted the refusal of the Council to act on the resolution presented to them, but added that this refusal 'is another added to the already innumerable existing proofs that the President and Council are alike indifferent to the honour, happiness, and respectability, of the commonalty of this chartered College'.

Shortly after this resolution was passed, a number of Bow Street officers entered the theatre, with the instruction to eject Wakley. A number of members came to Wakley's assistance, but the editor of the *Lancet* was finally removed after a violent struggle in the course of which he received a blow with a truncheon. Although Wakley had been evicted, most members remained in the theatre, and it was unanimously resolved to send a deputation to the Lord Chamberlain to complain of the order relating to naval surgeons. The deputation duly waited on the Lord Chamberlain, and the offending order was withdrawn.[23]

Four days after the violent meeting of 8 March, the *Lancet* published an 'Address to the medical profession of Great Britain and Ireland', in which it referred to the 'foul, unprovoked, and illegal assault' on the members of the College, which was committed 'by order of — we blush to say it — by order of their Council'. The address claimed 'thus have our rights been trampled upon, our lives endangered, our feelings outraged, and our profession insulted, by our own Council', and it went on to express the hope that 'no medical student will present himself for a diploma stained with the blood of his senior colleagues'.[24]

In the same issue, there was an announcement which stated that 'in consequence of the atrocious assault committed upon the Members of the College of Surgeons', a public meeting of the profession was to be held at the Crown and Anchor tavern in the Strand on 16 March. At this meeting, a plan would be introduced for the institution of a new medical college, 'founded upon the most enlarged principles, and in which all legally-qualified practitioners, whether physicians, surgeons, or apothecaries, will be associated upon equal terms, will enjoy equal rights, and will be recognised by the same title'.[25] As we have noted, this represented an important change of strategy, for since 1826 the efforts of the reformers had been directed to bringing about changes within the College of Surgeons, rather than with instituting a new college.

The meeting on 16 March aroused considerable interest and was attended by thirteen hundred members of the profession.[26] At this meeting, it was resolved that 'the establishment of a new medical college on principles in accordance with the progress of science, presents, at the same time, the most practicable means of obtaining a general and complete reform in the system of medical legislation, is calculated to afford the greatest security to the public health, and will most effectually increase the utility, and advance the rank and respectability, of the general body of the medical profession.' The wording of this resolution — that the new college should be established 'on principles in accordance with the progress of science' — is important, for many general practitioners claimed that the progress of medical science had effectively undermined any rationale for the tripartite separation between the different branches of practice, so long institutionalised in the structure of the Royal Colleges and the Society of Apothecaries. As the proposer and seconder of the motion pointed out, this tripartite separation was no longer acceptable to many members of the profession. Thomas King, who proposed the motion, argued that there was no natural distinction between medicine, surgery, and the dispensing of medicines, and he claimed that the 'divisions which at present distinguish the profession are in every respect detrimental to the welfare of our fellow-creatures and the advancement of science'. It was therefore imperative that the new college must embrace in its examination 'every department of medicine and surgery'.

A committee was appointed to draw up a plan for the

formation of the proposed London College of Medicine, as
it was to be called, and from their report it is clear that one
of the major objectives of the new college was to break down
the tripartite structure of the profession. The new college
was not to be a college of surgeons, or of physicians, or of
apothecaries; it was to be, in effect, a college of general
practitioners. Thus all persons legally qualified to practise
in any branch of the profession were deemed eligible candidates, without examination, for the diploma of the College,
and all those who possessed the diploma were to be denomin-
ated Fellows, and were to enjoy the title of Doctor.[27] Thus
would the new college 'cast aside the absurd distinctions
which now exist in the profession, as to names, such as
Physician, Apothecary, Surgeon, and Accoucheur'.[28] The
Lancet recognised that some physicians — the only group
which, at that time, enjoyed the right to use the title 'Doctor'
— would object to this scheme and would 'allege that it is
"infamous" to confer upon the general practitioner the title
of "Doctor"'. However, the *Lancet* argued there was no
reason why general practitioners should not have this right,
for the medical attainments of many general practitioners
were 'immeasurably beyond those of hundreds of individuals who are now invested with that mark of distinction'.[29]

Moreover, the college was to offer the first comprehensive
examination designed to meet the needs of general practitioners. Thus all students who presented themselves for
examination were to be examined in all branches of medical
science — anatomy, physiology, pathology, surgery, materia
medica, semeiology, and the 'practical application of those
facts and principles in the practice of medicine, as empirically
divided into medicine, surgery, and midwifery'. The Fellows
were to be free to practise all branches of medicine, and even
if candidates for the diploma wished to specialise in a single
branch of practice, 'public security will demand that . . .
[they] display a competent knowledge of the whole'.[30] The
public would then have the 'infinite satisfaction of knowing
that every possessor of the diploma . . . has proved that he is
well qualified to practise in every branch of medical science'.[31]

The new college was to be organised on democratic principles, with the governing Senate being elected annually by

the whole body of Fellows. In addition — and in marked contrast to the regulations of the College of Surgeons — medical students were not to be required to produce certificates of attendance at any particular institution, but were to be free to acquire their medical education in whatever institution they chose to attend. The question of where candidates had received their medical education was deemed to be immaterial; the real question was to be whether the candidate had a sufficient knowledge of medicine to pass the examination of the college. Thus what the *Lancet* called the 'plundering "certificate system"' of the College of Surgeons was to be 'completely exploded' in this new institution.[32] In short, the London College of Medicine was, as Sprigge has put it, 'to do everything as properly as the existing College did everything improperly'.[33]

The proposed new college was clearly seen by some medical men not only as a solution to the problems facing general practitioners, but also as a development which presaged the final break-up of the existing medical institutions. Thus one practitioner from Rotherhithe, for example, in welcoming the plan to form the London College of Medicine, wrote 'Farewell to our monopolizing colleges and corporations! Rotten in constitution, what can uphold them? The very walls, which have so long concealed from public view their fraudulent and tyrannising machinations, are already shaken to their foundations . . . At this moment they totter, and the hour is fast approaching when they will assuredly fall. I cannot help, Sir, expressing myself thus strongly . . . because I have seen the general practitioner trampled to the ground by these vampires of the medical world.'[34] Throughout the summer of 1831, the *Lancet* published a number of similar letters in support of the new college, and the journal reported frequently and optimistically on the progress and prospects of the new institution.

By the autumn, however, it was already becoming clear that all was not well with the new college, and that support for the new institution had not been as widespread or as sustained as the *Lancet* had originally hoped. On September 24, the journal announced that the committee of the College had decided to postpone the general convocation, due to be held on 29 September[35] and by October, the *Lancet* was already denying rumours that the London College of Medicine was foundering.[36] In the months that followed, references to the London College became less and less frequent in the pages of the *Lancet*; from November 1831 to August 1832, the new college was referred to less than half-a-dozen times. Eventually, in October 1832, the *Lancet* published a letter from a correspondent in which the writer said that he, and other readers, 'cannot fail to regard with considerable apprehension and anxiety, the ominous silence your pages have latterly evinced respecting the condition of the affairs and the future prospects of the London College of Medicine — as, for instance, the state of its funds, the number of its enrolled members, the means designed, and the period when it is intended to apply to the legislature in order to render it a corporate body; and, above all, the circumstances affecting the probability or non-probability of its eventually becoming such.'[37] The *Lancet* did not offer a reply. By this time, it was clear that there was insufficient support for the establishment of a new college. The plan to institute the London College of Medicine was quietly abandoned.

At first sight, the failure of the new college may seem surprising for, at least superficially, the new college would seem to have met all the requirements of the reformers, both in terms of providing a suitable education and licence for general practice, and in terms of giving general practitioners effective political control over their own affairs. Why, then, was there so little sustained support for the new college from members of the College of Surgeons, almost all of whom practised generally?

Unfortunately, the only original source of information relating to the London College of Medicine appears to be the *Lancet* for the period between March 1831 and October 1832, and that journal simply allowed the short-lived proposal for a new college to fade away without any comment and without giving any reason for its failure. Nevertheless, it is clear that the relative lack of support for the new college was closely associated with the development — or more precisely, with the relatively low level of development — of what may be called a 'general practitioner consciousness', for during this early part of the reform movement, the general practitioners continued to be divided amongst themselves, largely along corporate lines.

In this context, it is important to bear in mind that although the London College of Medicine was to be open to all legally qualified practitioners, the proposal for the new college was born specifically out of a conflict within the College of Surgeons, and there is little doubt that the new college aimed to attract its initial support largely from amongst the membership of the College of Surgeons. The members of that College were, however, in a structurally ambiguous situation, and this ambiguity was nicely captured in the phrase which was frequently used by the *Lancet* to refer to the members of the College of Surgeons: 'surgeons in general practice'. Thus, on the one hand, they were members of the College of Surgeons with a clear and legally recognised affiliation with that institution, whilst on the other hand, they were also general practitioners and as such had certain common interests with other general practitioners who were not members of the College of Surgeons. Thus the members of the College of Surgeons were faced with a dilemma: should they seek to reform the College, and to extend what they saw as their rights as members of the College; or should they, in effect, ignore their institutional affiliation to the College, and instead make common cause with other general practitioners – physicians, surgeons and apothecaries – in a new institution?

This problem almost certainly did not arise in such an acute form for those general practitioners who simply held a licence from the Society of Apothecaries, for few – if any – practitioners felt any real commitment to what had been, and to some extent still was, a trading corporation; 'Rhubarb Hall' was rarely seen as an institution worth preserving, even if it could have been reformed. The Royal College of Surgeons, however, was a different matter. Not only did the College enjoy the prestige conferred by the grant of a Royal Charter, but it also included amongst its members all the leading surgeons in England, many of whom sat on its Court of Examiners, a fact which gave the College's diploma a status which was respected throughout the country. The respect in which the College's diploma was held may be judged by the fact that evidence presented to the Select Committee on Medical Education in 1834 indicated that in the preceding five year period, more students had taken the examination for the diploma of the College of Surgeons than had taken the examination for the licence of the Society of Apothecaries;[38] despite the fact that since 1815 the latter had been a legal requirement for all general practitioners, whereas the former was purely voluntary, the College having no power to require anyone to take its diploma and no power to prevent anyone from practising surgery without it. Candidates continued to present themselves for the College diploma, not because they were required to do so by law, but because of the status accorded to a diploma signed by many of the leading surgeons of the period.

It was largely because of the high status enjoyed by the College of Surgeons that most members were not prepared — at least at this stage of the reform movement — to cut themselves off from the College; indeed, it is probably true to say that in the early years of the reform movement (the 1820s and early 1830s) most 'surgeons in general practice' continued to identify themselves in the first instance as members of the College of Surgeons, and only secondarily as general practitioners. It was for this reason that most members were not yet prepared to abandon their attempt to reform the College and to gamble on the establishment of a new institution, whose status would have been uncertain. As Wakley's biographer has pointed out, the members wanted the College of Surgeons reformed, 'but they did not want it destroyed and a new institution with no history and no prestige substituted for it'.[39] Despite the failure of this first attempt to establish a separate college, the plan to establish a college of general practitioners was to be revived in the 1840s by which time, as we shall see, it had come to command much more widespread support amongst general practitioners.

Throughout the early 1830s, the reform movement continued to be organised largely along corporate lines. Within the College of Surgeons, the members continued to criticise the unrepresentative character of the Council and to demand reforms which would give the members effective control of their own College whilst, at the same time, quite separate attempts were being made by the licentiates to reform the structure of the Royal College of Physicians.[40] From the middle of the 1830s, however, the nature of the campaign began to change as a growing number of practitioners became increasingly aware of the significance of the changes within the structure of the profession, and as more and more medical men began to conceptualise themselves specifically as general practitioners and to identify with others — whatever their corporate affiliation — who were similarly engaged in general practice. Medical men, in other words, were increasingly coming to define themselves not primarily as members of the College of Surgeons or as licentiates of the Society of Apothecaries but simply as general practitioners. One symptom of this growing awareness that general practitioners constituted a distinct group which cut across the traditional corporate lines was the emergence of associations of general practitioners committed to radical reform and formed with the explicit aim of uniting all general practitioners — whether physicians, surgeons or apothecaries — within a single organisation.

One of the earliest, and certainly one of the most radical, organisations to develop along these lines was the British Medical Association, which despite its title was primarily an association of general practitioners in the London area. This association, it should be noted, was a quite separate organisation from the association which is so well known within the profession today; the modern British Medical Association had its origins in a separate organisation of provincial practitioners formed in 1832 about which more will be said later.

From the beginning, the London-based British Medical Association set out to identify itself quite explicitly as a general practitioners' organisation; it was to be an association of 'the English general practitioners of medicine, constituting the great body of the profession', a body of practitioners whom, it was noted, had been facetiously termed the 'subordinates' of the profession.[41] Moreover, the Association was established specifically with the idea of campaigning for radical measures of medical reform; literary and scientific pursuits, which formed an important part of the activities of most medical associations, were specifically excluded from its statement of objectives.[42]

Within the Association, the relationship between the general practitioners and the medical corporations was immediately singled out as a major source of the general practitioners' grievances. The chairman of the new association, Dr George Webster, a general practitioner from Dulwich, said that 'had the constituted authorities, the colleges, the corporations, and the halls done their duty, we should not have been obliged to meet . . . to take the matter into our own hands, and form an association. But instead of protecting the profession, I fear they have frequently oppressed it.'[43] It was the medical corporations, he pointed out, which still strove to maintain those 'most unnatural divisions and degrading distinctions' which were institutionalised in what were usually called 'The Three Branches of the Profession', just as it was the medical corporations which had consistently denied general practitioners any participation 'in the smallest degree' in the management of their own affairs.[44] The medical corporations demonstrated, in short, 'the natural and unfortunate effects of irresponsible power — the rottenness of the whole system of medical policy'.[45]

The major object of the association was to campaign for a radical change of the whole structure of the profession, involving the abolition of the tripartite structure, the unification of all branches of practice, and the establishment of a single controlling body which would be elected by the whole profession, and within which all practitioners would enjoy equal status: 'if what are now termed the three branches of the profession were comprehended in one general faculty of medicine, with the power of electing their own senators or council, we should soon have, as the legitimate and necessary consequence, a wonderful change in the aspect of medical affairs, and without this it is in vain to expect either unanimity, harmony or friendly feeling.'[46]

In order to ensure that the new association would remain firmly under the control of general practitioners, it was decided that, although membership of the association was to be open to all qualified practitioners, the president of the association should always be a general practitioner, whilst similarly only those who had been actively engaged in general practice should be eligible for membership of the controlling Council of the Association.[47] In explaining the reason for this, the chairman pointed out that 'this is expressly to be a society of medical men who practise every branch of the profession, general practitioners. We commenced as such for we considered that the physicians already had *their* clubs; the surgeons had *theirs*; . . . all these had their own exclusive associations . . . this was to be a society of general practitioners, of the great body of the profession.'[48]

Not surprisingly, the formation of the new association was unreservedly welcomed by the *Lancet*: 'The principles on which it is founded are identical with the interests of the general practitioner.'[49] The rule which excluded hospital physicians and surgeons from holding any official position in the organisation was, said the *Lancet*, 'absolutely necessary, in order to obviate the complete subversion of those fundamental principles on which the Association must be established, if it be intended that it should be successful'.[50] General practitioners, it said, 'constitute, probably, full fifteen-sixteenths of the whole profession, and ought therefore, to take the lead in the management of *their own affairs*; and they must firmly retain the control of the Association in *their own hands*, or, we unhesitatingly predict, that they will be again and again betrayed'.[51] Shortly afterwards, the *Lancet* reiterated this point, saying that the general practitioners of England and Wales

> have been taught . . . by years of direful experience, that the mere university physician . . . and the mere hospital surgeon, constituting the 'pures' of the 'highest ranks' in the profession, have combined with the heads of their own colleges in order to oppress, stigmatise, insult, and degrade those whom they have had the insolence to denominate the 'subordinate' members of the profession. Could it be expected, then, that the Provisional Council of the Association would be so utterly incapable of fulfilling the high trust which was committed to their charge, as to allow the enemies of general practitioners to exercise a

single function of the governing body in the new Association? Certainly not, . . . The wrongs of general
practitioners are to be redressed — the measures of relief
are to be devised and enforced by general practitioners
themselves. . . All the general practitioners in the kingdom will now have their minds fortified by the assurance,
that their interests will not be sacrificed or betrayed.[52]

In the next three or four years, medical reform associations
began to develop all over the country, and the British Medical
Association assumed the leadership role in trying to coordinate the efforts of the various regional associations by coopting
their presidents and secretaries as members of the Council of
the BMA.[53] At the same time, the Association was also involved in working out in more detail its own plan for medical
reform, in organising petitions to be sent to Parliament, and
in sending delegations from the Association to see government ministers and other MPs believed to be sympathetic to
the cause of medical reform.[54]

The Association published its 'Outlines of a Plan of Medical
Reform' in July 1839. The central proposal was one which
aimed 'to unite all the legally qualified members of the
medical profession . . . into "ONE FACULTY", to be entitled
"THE BRITISH FACULTY OF MEDICINE"'. The governing
body of the Faculty was to be elected periodically by the
whole membership, and all members were to receive the same
title, to enjoy equal rights and privileges, and to have the
right to practise in all branches of the profession. The
Faculty was to be required to keep a register of all legally
qualified practitioners, and only those who were so registered
were to have the right to practise medicine.[55]

Early in 1841, the BMA convened a conference of all the
leading reform associations throughout the country in an
attempt to get agreement on a reform bill which, it was
hoped, could then be presented to Parliament. The Conference on Medical Reform, as it was called, was held at the
Exeter Hall, London, and involved seventeen meetings
between March and June 1841. In addition to the delegates
from the BMA, delegates were also sent from associations
of practitioners in Cornwall, Devon (South), Glasgow,

Gloucestershire, Nottingham and Taunton, from the Irish Medical Association, the East of Scotland Medical Association, the North of England Medical Association, and the Provincial Medical and Surgical Association. The last named association was later to play a very important part in the development of the medical profession, for after the London-based BMA had ceased to exist as a separate organisation when it joined with the National Association of General Practitioners in the mid-1840s, the Provincial Association changed its name in 1855 and, adopting the name formerly held by the London Association, finally emerged as the British Medical Association so well known today. It is, therefore, worth pausing briefly at this stage to say something about the early development of the Provincial Association, both because of its subsequent importance, and also because it played a controversial part in the Reform Conference of 1841.

Unlike the London Association, the Provincial Association had not been formed specifically to further the cause of medical reform, for its initial objectives were 'friendly and scientific' rather than medico-political and, in the first few years of its existence, the Association became involved only slowly and cautiously with the issue of medical reform. It was primarily for this reason that the *Lancet*, after initially welcoming the formation of the Provincial Association in 1832, became increasingly critical of its activities. Moreover, the *Lancet* quickly drew a link between the Association's relatively slow involvement in the reform movement and the fact that the Council of the Association was dominated, in its early years, by physicians and surgeons attached to hospitals in the provinces. Many provincial hospital physicians and surgeons were, it should be noted, considerably more liberal than their London counterparts, who were much more closely associated with the conservative hierarchies of the Royal Colleges. Nevertheless, the *Lancet* was insistent that it was not in the best interests of general practitioners that they should be led by physicians and surgeons; in the Provincial Society, it said, the physicians have 'in the very infancy of the society, obtained, apparently, the entire control of the association. We do not charge them with having usurped any authority. They may exercise their function, legitimately, and without even the breach of professional etiquette; but still we resolutely say, that it is not for the interest of general practitioners that they should be placed under the guidance of *physicians*, however estimable they may be in the relations of private life, however exalted they may be in professional reputation.'[56]

The Provincial Association did, however, slowly become more involved in the reform movement. In October 1839, the Council of the BMA formally welcomed 'the accession of the Provincial Medical and Surgical Association to the ranks of reform, and the establishment, in consequence, of a correspondence and co-operation between it and this Association'.[57] At its annual conference in the following year, the Provincial Association passed a resolution to the effect that 'steps should be taken to obtain medical reform on the principles of a uniform test of qualification and a representative system of government'.[58] However, although the Provincial Association had, by 1840, committed itself to the cause of medical reform, its position was considerably less radical than that of the BMA, and these divisions became particularly evident in the course of the London Conference on Reform in 1841.

The plan of reform which had been drawn up by the BMA formed the basis for discussion at the conference, and it quickly became clear that the delegates from the Provincial Association had important reservations about parts of that plan. It was argued by some of the Provincial Association's delegates, for example, that whilst the representative principle was desirable, they did not regard it as an essential feature of any reform. The Chairman of the BMA immediately accused the Provincial delegates of 'retrograding' on the decision taken at their annual conference, with the implication that they did not properly represent the interests of the general practitioners who formed the bulk of the membership of the Association.[59] More importantly, however, there was a fundamental disagreement over the extent to which the existing corporations should be respected in any plan of reform. The plan drawn up by the BMA would have effectively destroyed the Royal Colleges and the Society of

Apothecaries, for it would have taken away their major function — that of licensing practitioners — which would have become the responsibility of the new Faculty of Medicine; the vice-president of the College of Surgeons said that the plan of the BMA, if implemented, 'would operate as a dose of arsenic to the college'.[60] The delegates from the Provincial Association, on the other hand, insisted that 'existing medical institutions be respected, provided their existence can be rendered compatible with uniformity of qualification, equality of privileges to practise medicine, and a fair system of representative government'.[61] Throughout the whole proceedings, the Provincial Association delegates displayed a much more conciliatory attitude towards the Royal Colleges. As it became clear that a majority of those present were prepared to support the plan drawn up by the BMA, one by one the delegates from the Provincial Association resigned from the Conference. Although the reform movement had, by 1840, begun to break down the divisions along corporate lines within its own ranks, the Conference indicated that the reformers were still seriously divided, albeit along rather different lines.

Despite the failure of the Conference to reach agreement on a specific series of proposals, the issue of medical reform had, by this time, become firmly established on the political agenda. At a meeting of the BMA held in 1840, it was stated that in the previous session of Parliament, no less than 173 petitions containing the signatures of over 5,000 medical men — about a third of the entire profession — had been presented in favour of medical reform[62] and, from 1840 onwards, the House of Commons became an increasingly important focus for the activities of medical reformers. In August 1840, the first Medical Reform Bill was introduced into the Commons, and this was followed, early in 1841, by two further Bills. From this time onwards, the issue of medical reform was to be a frequent subject of Parliamentary debate, with the appointment of a Select Committee to investigate the whole question in 1847, and with the further introduction of no less than fourteen Reform Bills before the final passage of the 1858 Medical Act.

Quite clearly, it is not possible — nor necessary — to examine each of these Bills in detail. It will, however, be useful to look briefly at a few of these Reform Bills, for some Bills had important consequences for the development of the general practitioners' campaign, whilst others defined in a particularly clear way the major issues involved. In the next chapter, therefore, we will examine the Bills introduced by Sir James Graham in 1844-5 and the Bill introduced by Thomas Wakley in 1847; and in the following chapter we will examine in some detail the passage of the 1858 Act itself.

5.

The Parliamentary Campaign for Medical Reform

AS WE noted in the previous chapter, three medical reform Bills were introduced into the House of Commons in 1840-41. All of these Bills were private members' Bills, but by the early 1840s, the government itself was becoming increasingly concerned to regulate the medical profession more effectively, partly because of the growing employment of medical practitioners as Medical Officers under the new Poor Law. From the middle of the 1830s, both the London-based British Medical Association and the Provincial Medical and Surgical Association had been in frequent contact with the Poor Law Commissioners, and both Associations had consistently urged the necessity of amending those provisions of the 1834 Poor Law Amendment Act which related to the provision of Poor Law medical services.[1] In 1842, in response to a Parliamentary question on this issue, the Home Secretary, Sir James Graham, said it was not his intention simply to amend the law as it related to the Poor Law medical services, but also either in that session of Parliament or the following to introduce a much more general alteration in the laws regulating 'the whole system of medical practice throughout the kingdom'.[2]

Graham's Bill was finally introduced into the House of Commons on 7 August 1844. It was not Graham's intention that this particular Bill should become law for it was introduced towards the very end of the Parliamentary session in order to 'allay the fears of the profession' and to lay before the profession a concrete series of proposals for discussion.[3] While Graham's Bill did little to meet the demands of the general practitioners, the discussion which it provoked did give rise to a new organisation of general practitioners which,

for the next four or five years, was to push the reform movement in a new direction.

Graham's Bill 'for the better Regulation of Medical Practice
throughout the United Kingdom' provided for the establishment of a Council of Health and Medical Education which
would, amongst other things, have the duty of maintaining
a register of all qualified practitioners.[4] The Council was to
have as its president a principal Secretary of State and the
remaining membership was to consist of five university
professors of medicine or surgery together with six representatives from the Royal Colleges in England, Scotland and
Ireland, and six other persons nominated by the crown; no
provision was made for general practitioners to be represented
on the Council. Moreover, the register of practitioners was
to have three divisions: physicians and surgeons were to continue to be recognised as distinct 'orders' within the profession,
with general practitioners being recognised as a third — and
clearly subordinate — class with the rather cumbersome title
of Licentiates in Medicine and Surgery.[5]

Within Parliament, Graham's proposals were savagely
attacked by Thomas Wakley who, in addition to editing the
Lancet, had also been the MP for Finsbury since 1835.
Wakley said that petitions had been presented 'from all parts
of the Kingdom on the subject of medical legislation, and
what were the prayers of those petitions? Those prayers were
invariably that the petitioners might be invested with a controlling power with reference to those Medical Institutions
to which they belonged. . . . How were these petitions
answered? Were the petitioners to acquire additional power
by the proposition of the right hon. Baronet? Were they to
elect the Council [of Health]? No; but they were to be
subject to a Council appointed by the Government, and by
Colleges of the conduct of which they had been complaining.'
In an apparent reference to Sir Benjamin Brodie, president of
the Royal College of Surgeons who had acted as an adviser
to Graham, Wakley said that the Home Secretary had been
'earwigged, deceived, misinformed, and had had the subject
misrepresented to him by somebody who had gained access
to him, while the medical body had not been able to obtain a
hearing'.[6]

Outside Parliament, the reaction of general practitioners was equally hostile; and towards the end of 1844 the first steps were taken to form a National Association of General Practitioners in Medicine, Surgery and Midwifery, with the object of suspending any further consideration of Graham's Bill until the general practitioners had been 'legally recognised and placed in an independent position'[7] – by which the National Association meant that it wished to see general practitioners incorporated in their own college. The London-based British Medical Association merged with the National Association, and within three months the new Association claimed a national membership of over 4000 general practitioners.[8] A meeting of the National Association held in London in March 1845 attracted no fewer than 1000 general practitioners, who adopted 'almost unanimously' the Association's plan for the establishment of a separate College of General Practitioners in Medicine, Surgery and Midwifery.[9]

In his evidence before a Select Committee in 1848, James Bird, a prominent member of the National Association, explained why they had objected to Graham's Bill and had decided to campaign for a separate College of General Practitioners. Under Graham's Bill, general practitioners, or Licentiates in Medicine and Surgery as they were to be called, were to be examined in medicine by the Royal College of Physicians, assisted by the examiners of the Society of Apothecaries, and in surgery by the Royal College of Surgeons. Graham's Bill thus proposed to place 'the power of licensing and of framing the curriculum of study, and of testing, by examination, all future persons engaged in general practice, under the control of the College of Physicians and Surgeons'. The National Association objected to this proposal, however, for, as Bird pointed out, 'neither the College of Surgeons nor the College of Physicians has any sympathy with the general practitioners'. It was felt that, under Graham's proposals, the Royal Colleges would give the general practitioners 'no more qualification than they thought proper' whilst there was, within the Royal Colleges 'a disposition to keep them in an inferior position'. As we have already seen, general practitioners were excluded from any participation in the affairs of the Royal Colleges whilst, in addition, Graham's Bill made no provision for general practitioners to be represented on the Council of Health. General practitioners would thus continue to be left without any form of political representation within the profession; as Bird put it, there was 'no ostensible body to represent the interests of the mass of the profession'. It was largely on these grounds, he said, that the National Association had decided that there would be 'great advantage in the establishment of a new institution, that shall comprise within its fold, as it were, all those gentlemen who are engaged in general practice throughout the country ... on the condition that the College shall have the unfettered right and privilege of framing its own curriculum, and testing by examination all future candidates for general practice, not in medicine alone, not in surgery alone, not in midwifery alone, or pharmacy alone, but in all those branches that are essential to constitute an efficient general practitioner'.[10]

As we have noted, Sir James Graham's original Bill of August 1844 had never been intended to pass into law, but simply to stimulate discussion. However, in February 1845, shortly before the mass meeting at which the National Association adopted its plan for a separate College of General Practitioners, Graham introduced a slightly revised version of his earlier Bill. The registration clauses and the composition of the Council of Health were unchanged, but the new Bill did propose that the Council should institute an examination in midwifery, although this examination was apparently to be voluntary rather than compulsory.[11] In addition, the Bill included a new clause to the effect that all Licentiates in Medicine and Surgery should be members of the appropriate Royal College of Surgeons in England, Scotland or Ireland.

This new clause was important, for it indicated that the government was still hoping for some reconciliation between the general practitioners and the College of Surgeons which would obviate the necessity for the separate incorporation of general practitioners; in his speech to the Commons, Graham said that he would 'most deeply regret the separation of the general practitioners from the College of Surgeons'. Following the introduction of a new Charter which had been granted to the College of Surgeons in 1843, Graham hoped 'that the general practitioners and the College of Surgeons will be in a more close and honourable connexion than at any antecedent period'. He was, he said, 'most anxious to sustain the station, the honour, and the attainments of general practitioners' and he doubted 'whether we should be doing good, and should advance the honour and the character of the general practitioners, by dissolving the connexion between them and the College of Surgeons.'[12]

The National Association immediately sent a deputation to see the Home Secretary, who asked for an assurance that the Association really represented the views of most general practitioners, and that there was no possibility of a reconciliation between the general practitioners and the College of Surgeons.[13] The National Association was apparently able to persuade the Home Secretary on both counts. In relation to the latter issue, it was pointed out that, in addition to the practical difficulty of achieving any reform in the College of Surgeons, there was a further and perhaps more compelling reason why the College, even if reformed, could not adequately represent the interests of all general practitioners. According to Bird, 'There was a misapprehension existing as to our being reconciled to the College of Surgeons; if all the general practitioners were members of the College of Surgeons, there can be no doubt the energies and efforts of the association would be directed to ascertain the point whether it was practicable so to liberalise the council of the College of Surgeons as to satisfy the demands of its members; but the National Association contained amongst others many gentlemen who were not members of the College of Surgeons, and it was not to be supposed that the College of Surgeons could by possibility admit the whole of those parties, or that it was practicable to make it the kind of institution which was required by those who were engaged in general practice.'[14]

In other words, even if it had been possible to enfranchise within the College of Surgeons those whom the *Lancet* had called 'surgeons in general practice', this would still have left very many apothecaries in general practice, as well as a substantial number of Scottish-educated physicians in general practice, without any representation.

The deputation from the National Association subsequently had several interviews with the law officers of the Crown for the purpose of framing a charter for a new College of General Practitioners and, in April 1845, the heads of a charter were sent to the Home Secretary. By the time Graham's Bill received its second reading towards the end of April, it was clear that the National Association had managed to win the support of the Home Secretary. In the Commons debate, Wakley asked for confirmation of a report that Graham now considered it 'impossible that the general practitioners should be enfranchised in the College of Surgeons'; Graham replied that he would not say that the door was 'absolutely closed' in that direction, but that 'his fears against, greatly exceeded his hopes . . . of, any adjustment being at all possible'.[15]

Early in May, the Home Secretary asked the House to recommit the Bill which, by this time, had undergone some fundamental changes in order to meet the expressed wishes of the National Association, by this time clearly established as the major organisation representing general practitioners. Graham told the Commons that he viewed 'the differences which unfortunately exist between the general practitioners of England and Wales and the College of Surgeons' as 'irreconcilable', and that as a consequence he was persuaded it was necessary to incorporate the general practitioners in a separate college.[16] Accordingly, the Bill now proposed the establishment of a Royal College of General Practitioners in Medicine, Surgery and Midwifery, with the Council of the College having the right to nominate two general practitioners to the proposed Council of Health. All general practitioners would, in future, be examined by a joint board of the two older Royal Colleges, followed by a second examination at the Royal College of General Practitioners, and all general practitioners were to be required to become Fellows of the new College.[17]

Graham had opened his speech in the Commons by saying, 'if I could have anticipated the extensive difficulties of this subject, I should not probably have presumed to interfere with it'; and he concluded by saying that if his present Bill were to fail, 'I confess I shall absolutely despair.'[18] In making this comment, the Home Secretary was by no means exaggerating the difficulties involved in legislating for what was a deeply divided profession. Perhaps not surprisingly, Graham's revised Bill did not meet with the approval of the Royal Colleges. It came in for equally vigorous criticism from what was by now a minority of general practitioners who still felt that the solution to their problems lay in a democratisation of the College of Surgeons, and that any new college would be of a markedly inferior status. Somewhat ironically, in view of his earlier involvement with the abortive attempt to establish the London College of Medicine, it was Thomas Wakley who was the most prominent spokesman in Parliament for this group of practitioners. Wakley told Graham that under the terms of his revised Bill, the general practitioners would be 'thrust out of their own institution, for the purpose of exercising a miserable privilege elsewhere';[19] whilst the *Lancet* expressed the view that the general practitioners were finally to be freed from the shackles of 'Rhubarb Hall' (the Apothecaries' Society) only to become the new tenants of the National Association's 'Gallipot Lodge'.[20]

The more serious objections, however, came from the Royal Colleges. On June 18, the College of Physicians sent a memorial to Graham in which they claimed that certain clauses of Graham's Bill were likely to have the effect of lowering 'the standard of the general and professional acquirements of physicians'.[21] In relation to the general practitioners' claims, the College of Physicians objected to the proposal to give general practitioners two representatives on the Council of Health, whilst the College of Physicians also felt it was not proper that 'persons who have undergone a previous examination by physicians and surgeons, should be examined, subsequently, in medicine and surgery, by general practitioners' who clearly constituted, in the eyes of the College, an inferior body. The College of Surgeons also objected to Graham's Bill — in particular, the proposal to give the College of General Practitioners the right to examine in surgery.[22] Graham further amended his Bill in an attempt to meet the objections of the Royal Colleges, and the amended Bill was recommitted on 28 July.[23] By this time, however, it was too late in the Parliamentary session to proceed any further, and the Bill was dropped.

Although Graham declined to introduce a further Bill in the following session of Parliament, the campaign to establish a separate College of General Practitioners continued. Towards the end of 1847, the two Royal Colleges, together with the Society of Apothecaries, began to hold a series of meetings in an attempt to work out a coordinated response to the widespread demands within the profession for reform. In December 1847, the three corporations sent a letter to Sir George Grey, who had by this time replaced Graham as Home Secretary, and in his reply Grey said that it was important 'that the interests of the general practitioners should be considered' and he suggested that some representatives of the general practitioners should be included in the conference.[24] Accordingly, three representatives from the National Institute of Medicine, Surgery and Midwifery — a body which appears to have been a sub-group of the National Association of General Practitioners formed to advance the aims of the parent Association — were invited to join the conference.

Perhaps rather surprisingly, it appeared as though, within two months, representatives of all four organisations had reached agreement on a plan of reform, for in February 1848 the heads of the four delegations signed a document of 'Principles' on which a new Reform Bill might be based.[25] The 'Principles' proposed the establishment of a central Council responsible for the general control of medical education and practice, with one of the Principal Secretaries of State acting as president; the remaining twelve Council members were to be nominated by the crown. Most importantly, however, the statement argued for the establishment of a Royal College of General Practitioners of England. It was agreed that, in future, all general practitioners should be examined by both the Royal College of Surgeons and the proposed Royal College of General Practitioners. However, membership of the Royal College of Surgeons would no longer constitute, on its own, a qualification to practise; members of the College of Surgeons would, in future, only be entitled to be registered after they had also passed the examinations of the College of General Practitioners. The document which had been agreed at the conference thus clearly recognised the principle that in future all general practitioners should be required to undergo an examination in all branches of practice. The representatives of the National Institute had, it seemed, managed to persuade the medical corporations to accept a slightly modified version of the plan which had first been adopted by the National Association of General Practitioners in 1845.

Both the statement of 'Principles' and the draft charter for the proposed Royal College of General Practitioners were examined by a Select Committee in 1848. However, in the course of this examination, it quickly became clear that any agreement which had been reached at the conference was more apparent than real; there was continuing disagreement over whether the College of Surgeons would allow the College of General Practitioners to examine in surgery. Speaking on behalf of the National Institute, James Bird said that the Royal College of General Practitioners would 'take power to examine in all branches of medical and surgical knowledge'.[26] Bird was quite insistent on this point: 'It was most clearly explained at the conference that the examination before the College of General Practitioners would be in medicine, surgery and midwifery, or any other department of medical science that the council should think fit to order'[27] whilst later he added that the College would have 'the unfettered right to examine in medicine and in surgery'.[28] He was aware of the fact that the College of Surgeons had formerly objected to the College of General Practitioners holding its own examination in surgery but that objection was now 'completely cancelled'.[29]

However, when Benjamin Travers gave evidence on behalf of the Council of the College of Surgeons, he indicated quite unambiguously that the College continued to regard surgery as a distinct branch of practice, one which constituted the exclusive province of the College of Surgeons. Asked whether the proposed College of General Practitioners would have the right to examine in surgery, Travers replied, 'No, certainly not; decidedly not; it will be a *sine qua non* with us that they do not examine in surgery.'[30] If the new college were to examine in surgery, 'it would be rendering neutral, or at least superseding our vocation'; it would be 'going out of their province, and would be decidely invading ours'.[31] As we have seen, the idea that the College of Surgeons had its own particular 'province' and that the College should confine itself exclusively to that 'province', had traditionally been at the very heart of College policy, and the College was clearly unwilling to give up its exclusive jurisdiction in relation to surgery in favour of a college of mere general practitioners. The College of Surgeons, it seems, was prepared to allow the proposed College of General Practitioners to do nothing more than to take over the examining function, and presumably also the humble status of the Apothecaries' Society which, under the terms of the 'Principles' agreed at the conference, would lose its function of examining in medicine and pharmacy. Thus Travers said that the Council of the College of Surgeons 'understood, of course, that a member of the New College would be equivalent to a member of the Apothecaries Society, and it is upon that basis that we have hitherto legislated'.[32] The *Lancet*'s fears in relation to the new college were not, it seems, unfounded, for the College of Surgeons clearly intended that any College of General Practitioners should be nothing more than a 'Gallipot Lodge'.

Although discussions on the formation of a College of General Practitioners continued until early in 1850, the College of Surgeons continued to insist that it alone had the right to examine in surgery. Thus, at a meeting held on 16 March 1849, the Council of the College of Surgeons stated that it 'objects in the strongest possible manner to any authority for examinations in Surgery being granted to the Society of Gentlemen claiming incorporation as the National Institute of General Practitioners'.[33] Shortly afterwards the discussions between the medical corporations and the National Institute broke down without any agreement being reached;[34] after more than five years of intensive political activity, the plan to establish a separate College of General Practitioners was finally abandoned in the face of continual opposition from the College of Surgeons. Having refused for more than twenty years to enfranchise the 'surgeons in general practice' within the College of Surgeons, the Council of the College had now effectively blocked the alternative proposal for the establishment of a separate College of General Practitioners.

At this point, it may be appropriate to recap briefly on some of the major aspects of the general practitioners' campaign from the 1820s, and to indicate some of the recurrent issues which underlay the campaign throughout this period. The specific nature of the general practitioners' demands changed from time to time as different organisations assumed the leadership of the general practitioners' movement, but it is nevertheless possible to identify at least two general issues which tended to recur, in one form or another, in virtually all the different phases of the general practitioners' campaign. The first of these issues related to the exclusion of general practitioners from any participation in the affairs of the ruling bodies within the profession, and one of the most persistent demands of the general practitioners throughout this period was for some form of political representation which would allow them to play a part in regulating the affairs of the profession. In the 1820s, the members of the College of Surgeons had demanded a fundamental reform of the structure of the College, with the officers of the College being elected annually by the whole membership in order that each member 'may have a voice in the election of those persons who are to regulate the proceedings of the College'.[35] Following the failure of this early reform plan, there were a number of different plans to establish new institutions which would have the power of examining and licensing practitioners and would allow the general practitioners to participate effectively in their government; in both the London College of Medicine and in the British Medical Association's proposed Faculty of Medicine, for example, the governing Council or Senate was to be democratically elected by all those who held a licence from these institutions. Similarly in the 1840s, much of the support for the National Association's plan for the establishment of a separate Royal College of General Practitioners arose from the exclusion of general practitioners from all political representation within the existing medical corporations and their minimal prospects of ever being enfranchised.

There was one other form which political representation

for general practitioners could take, only briefly touched upon so far. It will be recalled that one of the grounds on which the National Association of General Practitioners had objected to Sir James Graham's original Bill of August 1844 was that the Bill made no provision for general practitioners to be represented on the proposed Council of Health. In Graham's revised Bill of May 1845, however, it was proposed to give general practitioners two representatives on this Council. Although the College of Physicians successfully objected to this proposal, the idea that general practitioners should be represented on any proposed central Council was to be revived in the 1850s, and was to remain as one of the general practitioners' major objectives.

Thus although the specific demands which were made by the general practitioners changed from time to time, it is clear that underlying all those different demands from the 1820s onwards was one fundamental principle, namely that any system of medical reform must ensure some form of political enfranchisement for general practitioners within the governing bodies of the profession, in order that the interests of those who constituted the great majority within the profession could be properly represented. The continued exclusion of general practitioners from any participation in regulating the affairs of the profession was one of the most deeply felt grievances on the part of general practitioners, and the demand for political representation within the profession's governing institutions was one of their most basic and persistent demands.

The second, related, issue concerned the fact that general practitioners had special educational needs which were not being met by the existing medical corporations. As we have seen, the medical corporations continued to reflect the traditional tripartite division of the profession into physicians, surgeons and apothecaries, with an equally rigid division between the three major branches of practice. The general practitioner was not a physician, nor a surgeon, nor an apothecary, for his professional practice was based on the integration of all those branches of practice. Indeed, it was precisely because the general practitioners integrated all branches of practice that they were rejected by the medical corporations, and denied any representation within them. None of the medical corporations was willing to provide an appropriate examination and licence for general practice, or even to recognise the importance of general practice, for each was concerned only with the particular branch of practice for which it was responsible, with none of them taking any clear responsibility for the teaching and examining of midwifery. For this reason it was important, from the perspective of general practitioners, that any new institutions which were established should not perpetuate this increasingly outdated tripartite structure but that, on the contrary, they should seek to break down the traditional divisions within the profession and that, above all, proper provision should be made for the education and examination of those who acted as general practitioners. Thus within the proposed London College of Medicine in the early 1830s, the intention was to 'cast aside the absurd distinctions which now exist in the profession'.[36] The examinations of the College were to integrate all branches of medicine, surgery and midwifery, and all practitioners who were licensed by the College — even those who intended to specialise in a single branch of practice — would first be required to undergo a comprehensive examination in all branches of practice for the security of the public. The British Medical Association similarly aimed to break down those 'most unnatural divisions and degrading distinctions'[37] which were institutionalised in the tripartite structure; within the Association's proposed Faculty of Medicine, all branches of the profession were to be integrated and all those who were licensed by the Faculty were to be free to practise in all branches of the profession. Finally, as we have seen, it was intended that the proposed Royal College of General Practitioners should take power to examine all future candidates 'not in medicine alone, not in surgery alone, not in midwifery alone, or pharmacy alone, but in all those branches that are essential to constitute an efficient general practitioner'.[38] Thus a second major theme of the general practitioners' campaign may be said to have been their rejection of the traditional separation between the different branches of the profession and, in particular, their demand that proper provision should be made for the education and examination of general practitioners in all branches of practice.

Whilst these two issues were present in the general practitioners' campaign almost from the beginning, a third issue, relating to the establishment of a medical register, came into particular prominence from the late 1840s and proved to be a further focus of disagreement between the general practitioners and the Royal Colleges. It is important to note, however, that this disagreement did not centre on the desirability of registration as such, for the necessity for some form of registration had been accepted by all sections of the profession and had been a feature of every Bill introduced into Parliament from 1840 onwards. Thus whilst it was the general practitioners who were particularly vehement in their demands for a register of qualified practitioners, since they felt this would give them some protection against the competition of unqualified practitioners, even the conservative Royal Colleges were not opposed to the principle of registration. In his evidence to the 1847 Select Committee on Medical Registration, for example, the president of the College of Physicians, J A Paris, stated that the College had no objection to a register;[39] whilst the College registrar, Francis Hawkins, went considerably further, and expressed the view that it was 'very desirable that the medical profession should be registered in a manner better than it is now'.[40] For the College of Surgeons, the president, William Lawrence, saw no objection to 'a registration of medical practitioners that should set forth the qualifications under which they practise',[41] whilst Sir Benjamin Brodie, a member of the Council of the College and a former president, also felt that a system of registration of all qualified practitioners 'would be a very good thing; it would be popular with the profession, and rather useful for the public'.[42]

There was, therefore, little serious disagreement within the profession on the desirability of registration. There was major disagreement over the precise form which the registration should take. As part of their attempt to break down the traditional divisions within the profession, the general practitioners wanted a single register which would simply list in alphabetical order all qualified practitioners and give all registered practitioners a similar legal status, with the legal right to perform the complete range of medical and surgical tasks. The Royal Colleges, on the other hand, whilst not being opposed to the principle of registration, insisted that there should be not one common register for all practitioners, but rather three separate registers, one for physicians, one for surgeons, and one for apothecaries; in this way, the three traditional 'orders' of the profession, each with its own exclusive, legally defined sphere of practice, would be maintained.

The issues involved in this debate were defined particularly clearly as the result of the introduction of a new medical reform Bill — the seventh since 1840 — by Thomas Wakley in April 1847. Wakley's Bill made provision for all qualified practitioners, whatever their former legal status, to be listed in a common register, with every registered practitioner enjoying similar legal rights — including the right to recover charges for advice, visits and attendance, the right of exemption from service on juries and inquests, and the right to practise medicine 'throughout that part of the United Kingdom for which his certificate was issued', that is to say, England and Wales, Scotland, or Ireland. Equally importantly, however, Wakley's Bill also included an interpretation clause which stipulated that 'the words "Medicine" and "medical", when used in this Act, shall also mean and include the words "Physic", "Surgery", and "surgical"'.[43] The provision for registration contained in Wakley's Bill, together with this interpretation clause, would thus have effectively undermined the tripartite structure of 'orders' within the profession.

In view of this fact, it is not surprising that the College of Physicians petitioned against Wakley's Bill.[44] The Council of the College of Surgeons similarly decided, at an extraordinary meeting held on 3 May 1847, to oppose Wakley's Bill, and the president and vice-presidents were instructed to communicate with the Secretary of State on the subject of the Bill.[45] At the Council meeting on 10 June, it was reported that the president and vice-presidents had petitioned the Commons against Wakley's Bill which, they argued, would have the effect of 'confounding the existing distinctions in the Profession, and reducing all its Members to one level'.[46]

Although Wakley subsequently withdrew his Bill, he did so only after successfully moving for the establishment of a Select Committee to inquire into the registration of medical practitioners. In their evidence before that Committee, the Royal Colleges made their position quite clear. Speaking on behalf of the College of Physicians, the president of the College held that the effect of Wakley's Bill, which at that stage had not yet been withdrawn, would be to create one class of medical practitioner. He argued that 'the highest grade would cease to exist', with the result that medicine would no longer be a learned profession.[47] Although not opposed to registration as such, he held that 'medical men should be registered in classes or grades'.[48] The registrar of the College of Physicians, Francis Hawkins, similarly held that 'if the registration were to be formed upon the principle of their [the three "orders" of the profession] being placed together, it would tend to destroy those distinctions which have been found to be beneficial to the whole profession, and also to the public.'[49] The effect of Wakley's Bill, he argued, would be to 'throw all the orders of the profession into one class . . . I think the attainments of those who have hitherto been the most highly educated in the medical profession would undoubtedly be lowered.'[50] Like the president of the College, the registrar argued that 'registration ought to be effected in grades' and he went on to suggest that 'such registration in classes might very simply be effected by means of the existing corporate bodies. The College of Physicians might register all physicians, the College of Surgeons might register all surgeons, and the Society of Apothecaries might register all apothecaries.'[51]

Wakley's Bill was attacked in similar terms by other representatives of the College of Physicians. Thus Henry Holland held that the Bill was 'pernicious'; it was, he argued 'exceedingly important for the profession and the public that there should be grades in the profession, and that any measure that might tend to abolish those grades, or even to weaken their influence, would be as injurious to the public as to the profession'.[52] The physicians' concern to maintain a distinct legal status which would clearly separate them from the 'lower orders' of the profession was, perhaps, most clearly expressed by the president of the College in relation to something which, to the modern reader, might seem a trivial change in the legal status of the physician but which to the College was clearly of considerable importance. For a number of years, both surgeons and apothecaries had had the legal right to sue a patient for recovery of charges. Physicians, as befitted gentlemen, were legally considered as attending patients for an honorarium and, as such, they were unable to maintain an action for fees; in this way, the professional activities of the physician were defined as lying outside of the context of normal commercial or market transactions. Wakley's Bill, however, proposed to give all registered practitioners similar legal rights, including the right of recovering payment of charges for their attendance. The College of Physicians was, as ever, alert to any threat to its exclusive status, even from such a minor change in the law. 'We object to that very much', said their President, 'we consider that the physician would under those clauses be converted into a tradesman; we should feel that we had lost caste by allowing those clauses to pass.'[53]

Like the College of Physicians, the College of Surgeons also objected to any form of registration which did not differentiate between the different 'grades' within the profession. Thus William Lawrence, president of the College of Surgeons, criticised 'those levelling principles of equality which are found to be injurious wherever they exist in practice',[54] and he went on to argue that 'If you have all on one level, it must be by depressing those who are higher to the level of those who are lower in public opinion and confidence.'[55] Lawrence considered that registration in classes or grades would be 'the only kind of registration which would give the public proper information'.[56] Sir Benjamin Brodie similarly held that the effect of Wakley's Bill would be 'to confound all grades of the profession together', a process which he held to be 'not at all desirable'.[57] George James Guthrie, a Councillor and former president of the College of Surgeons, did not object to a register of qualified practitioners, but held that 'they should be kept distinct as to their being physicians or surgeons, or surgeon-apothecaries.'[58] Using a particularly appropriate medical analogy, he went on to argue that 'a certificate should say the individual is qualified to practise as a surgeon or as a physician, or a general practitioner as the case may be; but it does not do so, and that is what the Colleges have objected to, as pounding us all up in the same mortar, in fact.'[59]

In relation to the question of medical registration, therefore, the crucial question was not whether there should be a register of qualified practitioners, for by this time all sections of the profession had accepted the need for some form of registration which would enable the public to differentiate between those practitioners who were qualified and those who were not. Rather, the central question was whether the three 'grades' of the profession should be registered separately, thus maintaining a separate legal status for physicians, for surgeons, and for apothecaries, or whether, as Guthrie had put it, all practitioners should be 'pounded up in the same mortar' in a common register.

In summary, therefore, we may say that the general practitioners' campaign for reform was characterised by two longstanding demands which were present almost from the very beginning of their campaign, whilst a third issue, which further divided the general practitioners and the Royal Colleges, came into prominence from the late 1840s. These two longstanding demands of the general practitioners were, firstly, that any programme of reform must recognise the existence of general practitioners by giving them some form of political representation within the profession and, secondly, that any proposals for reform must make adequate provision for the education and examination of general practitioners in all branches of practice; the third issue related to the disagreement between the general practitioners and the Royal Colleges as to the precise form which the registration of medical practitioners should take. Bearing these three major issues in mind, in the next chapter we shall examine in some detail the culmination of more than thirty years' agitation for reform — the Medical Act of 1858 — and we shall be concerned, in particular, to examine the extent to which the Royal Colleges on the one hand, and the general practitioners on the other, were successful in shaping the

Act in accordance with their own interests. To what extent, then, did the 1858 Act meet these three basic demands of the general practitioners in relation to political representation, education and registration?

6.

The 1858 Medical Act:
A Triumph for the Reformers?

THE Medical Act of 1858 is generally regarded as a major legislative landmark — perhaps the major legislative landmark — in the development of the medical profession, for in establishing the General Medical Council and in requiring the Council to maintain a register of all qualified practitioners the Act established an important part of the institutional framework of the modern medical profession in Britain. Clearly, therefore, some understanding of the processes leading up to the passage of the Act, and of the consequences of the Act, is important for a broader understanding of the development of the medical profession as we know it today. In this chapter, we shall be concerned with an analysis of the processes leading up to the 1858 Act and of the part played by the Royal Colleges and the general practitioners' organisations in shaping the Act, whilst, in the next chapter, we shall examine some of the major consequences of the Act for the subsequent development of the profession.

As we have noted, the first Medical Reform Bill had been introduced into the House of Commons in August 1840; throughout the 1840s other reform Bills were introduced at intermittent intervals. By the mid-1850s, it was clear that the medical reform movement within Parliament was growing in strength; further Bills were introduced in 1854 and 1855, whilst in the early part of 1856, two very different Bills were introduced into the Commons and were referred to a Select Committee, which subsequently devised and reported a Bill of its own. This flurry of Parliamentary activity clearly worried the Royal Colleges in London, for in the summer of 1856 they formed a semi-formal but confidential alliance which held regular meetings, and which played a major part in shaping and modifying subsequent Bills, including that which eventually became the 1858 Medical Act. In order to understand the part played by the Royal Colleges in shaping the 1858 Act, therefore, it is necessary to examine the development of this alliance, and the events which gave rise to it.

In February 1856, T E Headlam introduced into the Commons a Bill 'To alter and amend the Laws regulating the Medical Profession'; two months later a second Bill 'for Regulating and Improving the Medical Profession' was introduced by Lord Elcho. The precise details of these two Bills need not concern us here, but it is important to note that Headlam's Bill was considerably more sympathetic to the claims of the Royal Colleges than was that of Lord Elcho. Thus Headlam's Bill proposed not only the registration of practitioners in classes or 'grades', but also a significant extension of the powers of the Royal Colleges in relation to the examination and licensing of practitioners, for in future all practitioners were to be required to be examined by and to be enrolled in the appropriate Royal College. In marked contrast, the Bill of Lord Elcho proposed the common registration of all practitioners and in its provisions relating to the examination and licensing of candidates sought to protect the position of the universities — particularly the Scottish universities — rather than that of the Royal Colleges.[1]

The College of Physicians petitioned in favour of Headlam's Bill, subject to certain minor amendments and, in April 1856, the president and registrar of the College sent a memorandum to the Select Committee to which both Bills had been referred. In this memorandum, they indicated their support for the general principles of Headlam's Bill and their opposition to Elcho's Bill which, they claimed, proposed to grant 'perfect equality to all licences and diplomas', a principle which the College found unacceptable.[2] When the Select Committee reported, however, they recommended a Bill which was unlike either Headlam's or Elcho's.[3]

It was at this stage that the Royal Colleges, clearly expecting further legislation to be introduced in the next session of Parliament, began to form themselves into a well-organised pressure group. Rather curiously, the Annals of the College of Physicians contain relatively little information about the formation of this alliance between the Royal Colleges, but the minutes of the Council of the Royal College of Surgeons are rather more helpful and, from this information, it is possible to piece together the part played by both Royal Colleges in the development of this alliance.

At a meeting of the Council of the College of Surgeons held on 7 August 1856, the president of the College, Benjamin Travers, reported that he and six other prominent members of Council, 'having taken into consideration what in their opinion should form the basis of a Medical Bill', had held two meetings with the president, the registrar and four other representatives of the Royal College of Physicians. At these meetings there had been 'general concurrence with certain Elementary Propositions or Principles on which such Bill might be founded'. The Council of the College of Surgeons agreed that the president and the six other members of Council who had been involved in these meetings should constitute a committee with authority to confer with other interested parties.[4]

At the next meeting of the College Council, on 16 October, the president reported that three further conferences had taken place with representatives of the College of Physicians and that, at two of these meetings, a deputation from the Society of Apothecaries had also attended. It had been decided that, in an attempt to win support for the Bill being drawn up by the London corporations, a larger conference should be held at the end of October, and that representatives should be invited from all the Royal Colleges in England, Scotland and Ireland, from the London Society of Apothecaries, and from the Glasgow Faculty of Physicians and Surgeons.[5]

This conference was duly held at the Royal College of Surgeons in London on 21, 23 and 24 October 1856, with the president of the College in the chair. The minutes of the conference indicate that, on the opening day, proposals for a Medical Bill — presumably drawn up by the London corporations at their earlier meetings — were circulated, and that the whole of the conference was taken up with a consideration of this Bill. It was agreed that the observations of the various delegations should be marked 'confidential', and that 'the proceedings of these Conferences be considered strictly confidential'.[6] The London colleges appear to have been successful in persuading the other corporations to accept their proposals, subject to what seem to be a few minor amendments, and at a special meeting of the Council of the College of Surgeons, held on 30 October, the Council was informed that proposals for a Medical Bill had been discussed, and 'the heads of a Bill settled'.[7] Following this conference, the Scottish and Irish delegates departed, but further meetings took place between the two London Royal Colleges and the Society of Apothecaries, and on 11 December, the President of the College of Surgeons was able to report to his Council that 'the subject of the Bill was, in his opinion, progressing favourably'.[8]

With the principles of the Bill apparently agreed, the London corporations now needed to find a sympathetic MP prepared to introduce their Bill into the Commons. Headlam's Bill of February 1856, it will be recalled, had been broadly sympathetic to the claims of the Royal Colleges and, indeed, a number of clauses in Headlam's Bill had been taken directly and incorporated into the Bill drawn up by the Royal Colleges.[9] Headlam was accordingly approached, and agreed to introduce the Bill.

One final obstacle remained to be overcome before the Colleges' own Bill could be introduced into the Commons. Although no government Bill on this subject had been introduced since Sir James Graham's last Bill of 1845 — all subsequent Bills being private members' Bills — the Royal Colleges appear to have been worried that, on this occasion, the government might introduce its own Bill, perhaps based on the recommendations of the Select Committee of the previous session; for the chairman of the Select Committee had been W F Cowper, and Cowper had not only taken a keen interest in the subject but, as president of the Board of Health, he was also a member of the government. Accordingly, the heads of the three London corporations made representations to the Prime Minister, Lord Palmerston, in which they informed him that they proposed introducing a Bill of their own and asked that, in the light of this information, the government refrain from bringing in any Bill until the Bill projected by the corporations had been prepared and considered.[10]

It is not known whether, at this stage, Cowper was thinking of bringing in a Bill,[11] but on 27 January 1857, John
Simon, the Medical Officer to the General Board of Health,
wrote on behalf of Cowper to the registrar of the College of
Physicians, requesting a copy of the corporations' Bill at
the earliest opportunity, for Cowper apparently felt that he
'must be ready at the opening of Parliament to state his
intentions on the subject'.[12] No government Bill was subsequently brought forward, though one cannot, of course,
be certain whether this was a result of the representations
made by the London corporations or of some other considerations. In any event, the outcome was that desired by the
London corporations, for the absence of a government Bill,
for whatever reason, left the field clear for the introduction
of the corporations' own Bill.

On 16 February 1857, the Council of the College of
Surgeons held a special meeting at which the Draft Medical
Bill was considered and approved. Early in May, shortly
before the Bill was to be introduced into the Commons, a
further meeting was held between Headlam and representatives of the two Royal Colleges and the Society of
Apothecaries.[13]

The Bill which had been drawn up by the London corporations was given its first reading in the Commons on 13 May
1857 and, not surprisingly, the Bill itself clearly reflected
the interests of those who had drafted it. In particular, the
Royal College of Physicians, as the most prestigious of all
the medical corporations, appears to have played a dominant
part in the drafting of the Bill, for the interests of the College
were meticulously protected in every detail. The Bill
proposed to establish a governing Council for the profession,
to be composed of seventeen persons chosen by the corporations and universities in Britain, together with six persons
nominated by the crown. Separate registers were to be kept
for physicians and for surgeons and, significantly, the term
'physician' was defined in a very restrictive manner in order
to ensure that only those who practised as physicians in the
sense in which the College understood the term could be
so registered. Thus clause fifteen of the Bill stated that
in 'The Physicians Register', as it was to be called, were to

be listed the names of all those who were licensed to practise as physicians, 'and not engaged in the Art and Mystery of an Apothecary, or in the Practice of Pharmacy'.[14] The College was clearly being very careful to ensure that the status of the physician would not be diluted in any way.

It will be recalled that there was another aspect of the status of the physician about which the College of Physicians was particularly sensitive, relating to the proposal to give physicians the legal right to recover charges for attendance and advice. When this proposal had been included in the 1847 Bill of Warburton and Wakley, the College had objected strongly, saying 'the physician would under those clauses be converted into a tradesman'.[15] Nine years later, the president and registrar of the College reiterated this point in the memorandum which they submitted to Cowper and the other members of the 1856 Select Committee: the College was 'anxious that physicians should not have their social position lowered by having the power given to them of recovering charges'.[16] Given the prominent part played by the College of Physicians in drawing up the Bill which was introduced by Headlam, it is not surprising that the Bill proposed to leave the position of physicians unchanged in this respect; although it was proposed to give registered practitioners in general the right to recover charges, it was stated specifically that this right did not extend to those who were registered as physicians. The traditionally distinct and privileged legal status of the physicians as a separate 'order' within the profession was, under this Bill, to be preserved in all respects.

In addition, the powers of the College in relation to the examination and licensing of practitioners were to be considerably extended, for the Bill stipulated that, in future, anyone wishing to be registered as a physician would be required to have passed the examination of, and to have been enrolled as a member in, the appropriate Royal College of Physicians in England, Scotland or Ireland.[17] Thus whilst those persons who had obtained a university degree in medicine prior to the passage of the Bill could register on the strength of that qualification, a university degree obtained after the passage of the Bill would not, on its own, entitle anyone to be registered until that person had also been examined by, and enrolled in, the appropriate Royal College of Physicians. This provision would, of course, have greatly strengthened the powers of the Royal Colleges, and simultaneously weakened those of the universities, particularly the Scottish universities which, by this time, were producing large numbers of well qualified graduates. As we shall see shortly, there were other parts of the Bill which would have had the effect of further centralising control of medical education and licensing in the hands of the Royal Colleges, and particularly in the hands of the Colleges of Physicians in England, Scotland and Ireland.

Perhaps rather surprisingly, it seems that in the negotiations involved in the drafting of the Bill, the Royal College of Surgeons had agreed that 'The Surgeons Register' should contain the names of both surgeons and apothecaries, and that those who wished to register as surgeons would, in future, be required to pass three separate examinations, in medicine, surgery and midwifery. This provision was presumably designed as a concession to the demands of the general practitioners, but the particular institutional arrangements which were proposed in the Bill for carrying this provision into effect would have ensured that professional education became even more highly centralised under the control of the Royal Colleges, for the examinations were to be conducted by the medical corporations with no participation from the universities.[18] This provision would have ensured the continued dominance of the Royal College of Surgeons in relation to the practice of surgery, for it was stipulated that in England the examination in surgery was to be conducted exclusively by the College of Surgeons, and that all surgeons were to be required to pass the examination of, and to be enrolled in, the Royal College of Surgeons in London.[19] However, the greatest beneficiary of the new examination arrangements proposed in the Bill would undoubtedly have been the Royal College of Physicians, for the College was to be involved in the examinations in both medicine and midwifery which were to be obligatory for all those who wished to register as surgeons.[20] Thus the Bill not only proposed to maintain the class of physicians as a distinct 'order' within the profession and to give the College of Physicians a monopoly in relation to the licensing of physicians, but it also proposed that the College should be involved in the examination of *every single person* who wished to practise medicine, whether as a physician or as a surgeon. This imperialistic strategy on the part of the College of Physicians, had it succeeded, would have given the College far greater powers in relation to the entire profession than those ever enjoyed by any single corporation.

Finally, the Bill stipulated that any physician or surgeon who moved from one part of the United Kingdom to another would have to enrol as a Member or Licentiate in the appropriate College of Physicians or Surgeons for that part of the Kingdom to which he had moved, and any practitioner not so enrolling within three months was to be struck off the register.[21] Thus any practitioner — no matter how well qualified — following the well-worn path of medical migration from Scotland to England, would have been required to enrol in either the Royal College of Physicians or the Royal College of Surgeons in London. The control of medical practice in England by the two London colleges would have been almost total.

In the debate on the first reading of the corporations' Bill, two contributions were, perhaps, of special significance. Cowper, the president of the Board of Health, pointed out that the Select Committee of the previous year had, amongst other things, embraced the principle 'of fixing a minimum standard, without having attained to which no one could obtain a licence to practise. In order to come up to that standard it was necessary that a surgeon should know something of medicine, and that a physician should be in some degree acquainted with surgery.'[22] This basic principle was not, of course, met by the corporations' Bill, for it proposed to retain a class of 'pure' physicians.

The second significant intervention came from Lord Elcho, who suggested that 'It was possible . . . that there might be a unanimous feeling among the medical corporations in favour of this Bill, without a corresponding unanimity among the great body of the profession.' Elcho indicated his intention to bring in an alternative Bill, which he duly did on 15 May, two days after the first reading of the Bill drawn up by the medical corporations. Very briefly, the major features of Elcho's new Bill were the establishment of a controlling Council for the profession, the members of which were to be nominated by the crown rather than by the medical corporations and universities, a system of common preliminary and professional examinations to be conducted by boards representing both the universities and the corporations, and a single register for all practitioners.[23] Such a Bill was, of course, unlikely to find favour with the London corporations.

The College of Physicians in London immediately petitioned the House of Commons in support of Headlam's Bill — which was, of course, the corporations' own Bill — and against Elcho's;[24] whilst the medical corporations also published a joint statement entitled 'Reasons, on behalf of the Medical Incorporations, in favour of Mr Headlam's Medical Bill, and against that of Lord Elcho'.[25] On 10 June 1857, the president of the College of Surgeons reported to the College Council that 'the several Corporations were still acting with the utmost unanimity', and that they had had a meeting with the Prime Minister in order to express their opposition to Elcho's Bill.[26]

Headlam's Bill came up for its second reading in the House of Commons on 1 July 1857 and met some severe criticism. Mr Crawford, who was a co-sponsor of the Bill introduced by Lord Elcho, said that Headlam's Bill 'betrayed a greater anxiety to consult the interests of the corporations than he thought the House would sanction', and he indicated that he did not feel disposed 'to continue these corporations in the possession of privileges which were no longer suited to the spirit of our times'. The Bill was, he said, 'in no way calculated to advance the interests of the medical profession, though it would increase the privileges of certain corporations'.[27] Mr Black similarly pointed out that the Bill 'gave such immense power to the corporations', whilst he also objected to the Bill on the grounds that there 'ought not to be any class distinctions in the medical profession'.[28] Lord Elcho objected to the proposal to give the corporations 'powers which they had not heretofore possessed', and pointed out that Headlam's Bill proposed 'not that they should have a fair share of power — to which he should not object — but that they should have a complete monopoly'.[29]

The Bill also came in for criticism from Cowper, who indicated that he found it difficult to justify the proposal to deprive the universities of the power of licensing practitioners, and to centralise this power in the hands of the Royal Colleges. He also objected to the proposal to maintain a class of 'pure' physicians, saying that Headlam's Bill 'exempted the College of Physicians from the necessity of having an examination in the practice of surgery: so that, after this Bill passed, the physician would still be a man who with haughty and fastidious contempt for a necessary branch of the art of healing, might ignore what the humblest surgeon was compelled to know'.[30] The Royal Colleges, however, were not without their supporters; a number of MPs spoke in favour of the maintenance of what one of them called 'professional aristocracies', and when the vote was taken, Headlam's Bill was given a second reading by 225 votes to 78, a very comfortable majority of 147. Elcho took this as an indication of support for Headlam's Bill rather than his own, and immediately announced his intention of withdrawing his own Bill.

Thus far, things had gone very much according to plan, at least as far as the Royal Colleges were concerned. It soon became clear, however, that Headlam's Bill was running aground on what was for private members' Bills a familiar problem, for that session of Parliament was moving towards a close and it was clear that, unless the government was prepared to take up Headlam's Bill, there would be insufficient time in that session of Parliament for the Bill to pass. Early in July 1857, Headlam wrote to the College of Surgeons saying that although his Bill had passed a second reading, there was 'no chance of forcing the bill through this session'. He had, it seems, already approached the Prime Minister for support, but Lord Palmerston had 'too much on his shoulders', and had declined to take up the Bill. As a result, Headlam informed the College that he was dropping the Bill.

The next significant development came on 11 December 1857, when Cowper announced his intention of bringing in a Bill in the near future to regulate the qualifications of medical practitioners. Cowper, it will be recalled, was particularly well informed about matters relating to the medical profession, for he had been president of the Board of Health since 1855 and had also chaired the Select Committee of 1856 which had examined the Bills of Headlam and Elcho. It is reasonable to suppose that Cowper's announcement would not have been welcome news for the Royal Colleges, for in the debate on the second reading of the Bill which had been drawn up by the corporations and introduced by Headlam, Cowper had clearly indicated that he had little sympathy with some of the major provisions of the Bill; indeed, Cowper had gone so far as to describe the corporations' Bill as 'an ill-advised attempt to patch up the defects of the existing system',[31] implying that he himself had something much more radical in mind. Before Cowper could introduce his Bill, there was a change of government, for in February 1858 Lord Palmerston's government was defeated on another issue — the Conspiracy to Murder Bill — and Lord Derby became Prime Minister. Cowper was, of course, now simply a private member, but he nevertheless went ahead with the introduction of his Bill, which received its first reading on 23 March 1858.

Once it had become clear that Cowper was still going ahead with his Bill, the London corporations arranged a hastily convened series of meetings in order to coordinate their activities. On 4 March 1858, the Charter and Conference Committee of the Royal College of Physicians passed two resolutions, the first of which asked that a meeting of the three London corporations 'should forthwith be convened', whilst the second expressed the opinion that 'no time should be lost in asking the support of Government for the Medical Bill of last Session, which was framed and promoted by the General Conference of the United Kingdom, and the principles of which obtained the sanction of a large majority in the House of Commons'.[32] The College, in other words, wanted to see the reintroduction of the Bill which had been drawn up by the corporations, and introduced by Headlam in 1857. The proposed meeting of the three London corporations was duly held on 10 March, and on 15 March, the Council of the College of Surgeons held a special meeting to receive a report on this conference.[33] The Council suggested that support should once again be sought from the Scottish and Irish corporations, and this proposal was accepted by the two other London corporations at a further meeting on 16 March.[34]

All this activity on the part of the London corporations immediately prior to the introduction of Cowper's Bill suggests that they may well have been anxious about what the Bill might contain, and for good reason. Although Cowper knew a great deal about the medical profession, there is little doubt that the Bill itself was largely drafted by John Simon, whom Cowper had appointed as Medical Officer to the Board of Health in 1855, and with whom he had a close working relationship. Simon's involvement in drafting the Bill was well known to contemporaries, and is confirmed by an office memorandum written by Simon in 1858.[35] Since this memorandum sets out very clearly the principles and objects of the Bill, it is worth studying in some detail.

Simon began the memorandum by suggesting that there were five areas in relation to which there was general agreement within the profession on the need for reform. These five areas were:

1. the necessity for a legal definition to be given to the term 'qualified medical practitioner';

2. the need for an authentic register to be kept;

3. it should be a misdemeanour for any person falsely to assume a title implying that person to be legally qualified;

4. provision for removal from the register of any person found guilty of disgraceful offences;

5. registered practitioners should be entitled to practise throughout the United Kingdom.

Whilst Simon was probably correct in pointing out that there was general agreement on the necessity for reform in relation to each of these areas, it is equally correct to point out that, particularly in relation to the first two areas, there was no general agreement on the shape which those reforms should take. Thus whilst there may have been agreement on the need for a legal definition for the term 'qualified medical practitioner', there was none amongst the different sections of the profession on what form that definition should take, just as there was no agreement on the precise form which an 'authentic register' should take. Significantly, in relation to both of these major issues which divided the profession, Simon came down firmly in favour of the kind of argument which had long been advanced by many general practitioners, and equally firmly against the position adopted by the Royal Colleges.

In relation to the legal definition to be given to the term 'qualified medical practitioner', Simon set out his position in some detail: 'if the "qualified medical practitioner" is to be in any special sense recognised at law, and in even the smallest degree protected and privileged against competition, ample security must be taken, as regards future admission to the profession, that the legally-qualified medical practitioner shall be a well-qualified medical practitioner.'[36] Simon's conception of what constituted a well-qualified medical practitioner was, however, very different from the view traditionally held by the Royal Colleges. He pointed out that 'corporations of physicians and surgeons may award distinctive titles of honour to persons of riper age who show eminent qualifications for one or the other branch of practice', but he went on to argue 'such distinctive titles ought not, it is held, to be given except as super-additions to the primary and general title which should mark every member of the medical profession'. For Simon, it was unacceptable that, in future, any practitioner should be able to register as a legally qualified practitioner on the strength of a single qualification in one branch of practice only; it was, he wrote, 'an insecure arrangement for the public ... that candidates should receive any legal recognition as medical practitioners, founded on their exclusive knowledge of one department of medicine'. This view was, of course, bound to bring Simon and Cowper into conflict with the Royal Colleges, and particularly with the Royal College of Physicians, which had always argued that the different areas of medicine should be seen as separate and distinct branches of practice which were best left to equally separate and distinct groups of practitioners. Simon, however, was in no doubt about what was required: 'If legal status is to be given to the medical practitioner, it ought to be on the basis that from all future candidates there will be expected, first of all, the knowledge which would render them ... competent for general practice.'[37] On this first major area of intra-professional disagreement, Simon thus came down firmly in favour of the integration of the different branches of practice, something for which many general practitioners had long been arguing.

It was, therefore, a fundamental intention of Simon in drafting the Bill that in future all practitioners should be required to undergo a thorough education and examination in all major areas of practice. Moreover, Simon also made it clear that, if an adequate system of education and examination in all branches of practice was to be developed, the existing licensing authorities could not be relied upon to make the necessary reforms. Like the general practitioners, he viewed the medical corporations with suspicion, whilst his opinion of most university medical schools was not, it seems, very much higher. Thus he argued that the existing system did not give adequate security to the public, and the task of providing that security could not be left to what he called the 'mutually independent actions of 21 irresponsible authorities'.[38]

The objective of ensuring that all future practitioners would be properly qualified – in the sense in which Simon and Cowper understood the term 'qualified practitioner' – was to be achieved in the Bill by the creation of a General Council of Medical Education and Registration, to be given wide-ranging powers in relation to the control of medical education and examinations. The powers of the Council were defined in clause four of the Bill, which stipulated that the Council was to assume responsibility for 'Defining the Qualifications and conditions in respect of general and professional Knowledge and Course of Study ... which shall entitle Persons ... to be registered'.[39] In order to ensure that all practitioners would in future be qualified in all major branches of practice, the Council was to be given powers to require any two or more examining bodies in any part of the United Kingdom to cooperate in conducting joint examinations and to establish or to provide for the establishment of examiners in any branch of practice in which the Council felt that the existing examinations were inadequate. These powers to control and to direct the examinations of the existing licensing bodies were, as we have noted, wide-ranging, but they were central to the major objective of the Bill stated in the opening words of the preamble: 'Whereas it is expedient that the Qualifications of Persons seeking to enter the Medical Profession should be tested and declared by competent authorities'. Since the existing licensing authorities could not relied upon to make the necessary reforms, the Council was to be the major instrument for effecting reforms in the education and examination system and, if the Council was to be able to do its job properly, it was essential that the powers of the Council should be 'more than nominal', as Simon put it in his office memorandum of 1858.[40] Clause four of the Bill, which gave the Council the required powers, was at the very heart of the Bill, not only for Simon and Cowper, but also for the British Medical Association which had by this time clearly emerged as the single most important organisation representing general practitioners.

In relation to the second major problem which divided the general practitioners and the Royal Colleges — the question of the precise form which registration should take — Simon came down once more on the side of the general practitioners. Thus Simon argued firmly against the principle of registration in classes or 'grades', saying that 'it would be a task of extraordinary difficulty under the present circumstances of the profession, to define each of the three classes in the strict language of legislation'.[41] The Bill accordingly made provision for all registered practitioners, whatever their former legal status, to be listed alphabetically in a single register. Moreover, the Bill also proposed to give all registered practitioners the right to recover charges in a court of law, thus raising for the College of Physicians the awful prospect that in law the activities of the physician might be seen in the same light as those of a common tradesman.

The third of the general practitioners' demands involved the claim for some form of political representation within the profession and, on this point, the intention behind the Bill of Simon and Cowper was not entirely clear. Whilst

Simon clearly felt obliged to make provision for the medical corporations and the universities to appoint representatives to the new Council, he was understandably anxious that the Council should not simply 'guard the vested interests of corporate institutions',[42] and that the Council should carry out properly the major functions which were to be assigned to it under the Bill. Accordingly, the Bill also provided for the appointment of six independent members of the Council, to be nominated by the crown. Clause five of the Bill expressly stated that these six persons were not to be members of Council or office bearers in any of the corporations, though it is not clear whether the intention was that these additional six persons should be appointed from amongst rank-and-file practitioners, from amongst groups such as medical teachers not holding office in any of the corporations, from amongst lay persons, or — perhaps most likely — from amongst a mixture of these groups.[43] Whatever the intention behind clause five may have been, it did not exclude general practitioners from being appointed to the Council, whilst it clearly excluded the possibility that additional representation could be given to the medical corporations.

In summarising the major provisions of the Bill of Simon and Cowper, we may say that in relation to two of the demands of the general practitioners — the demand for an integrated examination system embracing all branches of practice and for a single register — their demands were more or less met in full by the Bill; whilst in relation to their third demand — for political representation — the door was at least left open, even if only slightly so, for general practitioners to be appointed to the Council. At the very least, therefore, it is probably fair to say that the general practitioners had considerably more reason to be pleased with the Bill than did the Royal Colleges.

Given the nature of Cowper's Bill, it is not surprising that when the Bill was introduced, it was welcomed by those organisations and individuals which had been in the forefront of the campaign for medical reform. On 10 April 1858, the *Lancet* expressed its support for Cowper's Bill, saying that 'Everything now is culminating to the point of success.'[44] The only significant reservation which the *Lancet* had in relation to the Bill was that it did not contain a penalty clause for unqualified practice, something for which the *Lancet* had long argued, but which was never likely to obtain majority support within Parliament. The following week the *Lancet* published a detailed analysis of Cowper's Bill and reiterated its support for the Bill,[45] whilst on 24 April the *Lancet* called on all medical reformers — 'those who have fought the battle over and over again, as well as others who have more recently joined the ranks of the veterans in the cause' — to unite and make 'one more grand effort' to promote the success of Cowper's Bill.[46]

The British Medical Association, representing the great majority of general practitioners, also welcomed the introduction of Cowper's Bill. At a meeting of the Association's Medical Reform Committee, held on 1 April, it was decided to ask Cowper to make a few minor amendments to the Bill, and to recommend the Bill with such alterations to the membership of the Association at large.[47] A further meeting of the Medical Reform Committee was held on 23 April, after which the Committee had a long interview with Cowper, who indicated his willingness to accept the alterations suggested by the Association, and to have the appropriate amendments made in the committee stage of the Bill. On behalf of the Medical Reform Committee, the chairman, Sir Charles Hastings, signed a petition to be presented to the Commons in favour of Cowper's Bill, and it was decided to ask all branches of the Association similarly to petition in favour of the Bill.[48] The *Lancet* described Cowper's acceptance of the alterations suggested by the Association as a 'graceful and important acquiescence in the wishes of the profession', and it said the duty of all sincere reformers was to support the Bill: 'If Mr. Cowper be properly supported there is now good reason to believe that his measure will be carried.'[49]

About three weeks later on 15 May, a large deputation from the British Medical Association saw Cowper once more, together with the new Home Secretary, Spencer Walpole, in order to reiterate their support for the Bill. Two points made by the BMA are of special significance. The first of these was made by Dr Budd and related to the proposed powers of the central Council: 'it would be desirable there should be a central council, which should not only fix the standard of education for medical practitioners, but that they should also have the power to enforce it; without that the powers of such a council would be useless.' The delegation clearly shared Simon's view that it was essential that the Council should be given adequate power, for Budd went on to say that 'they looked upon the point as the very essence of a measure calculated to benefit the profession and the public, and that they would rather not have the Bill at all if this power were withdrawn.'[50]

A second, related point was made by Dr Lankester, who pointed out that the College of Surgeons held an examination 'only applying to particular branches of the medical science; but what they contended for was, that every one taking the position of surgeon ought to have the same education as a physician; not merely to be enabled to understand the science of anatomy, but that he should have a thorough knowledge of all the branches of the healing art.'[51] In reply, Cowper mocked the traditional separation between the different branches of practice, apparently to the amusement of the deputation, and gave the Association the assurance that 'it was a principle of this Bill that for the future a physician should be versed in surgery as well as medicine, and *vice versa*'.[52] After many years of campaigning, the general practitioners could at last see the prospect of what a correspondent of the *Lancet* called 'an examining board which will act on the principle that medicine and surgery are one and indivisible'.[53]

The opponents of the Bill, however, had not been inactive; indeed we have noted that the Royal Colleges had already held a series of meetings, even before Cowper's Bill had been introduced. Following the first reading of the Bill, both Royal Colleges decided in April 1858 to petition against the Bill.[54] Whilst the Royal Colleges were inevitably opposed to the principle of common registration for all practitioners, they appear to have been even more anxious about the powers which it was proposed to give to the central Council. As we have seen, the Council was intended to be the principal instrument for effecting the necessary reforms within the profession and, in addition to compelling examining bodies to cooperate in conducting joint examinations, it was likely that the Council would also place other constraints on the independence of action of the Royal Colleges, the ruling bodies of which had never previously been responsible to anyone but themselves. In the petition drawn up by the College of Physicians, the College objected that it was proposed to give the Council 'not merely administrative power . . . but . . . power to make Orders and Regulations . . . relative to the construction of Examining Boards, the assignment of their privileges, and the discipline and government of the whole profession', and the petition made it clear that the College was opposed to the establishment of 'a Council possessed of powers so extensive'. The Royal Colleges, it should be pointed out, could not legitimately claim to be opposed to the principle of centralised control of medical education and examination, for it will be recalled that the Bill which they had themselves drawn up in 1856-7 had also involved a high degree of centralisation. In the case of the corporations' own Bill, however, that centralised control was to be vested in the hands of the Royal Colleges themselves, whereas under Cowper's Bill it was to be vested in an independent body. It is important to emphasise, however, that for both the BMA and the Royal Colleges, the powers which it was proposed to give to the new Council were at the very heart of the Bill; the major difference, of course, was that whilst the BMA deputation had insisted that the Council must have those powers, the Royal Colleges were utterly opposed to the establishment of a Council with such wide-ranging powers.

It is significant that at no time do the Royal Colleges appear to have had any direct contact with Cowper after his Bill had been introduced. Cowper's lack of sympathy with many of the basic policies of the Royal Colleges was, of course, well known from his comments in earlier Parliamentary debates, and it may well have been the case that the Royal Colleges decided there was little point in trying to persuade Cowper either to drop or to amend his Bill. Instead, the Royal Colleges appear to have decided on a two-pronged strategy which involved, on the one hand, ignoring Cowper and going direct to government ministers and, on the other hand, continuing to use Headlam as their major advocate on the floor of the House of Commons. We shall examine later the part played by Headlam but, for the moment, we shall concentrate on the more important link between the Royal Colleges and government ministers, in particular the new Home Secretary, Spencer Walpole.

As we have seen, both Royal Colleges decided in April 1858 to petition against Cowper's Bill, and by 17 April — a full month before the BMA saw the Home Secretary — a deputation from the College of Surgeons had already had an interview with Walpole.[55] This was followed ten days later by an interview with the Prime Minister, Lord Derby.[56] The original objective of the deputation appears to have been to try to persuade Walpole that the Government should reintroduce the corporations' Bill of the previous session, but in this they were unsuccessful. In the debate on the second reading of Cowper's Bill, Walpole indicated that the government saw this whole issue as a legislative nightmare; in explaining the government's unwillingness to bring in its own Bill, he pointed out that in the 1840s, even Sir James Graham 'with all his weight and authority in the House, and supported by one of the most powerful Governments which had been seen for years' had been unable to frame a measure acceptable to the conflicting parties.[57] If, however, the deputation was unsuccessful in trying to persuade Walpole to reintroduce the corporations' own Bill, there is good reason to believe that it was successful in persuading him that Cowper's Bill, at least in the form in which it had been introduced, should not be supported.

On 24 April, the *Lancet* reported that 'The Corporations have met, and a deputation from them has waited on the Home Secretary professedly to object to Mr Cowper's measure.'[58] The following week, the *Lancet* reported that the corporations had objected to the Council which Cowper's Bill proposed to establish, and went on to say that 'It is difficult to determine on what these grounds of objections rest, unless indeed upon a basis of unmitigated selfishness.'[59] The *Lancet* held that the objections of the Royal Colleges were 'not, indeed, very weighty — scarcely grave enough to merit any serious consideration', but it went on to warn its readers that 'they may still not be destitute of influence on the Government'.[60] That they were indeed not destitute of influence is clear from subsequent events.

Long before the BMA deputation saw the Home Secretary in May 1858, Walpole had already received a deputation from the College of Surgeons, which had clearly impressed upon the Home Secretary their objections to Cowper's Bill. It is significant, for example, that whilst Cowper and the BMA deputation appear to have been in complete agreement about the required legislative reforms, Walpole expressed doubts about two central aspects of the Bill. Thus he told the BMA deputation that objections had been raised to the principle of giving 'all the power to a central council sitting in London', whilst he also expressed the fear that Cowper's Bill did not keep up 'proper distinctions between the various classes of the medical profession'.[61] In making these comments Walpole was, of course, echoing the well-known objections of the Royal Colleges.

By the time Cowper's Bill came up for its second reading on 2 June, the situation within Parliament had once again become rather confused, for in the meantime Lord Elcho had introduced yet another Bill, whilst a third medical reform Bill had been introduced by Tom Duncombe, who had succeeded Wakley as the radical MP for Finsbury. Neither of these new Bills were acceptable to the Royal Colleges, who petitioned against both Bills.[62] This was not, of course, very surprising, for the Colleges had opposed both of Elcho's previous Bills, whilst the general flavour of Duncombe's Bill may be roughly gauged by its title: 'A Bill to define the rights of the members of the medical profession, and to protect the public from the abuses of medical corporations'.

The debate in the Commons on 2 June was a wide-ranging one, and involved a number of comparisons between what were held to be the advantages and disadvantages of each of the three Bills. Speaking about his own Bill, Cowper claimed that 'Upwards of a hundred petitions had been presented to the House from members of the medical profession in favour of the Bill', a fact which he claimed indicated that 'the great bulk of the profession, consisting of surgeons and apothecaries, approved of the Bill'.[63] Headlam, however, took this occasion to present to the Commons the petition against the Bill from the College of Surgeons.[64]

The major sponsors of the other two Bills, Elcho and Duncombe, also took part in the debate, but there is no doubt that the most significant contribution was that of the Home Secretary. After reviewing the merits of the three Bills, Walpole suggested that the House should take Cowper's Bill 'as the basis of their legislation on the subject, and duly consider the details in Committee'. However, Walpole went on to say that he must ask Cowper to reconsider two points in his Bill, which were really two different aspects of the same problem: 'the one was the enormous power given to the Council, which he feared would defeat the independent action of the medical bodies; and the other was that there was no provision for keeping alive the distinct and separate action of those bodies'. The powers it was proposed to give to the Council were, said Walpole, 'too large — they were, in fact, enormous; they would be able to overrule the independent action of the Universities and the existing medical bodies'. In making this statement Walpole was, of course, quite correct, for it had been precisely Simon's intention in drawing up the Bill that the Council should have power to overrule what he saw as the 'irresponsible' Colleges and universities, and this principle was, as we have seen, fully supported by the BMA. The Home Secretary was, however, insistent; if his suggestions were accepted, he said, he should 'be glad to give every consideration to the details of them in Committee'.[65] This was taken as an indication of Government support for a revised version of Cowper's Bill; Lord Elcho promptly withdrew his Bill, whilst the second reading of Duncombe's Bill was postponed, thus effectively ruling it out of consideration.

As a result of the Home Secretary's statement, Cowper's options had now become very limited. As an ordinary Private Member, he had virtually no chance of forcing the Bill through without the cooperation of the government. Walpole had made it clear that the price of government cooperation was the removal of the wide-ranging powers which the Bill proposed to give to the Council, and an amendment of the Bill along these lines would, of course, have undermined one of the central objectives of the Bill.

The date for the committee stage of Cowper's Bill was originally set for the following Tuesday, 8 June, but the committee stage was posponed on a number of occasions, and the Bill did not finally go to committee until a month later, on 6 July. A number of reformers were anxious about what might happen to the Bill in committee, for it was feared that the Royal Colleges would use their influence in order to undermine the fundamental objectives of the Bill during the committee stage. During the second reading of the Bill, for example, Lord Elcho had said that, when legislating on this issue 'one of the chief things to be guarded against was the rendering too stringent the powers of these corporations; and he would warn the House against the efforts which those bodies would be certain to make to carry out their aim when the Bill got into Committee'.[66] The *Lancet* similarly expressed the fear that when the Bill went into committee, opponents of the Bill 'will make the most strenuous efforts to reduce the Bill to a thing of shreds and patches, and destroy all the good it contains'.[67] As we shall see, these fears were by no means misplaced, for some important amendments which were to the advantage of the Royal Colleges were indeed made to the Bill during the committee stage. Few reformers seemed to anticipate, however, that the most important single change to the Bill would be made not in the committee stage, but before the Bill was even discussed at the committee stage, and this change in the Bill represented a major triumph for the Royal Colleges.

The long interval between the second reading of the Bill and the committee stage was used by the London corporations to exert additional pressure on the Home Secretary. It may be recalled that at the start of their campaign against the Bill, the Royal College of Surgeons had suggested that the London corporations should once again enlist the support of the Scottish and Irish corporations, and by early June, the London corporations were able to line up a powerful and impressive opposition which included representatives from virtually all the medical corporations in England, Scotland

and Ireland. A delegation representing all these corporations had a meeting with Walpole at the Home Office on 12 June.[68] The same issue of the *Lancet* that reported this meeting also reported that the principal objection to the Bill continued to revolve around the claim that the powers of the Council were 'likely to assume a despotic character'.[69] Like the British Medical Association, the *Lancet* had no such fears about the creation of a strong central Council. However, there is little doubt that in the period between the second reading of his Bill and the committee stage, Cowper came under strong pressure from the Home Secretary to modify his Bill in order to meet the objections of the Royal Colleges and eventually, and perhaps almost inevitably, Cowper succumbed.

On 22 June — just ten days after Walpole had received the deputation from the medical corporations, and two weeks before the Bill went into the full committee stage — Cowper introduced a number of alterations to his Bill.[70] The most important of these changes — changes which had in effect been forced upon Cowper by the Royal Colleges, acting through the Home Secretary — related to the powers of the central Council, for clause four of the original Bill, which would have given the Council its wide-ranging powers, had now been removed in its entirety. Whereas clause four would have given the Council direct authority to define the required course of study, to compel two or more examining bodies to conduct joint examinations, and to establish its own examiners, the Council was now left with greatly reduced and only indirect authority, such as the authority to require examining bodies to provide the Council with information relating to courses and examinations.

It is worth reiterating the point that clause four was, of course, absolutely central to Simon's major objective in drafting the Bill, and the principle of a strong Council had also received the full support of the British Medical Association; indeed, it will be recalled that representatives of the Association, in their meeting with Cowper in May 1858, had said that they 'looked upon the point as the very essence' of the Bill, and that 'they would rather not have the Bill at all if this power were withdrawn'. The removal of clause four had, in effect, removed the heart from the Bill.

Moreover, there can be no doubt about the processes which led to the removal of clause four. Some years later, John Simon, who was close to government ministers throughout the whole episode, said that he had 'no doubt' that clause four was lost in consequence of the opposition of some of the existing examining bodies. Although he did not specify which bodies, it is clear that the opposition to the Bill was led and coordinated throughout by the Royal Colleges in London. Simon added that the reduction in the powers of the Council was made 'under Mr Walpole's auspices' and he went on to point out that the issue was 'never discussed in the House'.[71] He might also have added that it was never the subject of a vote in the House. The Royal Colleges had achieved a notable success, not as the result of a public campaign, but as a result of private discussions with the Home Secretary; their victory had been achieved with a minimum of publicity and with virtually no public discussion of the issue.

In addition to removing clause four from the Bill, Cowper also made a number of other alterations, one of which — to the Bill's preamble — was symbolically important, for it recognised that, with the removal of clause four, the character of the Bill had been radically changed. The original preamble, as we noted earlier, began with the words 'Whereas it is expedient that the Qualifications of Persons seeking to enter the Medical Profession should be tested and declared by competent authorities'. Now that the Council had been stripped of most of its powers of control over the medical corporations, Cowper may well have felt — as Simon certainly felt — that the Council could no longer ensure that the qualifications of future practitioners would be tested by 'competent authorities', for Simon at least regarded the medical corporations as both incompetent and corrupt,[72] and it was surely no mere coincidence that the whole of the first part of the original preamble was removed at the same time as clause four was removed. The revised preamble now began 'Whereas it is expedient that Persons requiring Medical Aid should be enabled to distinguish qualified from unqualified Practitioners', thus implying that the major objective of the Bill had now become the establishment of a medical register rather than — as had been the original objective — the radical reform of the whole system of medical education and examinations through the creation of a strong central council, with the establishment of a register originally being a secondary consideration.

One other change which Cowper made was of particular significance, and this change also related to the loss of clause four. We have already seen that Cowper was opposed to the idea that, in future, practitioners should be allowed to register on the basis of a qualification in one branch of practice only, and this point was emphasised by Cowper in his meeting with the deputation from the British Medical Association. In the original Bill, this objective was to be achieved by giving the central Council the power to require examining bodies to conduct joint examinations, but this power was, of course, lost when clause four was removed from the Bill. However, at the same time that he was forced to remove clause four, Cowper also introduced a new clause — clause sixteen — which was clearly designed to make good at least some of the damage which had been done by the removal of clause four. This new clause stipulated quite simply that no person would be entitled to be registered in respect of any qualifications which he had gained after the passing of the Act 'unless he shall prove . . . that his Qualifications extend both to Medicine and Surgery'. The insertion of this new clause may be seen as an attempt to salvage at least one of the educational objectives of the Bill.

By the time Cowper's Bill came to the committee stage on 6 July it was, therefore, already a very different Bill from the one which Cowper had introduced back in March. In view of the changes which he had already made to the Bill, and in particular the removal of clause four, it is perhaps surprising that during the committee stage Cowper should have been attacked by Headlam on the ground that Cowper had 'steadfastly refused to meet the views of those who were opposed to some parts of the Bill'.[73] Headlam had, of course, worked in close cooperation with the Royal Colleges for the previous eighteen months, and his attack on Cowper was a clear indication that the Royal Colleges were not yet satisfied, despite the amendments which had already been made, and that further amendments would be introduced during the committee stage.

Not all these amendments, it should be noted, were accepted. Thus Headlam failed to win support for an amendment to the effect that no practitioners except those who had been examined by one or other of the Royal Colleges should be permitted to register under the Bill. This was, of course, a fairly blatant attempt to create a monopoly on behalf of the Royal Colleges and, in the event, it was defeated by 138 votes to 51.[74]

Three significant amendments to the already revised version of the Bill were, however, made during the committee stage. The most important of these amendments undoubtedly related to the complete elimination of clause sixteen, which was the new clause which Cowper had introduced at the time that he removed clause four, and which stipulated that all practitioners should, in future, be qualified in both medicine and surgery. The loss of this clause completely undermined the objective of Simon and Cowper of ensuring that in future, all practitioners would have the basic knowledge which 'would render them ... competent for general practice', for it allowed practitioners to continue to register on the basis of a single qualification in only one branch of practice.

The second significant amendment related to the provision in the Bill that all registered practitioners should have the right to recover in a court of law reasonable charges for their professional attendance and advice, and for medicines supplied to patients. The College of Physicians had argued that they would 'lose caste' if such a clause were passed, and Headlam successfully introduced an amendment to the effect that any College of Physicians could pass a bye-law prohibiting their Fellows or Licentiates from bringing any such legal action, and that such a bye-law could be pleaded in bar to any such action for recovery of fees. This amendment meant, of course, that in relation to one issue about which the College of Physicians was particularly sensitive, the physicians would continue to enjoy a legal status which was quite distinct from that of all other registered practitioners.

The third amendment of note related to the composition of the central Council. The Bill had originally provided for the appointment of six independent members of the Council to be nominated by the crown, and it was expressly stipulated that these six additional members should not include any person who was a member of Council or office bearer in any of the medical corporations. This stipulation was retained in the revised version of Cowper's Bill, but removed during the committee stage; the amended clause now stated simply that four of the additional members should be appointed for England, one for Scotland, and one for Ireland.

Cowper's Bill, with these amendments, was given a third reading in the Commons on 9 July, and then had a relatively quick passage through the Lords. A few minor amendments were made to the Bill during its passage through the Lords, but none of these were of major significance for the long-term development of the profession, and the Bill finally received the Royal Assent on 2 August 1858.

Before we consider the Act as a whole, it is necessary to examine, albeit briefly, the final outcome of the negotiations relating to the composition of the central Council, for this issue was not finally resolved until some time after the Act had been passed. Although the Act did not specifically provide for general practitioner representation on the new Council, and despite the change in the clause relating to the appointment of the six independent members of the Council, the general practitioners did not give up all hope of winning some form of political representation on the General Council of Medical Education and Registration, as the new body was to be called. Thus, five days after the Bill had received the Royal Assent, the *Lancet* pointed out that the seventeen medical members of the General Council were to be 'chosen' by the various corporations, and it went on to say that 'This we consider to be a defect, inasmuch as from their past history, it may be assumed that the medical corporations will make the selection of members of the Council as close and irresponsible as possible. It will be for the profession to make itself felt on this point, and if the corporations are wise, they will arrange the choice on a wide basis.'[75] A week later, the *Lancet* continued on the same theme, saying that 'The Act does not determine clearly in whom the power of election of members of the Council is vested. Is it, for instance, in the case of the College of Surgeons, in the "College", or ruling body? If the Act is to be taken literally, it is in the College itself, its Council, Fellows and Members.'[76] The *Lancet* clearly had in mind the possibility that the representative of the College of Surgeons might be elected by the whole membership of the College, thus ensuring that rank-and-file members of the profession had some form of representation on the General Medical Council.

This issue was followed up at a public meeting of members of the College of Surgeons, which was held at the Freemasons' Tavern in London on 5 October. Following this meeting, a letter was sent to the College Council on behalf of the members, requesting permission for a deputation representing the members to meet the Council in order to discuss the question of the election of the College's representative to the General Medical Council. The Council's reply was not, however, very helpful, for it simply indicated that the matter 'was under consideration by this Council'.[77]

On 26 October a further public meeting of practitioners was held in London, at which it was claimed that 'with regard to the election of a representative from the College of Surgeons, there was no doubt at all of the right of the members to elect such representative ... The members of the College have a clear right to vote, and it will be their own fault if they do not exercise that right, and for once get a voice in the affairs of their College.'[78] Following this meeting, a further letter was sent to the College Council in which it was claimed that, under clause four of the Act, the members, as part of the body corporate, were legally entitled to vote in the election of the College's representative to the General Medical Council.[79]

This letter was considered by the College Council at its meeting on 11 November. By this time, however, the Council had already taken legal advice on the matter, and this advice was to the effect that the College's representative should be chosen by the Council alone; accordingly, J H Green was duly elected as the College representative. All claims to any democratic participation by the members in the affairs of the

College were brushed aside, and the Council decided to reply to the members' demands simply by indicating that it had already 'under legal advice elected such representative in the General Council'.[80] The College Council had thus elected its own representative without any reference whatsoever to the members of the College; the last possible avenue for institutionalising general practitioner representation on the General Medical Council had been unambiguously closed, and the members of the College of Surgeons were still as far as they had ever been from having an effective voice in the affairs of their own College.

Having analysed in some detail the passage of the 1858 Medical Act, we are now in a position to return to the question which we posed at the end of the last chapter. The 1858 Act represented, of course, the culmination of more than thirty years' agitation for reform, but to what extent can the Act be seen as a significant triumph for the general practitioners who had been involved in this agitation? Or, to put the question another way, to what extent were the general practitioners on the one hand, and the Royal Colleges on the other, successful in shaping the Act in accordance with what they perceived to be their own interests?

In this context, it is important to emphasise that, in the form in which it was originally introduced, Cowper's Bill held out the promise of meeting most, if not all, of the longstanding grievances of the general practitioners. Thus the original Bill proposed the creation of a system which would have made it possible to ensure that in future, all practitioners would be examined in all major branches of practice, an objective which was to be achieved by the creation of a strong council which would have the power to overrule the independent action of what most general practitioners saw as the undemocratic, monopolistic and corrupt medical corporations. Both the objective of ensuring that all practitioners were examined in all branches of practice, and the means chosen to achieve this end — the creation of a council with wide-ranging powers — were very much in line with the demands of the general practitioners; indeed, in their interview with Cowper in May 1858 the deputation from the British Medical Association singled out these two aspects of the Bill as being of particular significance. In addition, the Bill proposed to establish a system of common registration of qualified practitioners, with all practitioners enjoying the same legal status and the same legal rights.

However, the amendments made to the Bill during its passage through Parliament meant that in the end the 1858 Act met only one of the specific demands of the general practitioners. Thus the powers of the General Medical Council were considerably reduced at the insistence of the Royal Colleges and the Home Secretary, while the clause which would have required practitioners to be examined in both medicine and surgery was removed during the committee stage of the Bill. In addition, as we have seen, the general practitioners failed to win representation on the new Council. Only in relation to the one issue of common registration, therefore, can it be said that the general practitioners were successful. Even here it should be noted that common registration did not imply a common legal status for all registered practitioners; for Headlam's successful amendment relating to the recovery of charges for professional services meant that, at least in relation to one area which it considered to be of importance, the College of Physicians had managed to ensure that the physicians would continue to enjoy a legal status which differentiated the physician from other practitioners, even within the context of a system of common registration. As far as the other demands of the general practitioners were concerned, it was to be a further twenty-eight years before the Medical Act of 1886 required all practitioners to be qualified in medicine, surgery and midwifery, thus introducing the principle of what Newman has called 'the safe general practitioner',[81] and before the profession as a whole, under the same Act, was given direct representation on the General Medical Council.

If, therefore, one compares the provisions of the Bill as it was introduced into the Commons, and the provisions of the Act as it was finally passed, it is difficult to avoid the conclusion that, in the lobbying which surrounded the Bill during its passage through Parliament, the Royal Colleges were able to exert considerably more influence, and with

considerably greater success, than were the general practitioners. Thus, of all the changes which were made to the
Bill, it is difficult to point to a single significant amendment
which was either demanded by or specifically to the advantage of the general practitioners; indeed, all the major amendments represented a series of retreats from those principles
of reform which were supported by the general practitioners,
and which were enshrined in the original Bill.

Given this situation, it is not perhaps surprising that the
reaction of most reformers to the Act was a relatively muted
one. This is not to suggest, of course, that there was any
significant group of reformers who were actually opposed
to the Act, for many practitioners anticipated — quite
correctly, as we shall see in the next chapter — that some of
the provisions of the Act, and in particular the establishment
of a medical register, would prove of considerable benefit
in raising the status and financial rewards of medical practice
in general, and of general practice in particular. Nevertheless,
it is fair to say that the Act did relatively little to meet those
specific demands which had been central to the general
practitioners' campaign for reform since the 1820s, and this
was recognised in much of the subsequent comment on
the Act.

Thus, for example, the *Lancet*, whilst welcoming the Act
as 'the first instalment of Medical Reform', pointed out that
'the new Act is deficient in many essential points', and that
it was 'altogether inadequate to meet the difficulties which
beset the subject of medical qualifications and the right of
practising'.[82] The following week, the *Lancet* noted that the
Act 'has produced in many quarters a feeling of uneasiness,
and in others those of actual disappointment'; amongst many
practitioners, it said, 'a strong feeling of disappointment
prevails because they have ascertained, or apprehend they
have ascertained, that certain advantages which they expected
would accrue, they now discover will not be conferred upon
them'.[83] George Webster, who many years previously had
been the chairman of the radical London-based British
Medical Association, welcomed certain provisions of the Act,
and in particular the fact that the establishment of a medical
register 'would afford a means of distinguishing the regular

practitioner from the impostor'. However, he went on to say that 'the new measure fell far short of the requirements of the profession', and that 'it was much to be regretted that the general practitioners were not likely to be represented in the Medical Council by members of their own body'.[84]

If, however, the new Act failed to meet the demands of the general practitioners on a number of essential points, few reformers felt inclined to criticise Cowper and, indeed, the *Lancet* showed considerable understanding of the problems which he had had to face in Parliament. Thus the *Lancet* congratulated Cowper on the 'patient attention' which he had given to the issue of medical reform, and it recognised the great difficulties with which he had been faced 'in conciliating the parties supporting and opposing it'.[85] Moreover, the *Lancet* went on to argue that 'it should be remembered, that Parliament legislated, not because it had any fancy for the subject of medical policy, but because it was absolutely nauseated and disgusted with the whole question. It was completely sickened and tired out, and allowed something to be done, which many who supported the Bill regarded as an evil, rather than encounter the annoyance of further medical agitation. Under such circumstances, it could not be expected that the enactment we have obtained would be a perfect measure, or even an approach to perfection.'[86] Whilst welcoming the fact that Parliament had, after very many years of agitation, finally passed what could only be regarded as an initial measure of medical reform, many practitioners also felt a keen sense of disappointment that the Act did little or nothing to remove some of the longstanding grievances of the general practitioners. This mixed reaction was, perhaps, most aptly summed up by George Webster in addressing a public meeting of practitioners in London on 26 October 1858: 'after many years of agitation and labour they had obtained a measure of reform which, such as it was, he felt they were bound to make the most of for the benefit of the profession and the public. They should get what they could out of the measure.'[87]

If the reaction of most reformers was a relatively mixed one, the chief architect of the Act, John Simon, appears to have been more impressed by the Act's omissions than by its achievements. Simon was particularly disappointed that, as a result of the opposition of the medical corporations and the Home Secretary, the newly created General Medical Council had been left with greatly reduced powers. Thus, in his evidence to a Select Committee which sat in 1878-9, Simon pointed out that 'the Bill, as introduced, gave powers of control to the General Medical Council. Under the Act as passed those powers were not given.' As a result, the Bill was 'mutilated in an essential part', and an 'essential intention was left unfulfilled'.[88] Five years previously, in a memorandum, Simon had described the Council as a 'timid experiment',[89] whilst in 1870 he was to declare that 'The General Council has been a failure'.[90] In making these comments, Simon clearly had in mind the fact that the Act had not given the Council the authority to control the actions of what he, along with many general practitioners, saw as not only deeply conservative but also corrupt medical corporations. Thus, in his presidential address to the Medical Teachers' Association in January 1868, Simon bitterly and eloquently denounced the corporations for their 'utter corruption', incompetence and abuses. Although he did not refer to the General Medical Council by name, the implications of his speech concerning the Council's inability to curb the abuses within the corporations were obvious.[91] Simon, it is clear, was by no means happy with the way in which his Bill had been emasculated during its passage through the Commons.

As far as the Royal Colleges were concerned, it may be suggested that they had cause for quiet satisfaction with the final outcome of the legislative process. It is true, of course, that the Royal Colleges had been forced to concede the principle of common registration — something they had traditionally opposed — but it is important to note that even before Cowper introduced his Bill, the Royal College of Surgeons, if not the Royal College of Physicians, was already modifying its traditional hostility to a system of common registration, and had already accepted the fact that, given the changes which had occurred within the profession, it would not be possible to establish a system which involved separate registration for the three traditional 'orders' within the profession. Thus it is significant that, in the Bill which the corporations had themselves drawn up in 1856-7, the College of Surgeons had already conceded the principle that surgeons and apothecaries should be listed together in a single register, even though the College of Physicians, as we have seen, had insisted on a separate register for physicians. In this sense, then, it may be said that the establishment of a common register represented more of a setback for the College of Physicians than for the College of Surgeons, but even in relation to the former, it must be remembered that Headlam's amendment relating to the recovery of fees allowed the College to retain a distinct legal status for physicians, even within the context of a system of common registration.

Moreover, there is little doubt that even if the Royal Colleges were opposed to, or at least unenthusiastic about, the principle of common registration, this was not the part of the original Bill to which they were most strongly opposed. Throughout the negotiations surrounding the Bill, both Royal Colleges saw the major threat to their privileged position as arising from the proposal to establish a central Council with wide-ranging powers. As we have seen, the Royal Colleges enjoyed a virtually unqualified success in limiting the powers of the Council. This was, of course, a major triumph for the Royal Colleges, and meant that as far as the College of Physicians was concerned, the physician would still not be required to familiarise himself with even the most elementary principles of surgery. More importantly, the limitations which had been placed on the powers of the Council meant that the Royal Colleges would continue to enjoy a very substantial measure of autonomy for, as a result of the complete elimination of clause four of the original Bill, the Council was not given powers to attack what Simon and many others saw as the abuses which had long characterised the medical corporations. Finally, it should be remembered that, notwithstanding the limitations which had been placed on its powers, the newly created General Medical Council was nevertheless an institution of major importance, for it represented the first step towards a proper system of regulating medical practice on a national level, and it is important to bear in mind that the medical corporations were amply represented on this new Council whilst the

general practitioners were left without any formal representation. In trying to gauge the extent to which the Royal
Colleges had been successful in shaping the Act in accordance
with their own perceived interests, it is significant to note
that when, on 12 August 1858, the president of the College
of Surgeons formally reported to his Council the passage
of the 1858 Act, he 'congratulated the Council on the
settlement, for the present at least, of the long agitated
subject of medical reform'.[92] If one recalls the almost unqualified hostility with which the Royal Colleges had greeted
Cowper's original Bill, then the fact that the president of
the College of Surgeons felt able to congratulate his Council
on the final outcome may itself be taken as an indication of
the degree to which the Royal Colleges had been successful
in emasculating Cowper's original Bill.

The activities of the Royal Colleges in the eighteen months
or so preceding the passage of the 1858 Act were, perhaps,
most aptly characterised by two editorials which were published in the *Lancet* in 1857-8. As we have seen, the Royal
Colleges had traditionally set themselves firmly against all
proposals which would have introduced any radical change
within the medical profession. However, by 1856, with the
medical reform movement gaining ground within Parliament,
it was becoming increasingly difficult for the Royal Colleges
simply to deny the necessity for reform and, in 1856-7, they
finally responded to the widespread demands for reform by
drawing up their own Bill which was introduced into the
Commons by Headlam in 1857. The *Lancet* was not, however, deceived by what appeared, at least superficially, to
be a sudden conversion of the Royal Colleges to the cause of
medical reform. In an editorial in January 1857, the *Lancet*
said that a 'most marvellous change has come over the once
anti-reforming, exclusive, and tyrannical corporations — a
change marvellous in its effects, but not so from the causes
which produced it. The year 1857 opens with the demand of
those very corporations for reform! ... This change has not
been effected by any love of reform on the part of the
corporate bodies. In heart and spirit, they have the same love
of absolute power ... which have existed from time
immemorial; but the progress of public opinion has cut the

ground from beneath monopoly, and if the corporations are to exist in any efficient condition, they must go with the times.'[93] In other words, the *Lancet* was suggesting that reform was slowly being forced upon the Royal Colleges, and that by implication the Royal Colleges would seek to minimise the extent of that reform in an attempt to maintain their traditionally dominant position within the profession. This point was made again — but this time more explicitly — in an editorial published in May 1858, after Cowper's Bill had been given its first reading in the Commons. The *Lancet* argued that the objections to the Bill 'do not come from the profession at large, but emanate from selfish corporations. They know and feel that reform must come, and their anxious wish is that that reform shall be as limited as possible, so that they may retain the monopoly which they have so long enjoyed, and thus thwart any measure of a comprehensive and liberal character.'[94] If the *Lancet*'s observations were correct — and given the history of the Royal Colleges, one has to say that they were, at the very least, plausible — then one also has to say the Royal Colleges enjoyed considerable success in ensuring that reform, when it finally came, was 'as limited as possible' and that, as a consequence, the continued dominance of the Royal Colleges within the profession was also ensured.

PART III

The Development of Medicine as a Modern Profession

Occupational Closure and the 1858 Medical Act

DESPITE the way in which Simon's original Bill had been emasculated during its passage through Parliament, the 1858 Medical Act was nevertheless to prove of major importance for the subsequent development of the medical profession in Britain. In the first place, and despite the limitation which had been placed on the powers of the Council, the creation of the General Medical Council did represent a significant step away from the traditional system of regulating the affairs of the medical profession on a purely local level, and towards the establishment of a structure for coordinating and regulating medical education and medical practice on a national level, that is to say throughout the whole of Britain. In this respect, the reformers were to be proved correct in their assertion that the 1858 Act could only be regarded as the first instalment of reform, for subsequent measures — particularly the 1886 Medical Act, which required all future candidates to undergo an examination in medicine, surgery and midwifery — were to accelerate the process of standardising the qualifications of all medical practitioners under the central control of the General Medical Council. In the short term the Council had not been given powers to curb the abuses within the medical corporations; nevertheless in the longer term, the General Medical Council was to emerge as the lynchpin of the modern system of professional self-regulation or self-government. The detailed analysis of the subsequent development of the power and influence of the Council is, however, beyond the scope of the present work.

In the second place, whilst it would not be correct to say that the 1858 Act formally abolished the traditional tripartite professional structure — for example, the Act, unlike the

original Bill, did nothing to require all newly qualified practitioners to have passed an examination in all branches of
practice — it did have the effect of further weakening the
significance of the traditional divisions within the profession,
in particular by the establishment of a common register for
all practitioners. In this context, it is important to note that,
with the exception of Headlam's successful amendment
relating to the recovery of charges by physicians, the Act
did not seek to define the separate privileges of physicians,
surgeons and apothecaries, as previous legislation had done,
but rather to define those common privileges which all
practitioners shared by virtue of being duly qualified or
registered practitioners as defined in the Act. In thus
emphasising those things · which all practitioners shared,
rather than those which had traditionally divided the profession, the Act marked a significant step in the development
of a more united profession. Moreover, in giving legal
definition to the term 'qualified medical practitioner', and
in drawing a sharp differentiation between those practitioners
who were qualified and therefore entitled to register under
the Act, and those who were not, the Act clearly established
the legal and other institutional bounderies of the regular
medical profession. In this sense, we can accept Horner's
observation that the immediate effect of the 1858 Act 'was
to draw all three grades of our calling into one fold, set up a
legal fence between them and the wholly unqualified, and
thus bring into being a "medical profession" for the United
Kingdom'.[1]

As Horner's comment indicates, one of the most important
provisions of the 1858 Act, in terms of its significance for
the subsequent development of the medical profession in
Britain, was that which related to the establishment of an
official register of qualified practitioners. The establishment
of a register of qualified practitioners is, of course, an
important process in the development of all modern professions. In view of this, the establishment of a system of
medical registration and the consequences of registration are
processes which merit more detailed analysis. The remainder
of this chapter is, therefore, concerned with an analysis of
these issues.

As previous chapters have indicated, there are many aspects of the campaign for medical reform which cannot be adequately understood without some understanding of the deeply-rooted tensions and divisions within the medical profession in the first half of the nineteenth century. It would, however, be quite wrong to convey the impression that there was *no* issue on which the medical profession as a whole was relatively united. There was one issue — the perceived necessity for some form of medical registration — in relation to which there was widespread agreement within the profession, even if there were important differences over the precise form which that registration should take. The establishment of a register is an important landmark in the development of any profession and, in view of this, it is not altogether surprising that the 1858 Medical Act is perhaps best remembered today not for the bitter intra-professional squabbling which preceded it, but for the fact that in establishing the General Medical Council and requiring the Council to maintain and to publish a register of qualified practitioners the Act laid down the foundations of the institutional structure of the modern medical profession.

The 1858 Act, particularly as it relates to the establishment of the General Medical Council and to the Council's duty to publish a medical register, has been the subject of a good deal of comment by both medical historians and, more recently, sociologists. In general, two rather different approaches to understanding the significance of medical registration may be identified in the literature. The first of these, which is the more traditional approach, has emphasised the benefits of registration to the public, whilst the benefits accruing either to the profession as a whole, or to particular segments of the profession, have received relatively little attention. A clear example of this approach may be found in the work of Dr Poynter, who has suggested that 'The important thing to remember is that the Act was not framed for the benefit of the profession ... but was one designed to protect the people in their individual and corporate capacity';[2] whilst A P Thomson, in a paper written to celebrate the centenary of the General Medical Council, has similarly argued that 'the Council came into existence for the protection of the public'.[3] It is, perhaps, not surprising to find this same position echoed by the General Medical Council itself. Thus in 1970, the Council pointed out that the preamble to the 1858 Act stated that it was 'expedient that persons requiring medical aid should be enabled to distinguish qualified from unqualified practitioners', and went on to argue that 'the whole of the Council's functions flow from that original objective. . . . It can be said that the general duty of the Council is to protect the public, in particular by keeping and publishing the Register of duly qualified doctors.[4]

In recent years, however, this approach has been challenged by the work of a number of social scientists who have begun to develop a more sceptical analysis of the significance of registration. Thus, in their work on the medical profession in Britain, Noel and José Parry have suggested that registration may best be viewed as part of 'an occupational strategy which is chiefly directed towards the achievement of upward collective social mobility and, once achieved, it is concerned with the maintenance of superior remuneration and status'.[5] The importance of registration, they suggest, lies in the fact that it enables practitioners to achieve 'a degree of monopoly with respect to the provision of particular types of services in the market'.[6] Perhaps the most fully developed and detailed analysis of medical registration as a monopolisation strategy, however, is contained in J L Berlant's *Profession and Monopoly*, which revolves almost exclusively around an examination of the monopolistic gains associated with professionalisation. Thus Berlant sees the establishment of a medical register under the 1858 Act, together with a number of other aspects of the professionalisation of medicine, as part of a broad monopolisation strategy. The campaign for registration, he suggests, was designed to reduce competition from outside the profession, whilst the development of medical ethics — examined in detail in the next chapter — served to regulate competition within the profession.[7]

Bearing these two contrasting perspectives in mind, in this chapter we shall examine the demands from medical men for the establishment of an official register of qualified practitioners. On the basis of this examination, it will be suggested that the campaign for medical registration did indeed have strong monopolistic elements, and that a major thrust of medical politics in the first half of the nineteenth century was concerned with the perceived need to restrict entry into what was seen as an overcrowded profession. Thus it will be argued that medical practitioners were concerned both to control the number of qualified practitioners entering the profession and to reduce the competition from practitioners who were not qualified. It will further be argued that most practitioners were clearly aware of the effect which this process of occupational closure would be likely to have in terms of raising both the status and the incomes of medical men, and that the establishment of a medical register under the control of the General Medical Council proved to be a very effective way of restricting entry to the profession. In order to understand this point more fully, it will be useful to examine briefly what many medical men saw as the problem of overcrowding within the profession, especially from the 1830s.

In the early 1830s, the *Lancet* argued that 'the members of the medical profession are not a body of wealthy individuals'[8] and, as we have seen, there is indeed considerable evidence to indicate that whilst the incomes of consultants were often very high, many general practitioners were forced to live on extremely modest incomes. The two most frequently identified causes of what medical practitioners saw as the depressed level of medical incomes were an oversupply of qualified practitioners and what was seen as unfair competition from those who were not qualified. In relation to the first point the *Lancet* held that one reason why medical incomes were depressed was because 'the colleges are tempted by their charters to admit such a number of practitioners, that sufficient rewards cannot be afforded to them'.[9] The evils of excessive competition, arising from an oversupply of qualified practitioners, were also pointed out by the author of an article published anonymously in the *Quarterly Review* in 1840. The author — believed to have been Sir Benjamin Brodie — argued that 'the supply of medical practitioners is in fact not only very much beyond the demand, but very much beyond what is necessary to ensure a just and useful degree of competition ... and to this cause may mainly be attributed the present restless and uneasy state of the profession. In this, as in all other pursuits, a certain degree of competition is required for the security of the public; but in the medical profession it is easy to conceive that the competition may be not only beyond what is really wanted, but so great as to be actually mischievous.'[10] Moreover, the view that the profession was overcrowded was not confined to medical practitioners. In the debate on the second reading of his Bill in the House of Commons in 1858, William Cowper held that 'at present there were more young men entering the profession than could gain a livelihood by it',[11] whilst, as Musgrove has pointed out, the term 'overcrowded professions' was freely applied to both the medical and legal professions in vocational handbooks of the period.[12]

Such complaints about overcrowding within the profession recurred frequently in the 1830s and 1840s. One should, of course, treat contemporary comments on overcrowding with some caution, for such complaints are almost as old as the professions themselves. Nevertheless, there are grounds for thinking that, at least in this case, there may have been some substance in these complaints; for in the 1820s and early 1830s there was a very rapid increase in the number of persons who took out a licence to practise medicine. Thus the Royal College of Surgeons estimated that in 1824 some 5000 persons held the diploma of the College; by 1833 this number had increased to 8125, an increase of more than 62 per cent in a ten year period.[13] A similar story emerges if we examine the number of medical men who took out a licence from the Society of Apothecaries. Thus in the five year period from 1815-16 to 1819-20, the Society granted an average of 214 certificates per year; in the period from 1820-1 to 1824-5, this increased to an average of 340 per year, and between 1825-6 and 1829-30 there was a further increase to an average of 408 per year, almost double the figure for the period from 1815 to 1820.[14] It may well have been the case that this rapid increase in the number of qualified practitioners did indeed result in a degree of overcrowding, at least for the two or three decades from the 1830s.

Peterson is in little doubt that the profession was overcrowded, for she argues that one reason why medical men, especially those in public employment and sick clubs, were so dependent on their lay employers was 'because of the overcrowding of the profession and the consequent competition among medical men for practice wherever it could be found'.[15]

It seems probable, therefore, that the profession may have been overcrowded, and the belief that it was overcrowded was certainly widespread among contemporary medical men. Moreover, any restriction of entry to the profession could only affect medical incomes in an upward direction, and thus could only be advantageous, in a pecuniary sense, to medical practitioners. The effect of restricting entry to the medical profession had, in fact, been dealt with by no less an authority than Adam Smith, in a letter to William Cullen in 1774. Cullen, who was at that time president of the Royal College of Physicians of Edinburgh, had asked Smith for his views on the practice of some Scottish universities of selling medical degrees, often without requiring any residence. In his reply, Smith criticised those institutions for taking part in what he called 'a most disgraceful trade' in degrees, but he went on to point out that the 'facility of obtaining degrees, particularly in physic, from those poor universities, had two effects, both extremely advantageous to the public, but extremely disagreeable to the graduates of other universities, whose degrees had cost them much time and expense. First, it multiplied very much the number of doctors, and thereby no doubt sunk their fees, or at least hindered them from rising so very high as they otherwise would have done. Had the universities of Oxford and Cambridge been able to maintain themselves in the exclusive privilege of graduating all the doctors who could practise in England, the price of feeling a pulse might by this time have risen from two or three guineas, the price which it has now happily arrived at, to double or treble that sum . . . Secondly, it reduced a good deal the rank and dignity of a doctor.'[16]

The effect of monopolistic practices on price levels was, of course, widely appreciated in the nineteenth century, and it is clear that the logic of Adam Smith's argument was not lost on the medical profession; for by the 1840s there was a general consensus amongst medical men on the need to restrict entry to the profession, and the issue was discussed frequently and openly in the medical journals. Thus the *Lancet* held that 'It is admitted on all hands that many of the evils under which the medical profession now labours, are owing to the teeming multitude of practitioners. This necessarily involves an impoverished state of the profession, and has, doubtless, contributed largely to that depression of intellect and morals among its members. . . The means of restraining this superfluity of doctors, and rendering the number of the profession more proportionate to the population, become, therefore, very important objects of medical legislation.' The *Lancet* then went on to review a number of schemes for restricting entry to the profession, including the imposition of a direct numerical limitation, a plan which was rejected as being 'incompatible with the institutions of a free country, and extremely difficult to reduce to practice under any circumstances'. Eventually, the *Lancet* argued that the best way to restrict entry was by 'making the standard of qualification high, as well in medicine as in letters and science'. If this scheme were adopted, 'the numbers of the profession would be effectually limited without any injurious exclusions; the character of the profession would be greatly elevated, and the public welfare would be promoted'.[17] This was, of course, a relatively sophisticated statement of what was essentially an economic argument for restricting entry to the profession; the rather less sophisticated form of this argument was neatly expressed by a correspondent of the *Lancet* who pointed out, albeit rather bluntly, that 'a fair system of undisputed remuneration' depended upon 'an effective system of registration'.[18] There can, in fact, be little doubt that one dimension of the campaign for medical registration involved a quite conscious attempt on the part of medical practitioners to restrict entry to the profession; nor can there be much doubt that practitioners were fully aware of the likely effect of this on the level of their own incomes. It is difficult to disagree with Musgrove's comment that the 'movement towards registration and the stipulation of minimum training requirements is an indication of a felt need to restrict entry'[19] and, as we shall see later, there is some evidence to suggest that the 1858 Act met this felt need very adequately.

A second aspect of the campaign for registration which involved a clear element of monopolisation was the attempt to prevent unqualified practice, and here, once again, economic considerations were of major importance. Thus in 1843, the *Lancet* argued: 'That "the profession is overstocked" we daily hear exclaimed, and the assertion is true. The "profession" is overstocked, and with a superabundance of unqualified men, mere speculators in drugs and chemicals.' *Quacks* The result was that 'educated practitioners are deprived of their legitimate means of obtaining a subsistence'. Medical men, continued the *Lancet*, 'who scorn to make their liberal profession a trade, complain of this usurpation of their rightful field of profit, and of this degradation of medicine, in vain'.[20] A few years later, a petition in favour of Wakley's Bill of 1847, discussed earlier, held that 'a very grievous injury is inflicted upon those members of an honourable profession who have complied, at a great cost, both of time and money, with the provisions of the law, and the regulations of the Colleges and Examining Boards, but who are now left without adequate protection in the exercise of their profession'.[21] The view that medical education was an investment, and that unqualified practitioners were denying qualified practitioners a legitimate return on that investment was, in fact, a recurrent theme. This idea was, for example, very precisely expressed by one contributor to the *Lancet*, who held that 'no person should risk the expenditure of time, labour, and money necessary to the attainment of his qualification or licence to practise, unless he felt himself to be effectually guarded by the laws against the competition of unlicensed and ignorant, though impudent and plausible empirics'.[22]

Whilst demands for the suppression of unqualified practice were almost invariably accompanied by the claim that unqualified practitioners were taking income away from those who were qualified, these purely economic arguments were sometimes coupled with other arguments relating to the protection of the public; indeed the profession had to put forward arguments of the latter kind if it hoped to persuade the legislature to grant a monopoly of practice to those who were qualified. The contributor to the *Lancet*, cited above, argued that if unqualified practice were made illegal, this would not only secure 'the rights and privileges of medical men', but would also serve to protect 'the public health'.[23] The purely scientific arguments in favour of limiting practice to the qualified were not, however, very strong. Thus, as Peterson has pointed out, much of the available medical treatment was of questionable value, even by the standards of the day,[24] whilst what little authority medical men had 'came not from their medical knowledge but had its origins in connection, social origins, or social style'.[25] Most importantly, however, medical men themselves, as Peterson has correctly noted, 'seemed to see the issue more in terms of protection from competition than in terms of the superior claims of medical science'.[26]

In demanding protection from competition, the rank and file of the profession was, of course, demanding what was in effect the creation of a monopoly, although most practitioners were understandably reluctant to express their demands in those exact terms. Indeed, one practitioner, the author of a series of articles published in the *Lancet* in 1841-2, explicitly attempted to defend the profession against such charges. Thus the author, D O Edwards, criticised what he called 'a belief too prevalent in society, that the medical profession are a sordid exclusive caste, who seek by vexatious barriers and invidious distinctions to secure a monopoly of the healing art'.[27] A 'monopoly of the healing art' was, however, precisely what many rank and file members of the profession were demanding, but in relation to this issue — whether qualified practitioners should be given a legal monopoly with penalties for unqualified practice — a clear division emerged within the profession itself.

Whilst there were, doubtless, some unqualified practitioners who made a handsome living by practising amongst the middle and upper classes, there was considerable agreement amongst contemporary observers that the great majority of unqualified practitioners were practising amongst the lower classes of mid-Victorian society.[28] Nor is this particularly surprising, for these people had the greatest difficulty in paying even the relatively modest fees of the general practitioner; as one MP observed in the debate on

Sir James Graham's bill in 1844, it was primarily the poor 'who were in the habit of asking the druggists to prescribe, in order to avoid the expense of a doctor'.[29] As such, of course, the incomes of general practitioners were most affected by the competition of unqualified practitioners, for they were often competing for the same market amongst the ranks of both industrial workers and rural labourers. By contrast, consultants normally drew their private patients from the higher social classes, and hence their practices and incomes were considerably less affected by the activities of unqualified practitioners. Thus, to the extent that unqualified practitioners were taking income away from those who were qualified, it was the general practitioners, rather than the consultants, who suffered most.

This difference between the everyday work situations of general practitioners and consultants was of major importance in shaping the attitudes of these two groups towards the question of whether or not qualified practitioners should be given a legal monopoly of practice. Not surprisingly, the general practitioners were most vociferous in their demands for the imposition of legal penalties for unqualified practice. For example, one of the reasons why general practitioners opposed Sir James Graham's bill of 1844 was because it did not make unqualified practice illegal;[30] and Thomas Wakley, defending as ever the interests of general practitioners, told the House of Commons that 'it was the paramount duty of that House to prevent any person from practising who was not duly qualified'.[31]

Consultants, on the other hand, as Peterson has noted, 'had little interest in the control of unqualified practice, inasmuch as it had little effect on their positions, prestige, or practice'.[32] They were accordingly able to adopt a less punitive attitude towards unqualified practitioners. In the article believed to have been written by Sir Benjamin Brodie published in the *Quarterly Review* in 1840, the author argued against giving a legal monopoly of practice to those who were qualified. The question to be decided was, he said, 'Should those who have passed their examination, and received their licence, have a monopoly of practice? Should there be penal laws to prevent their being interfered with by the competition of the ignorant, the uneducated, and un-licensed? Or is it sufficient that the public are supplied with a list of those who are supposed to be qualified practitioners, it being then left to individuals to procure medical assistance where they please?'[33] He recognised that it was 'natural that licensed practitioners, who have expended considerable sums of money, and no small portion of their lives, in their education, should be jealous of the competition of others',[34] and he also recognised that it was not so much consultants as 'those who belong to the class of general practitioners, that require the especial attention and protection of the legis-lature'.[35] Nevertheless, he was firmly of the opinion that the profession ought not to seek legislation to suppress unqualified practice: the 'empire of opinion will do more than legislative enactments'.[36]

Such arguments found no sympathy amongst the rank and file of the profession, some of whom pointed out in no uncertain terms the difference between their own social situation and that of consultants. Thus, referring specifically to the article in the *Quarterly Review*, one practitioner wrote that 'Court physicians and surgeons are better acquainted with the avenues of palaces than the thresholds of cottages. They are utterly ignorant of the kind of practice which is witnessed in rural districts and in poor neighbourhoods.' If they had more knowledge of such things, claimed the writer, 'they would not talk so coolly of "leaving quacks to their fate". As it is, the fate of the pretender is often much better than that of the genuine therapist.'[37] Another correspondent of the *Lancet* pointed out, in very sarcastic tones, that the London consultants who controlled the Royal Colleges had never supported the campaign to make unqualified practice illegal: 'On this point the Colleges *have* never sympathized with us; they *do* not — they *will* not. They affect not to believe in the existence of the evil: Cruikshank's caricature of the well-fed flunkies lazily asking, "What are taxes?" might with equal fidelity represent two of our wealthy self-elected rulers asking one the other, "What are quacks?" '[38]

Those practitioners — mostly general practitioners — who wished to have unqualified practice declared illegal were, however, unsuccessful, perhaps in part because the campaign received no support from the Royal Colleges; but also because, as Cowan has pointed out, in a period in which the dominant ideology was that of *laissez-faire*, the House of Commons regarded anything which smacked of monopoly with a good deal of suspicion.[39] Thus, whilst the Medical Act of 1858 made it an offence for any person to 'wilfully and falsely pretend to be' a qualified or registered practitioner, it did not make unqualified practice as such illegal. The Act did, however, create a monopoly of practice for registered practitioners in all public institutions. Thus no unregistered practitioner was to be allowed to hold any appointment as a medical practitioner in the army or navy, or in 'any Hospital, Infirmary, Dispensary, or Lying-in Hospital, not supported wholly by voluntary contributions'. In addition, unqualified practitioners were excluded from holding any appointment in 'any Lunatic Asylum, Gaol, Penitentiary, . . . Parochial or Union Workhouse or Poorhouse, Parish Union, or other public Establishment'; nor were they allowed to hold any medical appointment 'to any Friendly or other Society for affording mutual relief in Sickness, Infirmity, or old Age, or as a Medical Officer of Health'.[40]

Although many general practitioners were dissatisfied with the fact that the 1858 Act did not make unqualified practice illegal, the exclusion of unqualified practitioners from all government medical services was, in the long term, to assume greatly increased importance with the continual expansion of the public sector of health care in the late nineteenth and twentieth centuries. Thus, as Carr-Saunders and Wilson pointed out in 1933, the effect of the National Insurance Act of 1911 was to increase 'very substantially' the value of registration, for the 1911 Act stipulated that only registered practitioners could be accepted on the medical list.[41] Moreover, although the 1858 Act did not, except in the area of government services, create a legal monopoly of practice for those who were qualified, it did impose certain disabilities on unregistered practitioners. Thus unregistered practitioners could not certify any statutory documents, and they were not entitled, as were registered practitioners, to recover at law any charges for medical services which they had rendered. In addition, as Berlant has noted, the Act also conferred an advantage on registered practitioners 'by providing them with apparent state approval; that is, the prestige of the state was thrown behind members of the organised medical profession'.[42]

In conferring these advantages on those who were registered, the Act followed closely the principle laid down by Sir James Graham in 1844, when he argued that the law should not be used to prohibit unqualified practice, but it should be used to 'discourage it by securing exclusive advantages to the regular practitioner'.[43] Thus the effect of the 1858 Act was not only to exclude unregistered practitioners from the steadily expanding public sector of medical care but also, in the private sector, to give registered practitioners what Berlant has described as 'a competitive advantage in the open market'.[44] Moreover, the competitive advantages enjoyed by registered practitioners were, like the monopoly of government service, to become increasingly important, so that the long term effect of registration was to create what became virtually a *de facto* if not a *de jure* monopoly of medical practice for registered practitioners.

If, however, these competitive advantages accruing to registered practitioners were to become more apparent with the passage of time, the impact of the 1858 Act on the level of recruitment to the profession appears to have been one which took effect almost immediately. Thus, in the twenty years or so following the passage of the Act, the growth in the number of medical practitioners in England and Wales was quite minimal, and was far outstripped by the growth of the total population. In 1861, there were 14,415 medical practitioners in England and Wales. In the decade from 1861-71, this number increased by just 269, or 1.8 per cent, and in the period from 1871-81, there was a further increase of 407, or 2.7 per cent.[45] Thus, over the twenty year period from 1861-81, the number of medical practitioners in England and Wales increased by under 5 per cent, compared with a 24 per cent increase in the employed male population, and an increase in the total population of no less than 29 per cent over the same period.[46]

In the two decades following the 1858 Act, there was therefore, a marked reduction in the provision of qualified medical care to the population. In 1861, there was one medical practitioner for every 1392 persons, or 7.1 doctors per 10,000 population; by 1871 this had been reduced to one practitioner for every 1547 persons, or 6.4 doctors per 10,000 population; and by 1881 there had been a further reduction to one doctor for every 1721 persons, or 5.8 doctors per 10,000 population.[47] It is true that in the two decades from 1881-1901 there was a considerably more rapid expansion of the profession, perhaps partly due to the fact that by the late 1870s and early 1880s there was a clearly recognised shortage of doctors; but as late as 1911 there were still fewer medical practitioners in relation to population than there had been fifty years previously.[48] What is particularly pertinent within the context of the present discussion, however, is that a situation which was generally recognised as being characterised by a surplus of doctors prior to the 1858 Act had, within two decades of the passing of the Act, become one in which there was a serious shortage of qualified practitioners. Thus in his Carmichael Prize essay of 1879, Walter Rivington drew attention to 'the decrease in the supply of medical men', and he pointed out that William Farr, at that time superintendent of the statistical department in the Registrar General's Office, had also expressed his concern that qualified medical care had become steadily less available; indeed, Farr held that the shortage of medical practitioners was such that there was 'an imminent danger' that qualified medical care might become 'quite inaccessible to vast numbers of people'.[49]

The shortage of qualified practitioners was also an issue which concerned the 1882 Royal Commission which had been appointed 'to Inquire into the Medical Acts'. Some of the evidence which the Commission received made it quite clear that the *Lancet* had not been mistaken when, many years previously, it had argued that the most effective way to restrict entry to the profession was by raising the standard of qualification. Thus although the General Medical Council had not been given power to compel the Royal Colleges to conduct joint examinations, the Council had taken action to increase the stringency of medical examinations, and this action was followed by a sharp decline in the number of entrants to the profession. In his evidence to the Commission,

Professor Humphrey, who was Professor of Anatomy at Cambridge University, noted that medical men 'had decreased in number relatively',[50] and he agreed that there was a 'danger of the examinations becoming too strict'.[51] He pointed out that there had been a 'greatly increasing proportion of rejections' of candidates for a licence to practise medicine, a proportion which had increased from 14 per cent in 1867 to 23 per cent in 1875.[52] When asked directly whether he felt that 'this increasing stringency of examinations has interfered with the public interest by diminishing too much the supply of medical men', Humphry replied 'I believe it is so to some extent. When the examinations were increased, after the recommendations of the General Medical Council ... were adopted, there was a sudden diminution of members in the profession.'[53] The link between the 1858 Medical Act and the subsequent shortage of qualified practitioners could not have been made more explicit. The Act had proved to be, as most practitioners had hoped it would, a most effective way of restricting entry to the profession.

There is some evidence to suggest that, perhaps not surprisingly, this restriction of entry to the profession was associated with a significant improvement in both the earnings and the status of medical practitioners. Thus St. Thomas's Hospital, in the evidence which it submitted to a Government Committee in 1878, pointed to the 'steady and progressive decrease of the number of medical practitioners in the United Kingdom, proportionately to the population', and went on to note that 'It is certain that within the same period the remuneration of medical men occupied in civil practice has greatly increased ... The social status and influence of civil medical practitioners has undoubtedly increased with their increased earnings.'[54]

Systematic information on the level of incomes of medical practitioners is rather difficult to obtain, and for this reason the report of the 1878 Committee is of some importance. The Committee had been established as a result of growing concern about the declining number of recruits to the Army Medical Department and, as part of its investigation, the Committee compared conditions of work and incomes in military and in civilian medical practice. In order to estimate the average level of incomes in civilian medical practice, the Committee invited submissions from medical schools and universities, and also from individual practitioners. Most estimates of income from civil practice showed a substantial amount of agreement and all of them further agreed that medical incomes had risen in the previous two or three decades. In the evidence which it submitted to the Committee, St. Bartholemew's Hospital estimated the average income of a country general practitioner as between £600 and £1000 per year after ten years in practice, with the incomes of general practitioners in urban areas being somewhat higher. This estimate was broadly in line with that submitted by St. Thomas's Hospital, which held that the majority of young men 'of superior education' will be found 'at the end of ten years from their entry into practice to be earning from £500 to £1500 a year, or more'.[55] The Westminster Hospital similarly held that 'our men are very soon able to marry and earn incomes varying from £500 to £1000 a year'.[56] Dr Hewitt from University College declined to give specific figures but, like other witnesses, he was clearly of the opinion that the financial prospects of newly qualified medical men were by this time relatively good: the 'well educated industrious student finds little difficulty in the present day in establishing himself in civil practice, and if his abilities are of an average character he is certain within a short time to obtain a tolerably good income'.[57]

The general conclusion reached by the Committee was that 'Taken one with another, a medical man obtains in civil life a net income of £300 a year within 5 years of commencing practice. After 10 years he is unlucky if he does not net £500 a year, and thence his income gradually rises to an average of £800 to £1000. Of course, in exceptional cases these rates of income are very far exceeded.'[58] Even if one allows for the fact that the desire of medical witnesses to encourage the government to raise military surgeons' salaries may have led them, perhaps unconsciously, to inflate their estimates of earnings in civilian practice, it is clear that the financial situation of medical men in the late nineteenth century was a steadily improving one, and one which was able to offer what Dr. Hewitt called 'a tolerably good income' for the practitioner of average ability, and very much more than this for the practitioner of outstanding ability.

It should be pointed out that this increased prosperity amongst medical men was not equally shared by all practitioners. As we noted in chapter three, pockets of financial hardship persisted particularly amongst practitioners who worked in the poorer urban areas until the end of the century. Nevertheless, it is clear that the financial situation of most medical men in the second half of the nineteenth century was a rapidly improving one and that, as a number of contemporary observers noted, there was a clear link between the improvement in the incomes and status of medical men and the restriction of entry to the profession which followed the passage of the 1858 Medical Act. In this sense it may be argued that the profession as a whole did indeed enjoy considerable monopolistic gains from the establishment of a medical register under the control of the General Medical Council.

In conclusion, therefore, we may suggest that those writers who have argued that the 1858 Act was passed for the benefit of the public have offered at best a grossly oversimplified account of the significance of registration, for they have ignored not only the fact that the profession derived significant monopolistic advantages from registration but equally importantly the fact that these monopolistic advantages were clearly recognised within the profession from the very beginning of the campaign for registration.

8.

The Development of Medical Ethics
in the Nineteenth Century

THE development of the general practitioners' campaign for medical reform constituted one of the more dramatic and publicly visible aspects of change within the medical profession in the first half of the nineteenth century. During this same period, however, numerous other changes were taking place within the medical profession, and many of these changes were also to play an important part in the long term development of medicine as a modern profession. One such area of change involved the development of a modern code of medical ethics.

The existence of a code of professional ethics has frequently been held to be one of the major distinguishing characteristics of modern professional occupations. If this is indeed the case, it is clearly important to examine the conditions under which a modern code of medical ethics developed in the nineteenth century. The object of this chapter is, then, to provide an analysis of the origins and early development of modern medical ethics by relating this development to other structural changes within the medical profession in the nineteenth century.

Medical ethics as such were not, of course, the creation of nineteenth century medical men; indeed, the most famous of all codes of medical ethics — the Hippocratic Oath — probably dates from as early as the fourth century BC.[1] There was, of course, no body with the power to enforce the ethical rules contained in the Hippocratic Oath, but Leake has suggested that the oath may nevertheless have had some influence on the practice of medicine. Prior to the end of the eighteenth century, he says, 'the medical profession tried generally to handle its ethical problems on the basis of the

Greek tradition of good taste and personal honor'.[2] Within the present context, however, our concern is to understand the development of specifically *modern* codes of medical ethics, and this means that our analysis must focus not on ancient Greece, but on nineteenth century England, for it was here that the foundations of modern codes of medical ethics were laid.

Amongst medical historians, there appears to be widespread agreement that the work of the Manchester physician Thomas Percival, whose *Medical Ethics* was published in 1803, marks a particularly important break point between ancient and modern codes of ethics. Thus, for example, Leake has pointed out that Percival, more than any other person, effected the 'transition from the broad principles of Greek medical ethics to the current complicated system'.[3] This view of the significance of Percival's work is shared by most other writers on the subject. Thus Barton has suggested that Percival 'compiled the first modern code of medical ethics',[4] whilst McConaghey has similarly argued that the 'rules of conduct of modern times stem from the small book published in 1803 by Thomas Percival'.[5] For Forbes, Percival's work represents a 'prominent landmark in the progress and evolution of medical ethics', and he goes on to suggest that 'No later work has modified in any material degree the precepts and practice defined by Percival for the conduct of a physician'.[6]

Percival's work is, therefore, of central importance for anyone wishing to understand the development of modern medical ethics. However, whilst it is difficult to overestimate the importance of Percival's book, it would be quite wrong to see it in an almost asocial sense purely as the work of a gifted individual; for Percival's work is simply the most famous of a number of publications by medical men in the first half of the nineteenth century, all of which indicate a major concern with ethical problems in the practice of medicine. Amongst these other works one might mention in particular W O Porter's *Medical Science and Ethicks*,[7] published in 1837, and Abraham Banks' *Medical Etiquette*,[8] published in 1839. This concern with ethical problems also found expression in articles and editorials on medical ethics in all the major medical periodicals, as well as in very many letters from readers dealing with similar problems. Finally, mention must be made of associations, like the Manchester Medico-Ethical Association,[9] which were founded specifically to deal with ethical problems, and of the development of medico-ethical committees in medical associations founded for more general purposes, such as the British Medical Association, which established its own medico-ethical committee in 1853.[10]

Clearly, therefore, Percival's concern with ethical problems in the practice of medicine was a concern which he shared with many of his contemporaries. Our problem then, is to explain why practitioners in England were so concerned with medico-ethical problems at this time. Why should so many practitioners have been concerned to set out the ethical principles which, in their view, should regulate the practice of medicine?

In general terms, the attempt to formulate codes of professional ethics and to establish institutions to enforce those codes may be seen as an attempt by professional men themselves to cope with certain recurrent problems with which they are faced in the day-to-day practice of their profession. It is important to appreciate that these problems are not individual problems, but are shared by many members of the occupational group in question. Thus, to ask why practitioners in England at this time were concerned with medical ethics is to ask what sort of problems they habitually faced in the practice of medicine. It is this question which we shall attempt to resolve in this chapter.

Before we attempt to resolve this question, it may be useful to outline briefly what has for many years been the dominant approach to understanding the development of codes of professional ethics. This approach, characteristic of the vast majority of those who have written on the subject, suggests that the development of professional ethics can only be understood within the context of an analysis of relationships between practitioners and their clients. In their classic study of the professions, first published in 1933, Carr-Saunders and Wilson argued that 'Just as the public may fail to distinguish between competent and incompetent, so it may fail to distinguish between honourable and dishonourable practitioners. Therefore the competent and honourable practitioners are moved mutually to guarantee not only their competence but also their honour. Hence the formulation of ethical codes.'[11] A few years later, TH Marshall suggested that 'Ethical codes are based on the belief that between professional and client there is a relationship of trust, and between buyer and seller there is not.'[12] Since the time that these words were written, the idea that an understanding of practitioner-client relationships is central to an understanding of professional ethics has become so widely accepted that it may now almost be described as a sociological orthodoxy. Characteristically, those who pursue this line of argument suggest that for a variety of reasons — primarily his ignorance — the client is unable to judge the quality of the professional services which he receives. As a result, the client is held to be very vulnerable to exploitation by the unscrupulous practitioner, and the development of professional ethics is seen as a response to this problem of social control. Thus the professional group itself underakes to guarantee the integrity of its members by the development and enforcement of codes of professional ethics. In this way, the risk of exploitation of the client is minimised.[13] Specifically in relation to medical ethics, this type of explanation appears to be accepted by most medical historians and, not surprisingly, by medical practitioners themselves.

This approach, however, has been developed without reference to any detailed empirical investigation of the development of codes of professional ethics. How well, then, does this approach enable us to understand the development of modern codes of medical ethics? Given the importance of Percival's work in this context, it may be appropriate to begin with an examination of some of the characteristics of his book.

A careful examination of Percival's *Medical Ethics* provides little evidence to suggest that Percival was concerned primarily with ethical problems in the doctor-patient relationship. Indeed, one of the most striking features of the book is the relatively small amount of space which he devotes to a discussion of these problems. Excluding Percival's last chapter, which is on medical jurisprudence rather than medical ethics, of the forty-eight remaining pages only half-a-dozen or so are devoted to a consideration of ethical problems in the doctor-patient relationship. Moreover, his advice to practitioners on how to behave towards patients is, for the most part, of a highly general kind which is very much in keeping with the Greek tradition; there is thus nothing specifically modern about it. Thus, for example, Percival advises medical practitioners to 'unite tenderness with steadiness' and 'condescension with authority'.[14] All patients should be treated 'with attention, steadiness and humanity'.[15] Percival gives little advice on how to cope with more specific problems in the doctor-patient relationship — although he does suggest that there should be no discussion of a case in front of the patient;[16] that medical men should observe 'secrecy and delicacy' with female patients;[17] and that the 'familiar and confidential intercourse, to which the faculty are admitted in their professional visits, should be used with discretion and with the most scrupulous regard to fidelity and honour'.[18]

Perhaps the most striking feature of Percival's book is that, whilst relatively little space is given to a consideration of ethical problems in doctor-patient relationships, a great deal of space is devoted to establishing a set of rules for regulating relationships *between* practitioners. Moreover, the advice which Percival gives to practitioners in this context is much more concrete and more detailed. Consider, for example, the following advice to practitioners concerning the proper conduct of consultations: 'In consultations on medical cases the junior physician present should deliver his opinion first, and the others in progressive order of their seniority. The same order should be observed in chirurgical cases.'[19] Consultations involving both physicians and surgeons are slightly more complex, and Percival's advice is accordingly more detailed: 'In consultations on mixed cases, the junior surgeon should deliver his opinion first, and his brethren afterwards in succession, according to progressive seniority. The junior physician present should deliver his opinion after the senior surgeon and the other physicians in the order above prescribed.'[20] Moreover, to resolve any uncertainty which may arise in situations where the lines of seniority are not clearly established, Percival even sets out a method for assessing the relative seniority of the practitioners involved in the consultation.[21]

The fact that Percival's book is concerned primarily with regulating relationships between practitioners has been clearly pointed out by Leake, who makes a distinction between medical etiquette and medical ethics. Medical etiquette, he argues, 'is concerned with the conduct of physicians toward each other, and embodies the tenets of professional courtesy. Medical ethics should be concerned with the ultimate consequences of the conduct of physicians towards their individual patients and toward society as a whole.'[22] He goes on to note that 'The term "medical ethics", introduced by Percival, is really a misnomer ... it refers chiefly to the rules of etiquette developed in the profession to regulate the professional contacts of its members *with each other*.'[23] That Percival's book deals primarily with intra-professional relationships is not very surprising, for the book was written in an attempt to resolve what was a purely intra-professional dispute. In 1789, the resources of the Manchester Infirmary were severely strained by an epidemic of either typhoid or typhus, and during the emergency the trustees of the hospital decided to double the staff. The physicians and surgeons who were already on the staff of the hospital took this as a reflection upon their efforts and resigned. In the confusion attending the change of staff, there was apparently a good deal of ill-feeling amongst the practitioners attached to the hospital; and Percival, who was physician extraordinary to the infirmary and a much respected practitioner in the area, was asked to draw up a 'scheme of professional conduct relative to hospitals and other medical charities'. The result was a small book which was printed for private distribution in 1794, and which appeared in a revised form in 1803 as Percival's *Medical Ethics*.[24] Leake has pointed out that the 'circumstances under which Percival's "Code" was written, made it necessary for him to place considerable emphasis on medical etiquette';[25] while Lester King has similarly observed that the book was designed 'specifically to establish greater harmony among the physicians who had the care of the indigent sick, and was in no sense an attempt to explore any vague ethical generalities'.[26]

Despite the specific circumstances under which Percival was writing, his book was by no means unique in terms of the kinds of problems with which it dealt, for his concern to regulate relationships between practitioners in a more ordered fashion was clearly shared by many of his contemporaries. Thus Abraham Banks' *Medical Etiquette*[27] was, as its title suggests, concerned almost entirely with the regulation of intra-professional relationships. Indeed, the only point at which the doctor-patient relationship becomes problematic for Banks is when one practitioner is called in to attend the patient of another, and only because more than one practitioner is involved in the management of the case. A similar story is told by the letters to the *Lancet*, in which allegations of unprofessional behaviour focus almost entirely around the conduct of consultations and the poaching by one practitioner of the patients of another.[28] Another problem which frequently gave rise to intra-professional disputes concerned the division of fees in cases where the regular practitioner had been unable to attend a patient, and another practitioner had been called in. This problem was, in fact, the very first problem dealt with by Banks in his book,[29] and in 1845 the *Lancet* reported that a meeting of practitioners had been arranged in London in order to establish some rules governing fee-splitting in such cases. The *Lancet* commented that 'Some general arrangements of this nature had long been needed', and it went on to express the hope that such an arrangement would help to remove 'the stigma cast upon the profession, that it displayed no more cohesion than a rope of sand'.[30]

In fact, virtually all of the literature from this period strongly suggests that relationships between practitioners were much more sensitive and — from the profession's point of view — much more in need of regulation than were relationships between practitioners and their patients. Occasionally, those tensions between practitioners gave rise to open hostilities. Thus in 1837, the *Lancet* carried an editorial on a dispute between some medical practitioners in Newport and Monmouth. In the course of this dispute, which was publicised in the *Monmouthshire Merlin* of 25 November, the practitioners involved took to 'placarding' one another, that is distributing handbills critical of their opponents.[31] In 1845, the *Lancet* devoted another editorial to a conflict which had broken out between two medical men in Frome, Somerset. This dispute, like many others during this period, arose as a result of a consultation between two practitioners, both of whom had published pamphlets criticising the other. The *Lancet* observed that one of the practitioners 'heaps insult upon insult on his opponent, on his opponent's brother — whose part in the case was merely that of a spectator — and even attacks the entire medical profession of Frome'.[32]

These well-publicised conflicts merely represented the tip of the iceberg however, for conflicts between practitioners were endemic at this time, and it seems to have been appreciated by medical men themselves that the major problems with which they had to contend arose from the internal divisions and tensions within the profession. Thus Abraham Banks drew attention to the 'prevalence of illiberality in country towns and villages; the jealousy existing between individual practitioners, who frequently, under the mask of candour and professed friendship, undermine each other's reputation, and never lose a chance of sinking one another in public estimation, when this can be done with seeming good grace and kindness'.[33] That relationships between practitioners in country towns and villages were frequently strained will come as no surprise to those who are familiar with Trollope's description of the medical 'war in Barsetshire' in *Doctor Thorne*. Dr Fillgrave, it will be remembered, did not consider Dr Thorne 'fit society', and declined to meet him in consultation, following which there was a bitter exchange of letters between the two practitioners in the *Barsetshire Conservative Standard*, and also in the newspapers of Bristol, Exeter and Gloucester.[34] Readers of George Eliot may similarly recall the hostility expressed towards the unfortunate Dr Lydgate by his fellow practitioners in *Middlemarch*.[35] If relationships between practitioners in the provinces were frequently strained, those between practitioners in London were often characterised by even greater extremes of bitterness. As an example, one might cite the *Lancet*'s description of hospital consultants and of those who controlled the Royal Colleges as 'crafty, intriguing, corrupt, avaricious, cowardly, plundering, rapacious, soul-betraying, dirty-minded BATS'.[36] Clearly it was this kind of intra-professional conflict with which Banks was concerned; his object, he said, was 'to promote concord and harmony amongst the several branches of the profession'.[37] A similar point had been made two years earlier by W O Porter in his *Medical Science and Ethicks*, in which he called upon all doctors to follow the golden rule: 'Do unto all men as you would that they should do unto you'.[38] He hoped that we 'should not then be exposed to feel, or witness, or even hear of those feuds, which sometimes arise between members of the profession, so injurious to the interests of all concerned, and so derogatory to that high character, which it is our duty to preserve, and should be our chief aim to raise in the estimation of the public'.[39]

This same point was repeated again and again by those writing on medical ethics. Thus in 1845, a correspondent of the *Lancet* called for the introduction of 'a standard or rule to guide doctors in their professional activities'. However, he went on in a somewhat despondent manner: 'Or, is this subject too delicate, and must we continue to live on, hoping for better feelings and deportment in those who have hardly a fair word to use for their brother? Perhaps it is doubtful, after all, whether any set of rules would unite a body so disaffected as ours.'[40] Perhaps most telling, however, are the comments of the author of an article on medical ethics published in the *London Medical Gazette*. The author, W B Kesteven, pointed to the 'urgent need of a generally acknowledged principle whereon to base the rules of medical ethics', and claimed that 'it is doubtless the want of some such principle that permits the jealousies, bickerings, and calumnies which distress and divide the different branches and interests of the profession'.[41] He then went on to ask, 'Is it not an unenviable paradoxical notoriety, that a profession pre-eminently benevolent and . . . eleemosynary to all beyond its own immediate sphere, should towards its own members be proverbially uncharitable and litigious? Alas! will the time never be that men shall apply to its members the eulogium so unwittingly extorted from the pagans of old, "See how these Christians love one another?" Or rather, how long shall it be that the world shall continue to say, "See how these doctors hate one another?"[42]

This argument is particularly telling, not least because it draws attention to the fact that relationships between doctors and the wider society, including patients, were frequently characterised by benevolence and charity on the part of practitioners. The same point was made in an editorial in the *Lancet* in 1842[43] and, indeed, this seems to have been something in relation to which the medical profession took considerable pride. The everyday problems facing medical practitioners, it is clear, arose not in their relationships with their patients, but in their relationships with their professionaal colleagues, relationships which all too frequently were characerised by tensions, hostilities, accusations and counter-accusations. The development of medical ethics, it is suggested, can best be understood as an attempt to regulate these tension-ridden relationships so as to reduce the amount of potentially very damaging intra-professional conflict.

There appear to have been two major processes associated with this endemic conflict within the medical profession, and both of these processes found a clear and direct expression in the literature on medical ethics during this period. The first of these processes related, perhaps not surprisingly, to the tensions associated with the breakdown of the traditional tripartite professional structure, which has already been analysed in earlier chapters. Building upon this earlier analysis, we are now in a position to draw out the relationship between these changes within the structure of the profession and the development of codes of medical ethics.

As we have already seen, in the first half of the nineteenth century the traditional tripartite structure of the profession was steadily breaking down. We have also seen, however, that an institutional structure appropriate to the newly emerging professional differentiation was slow in developing, for whilst medical men were increasingly being divided into consulting and general practitioners, the institutional structure of the profession continued to reflect the more traditional differentiation between physicians, surgeons and apothecaries. This resulted in a very confused situation, in which the definitions of appropriate roles and relative statuses within the medical profession became very unclear. As a correspondent of the *Lancet* pointed out in 1841, 'Everything connected with our profession is, at present, in a state of disorder and uncertainty; its laws are in abeyance; and young men, about to commence their medical studies, are quite at a loss what to expect, or what plan of education to pursue.'[44] The medical profession in the first half of the nineteenth century was, as Leake has bluntly but accurately characterised it, 'a mess', and within this fluid and ambiguous situation, different types of practitioners 'jockeyed for positions of prestige and power'.[45]

This jockeying for position was related largely to the prevailing confusion surrounding the division of labour within the profession, a problem which, as we have seen, was intimately related to the different statuses attributed to different kinds of medical work. Thus whilst more and more medical men were combining the practice of medicine, surgery, midwifery and pharmacy, the old established elite groups within the profession did everything in their power to maintain a clear separation between the work of the physician, the surgeon and the apothecary, and to stigmatise the work of the general practitioner. The sort of intra-professional hostilities which arose at the local level within this situation are well portrayed in George Eliot's *Middlemarch*, a novel which is of some significance to medical historians since, as Harvey has noted, it delineates 'with historical precision the emergence of a new *kind* of doctor',[46] the general practitioner. Harvey correctly points out that Lydgate 'represents this new type and the hostility he arouses in the physicians of Middlemarch . . . reflects in large part that uneasy awareness that the traditional orders, jealously guarded, are being subverted.'[47] One might add that this 'subversion' of the 'traditional orders' was also an important factor underlying the conflict between Dr Thorne and Dr Fillgrave so graphically described by Trollope.

In many ways, the local conflicts portrayed in *Middlemarch* and in *Doctor Thorne* may be seen as microcosms of the developing conflict on the national level. The attempt on the part of the Royal Colleges to maintain the traditional divisions within the profession and to stem the rise of the general practitioner gave rise to a long struggle for medical reform which was bitterly fought on both sides, and which gave rise to extremes of vituperation and personal insult, in which the *Lancet* in particular excelled. In 1858, the *Westminster Review* not inaccurately described the history of the medical reform movement as a history of 'the irreconcilable divisions and quarrels of the profession itself',[48] whilst two years previously, the same journal had referred to 'the dissensions which have so long festered' within the medical profession.[49] The widely held picture of a profession as a harmonious community is not one which can readily be applied to the medical profession in the first half of the nineteenth century; indeed, as Poynter has noted, the medical profession during this period was 'a profession in chaos ... split from top to bottom by jealous rivalries and competing interests'.[50]

This analysis provides a major key to understanding why relationships between practitioners were so frequently characterised by ill feeling and disharmony. It also helps us to understand why the problem of defining what kinds of medical work should be undertaken by what kinds of practitioners figured prominently in the literature on medical ethics, for this issue constituted a major source of the intra-professional disputes which so bitterly divided the profession during this period. Thus only in these terms, it is suggested, can we properly understand Percival's lengthy discussion of the relationships which, in his view, ought to prevail between the different 'grades' of practitioners. Of Percival's three chapters on medical ethics, the whole of the third chapter is devoted to a discussion 'Of the Conduct of Physicians towards Apothecaries', whilst other statements on the relationships between physicians, surgeons, and apothecaries are scattered liberally throughout his work. In his advice on the conduct of mixed consultations, cited earlier, Percival showed a clear understanding of the nice status distinctions between physicians and surgeons in his recommendation that the most junior physician present should deliver his opinion after the most senior surgeon had delivered his.

On issues of this kind, Percival was a conservative —according to Sir George Clark, 'the best conservative opinion' of his time[51] — and accordingly he advised his fellow practitioners to maintain the traditional division of labour within the profession. Thus in his chapter on hospitals, he advised, 'A proper discrimination being established, in all hospitals between the medical and chirurgical cases, it should be faithfully adhered to by the physicians and surgeons on the admission of patients.'[52] Similarly, in the chapter on private practice, he recommended that 'in large and opulent towns the distinction between the provinces of physic and surgery should be steadily maintained. This distinction is sanctioned both by reason and experience. . . . Experience has fully evinced the benefits of the discrimination recommended, which is established in every well regulated hospital, and is thus expressly authorised by the faculty themselves and by those who have the best opportunities of judging of the proper application of the healing art. No physician or surgeon, therefore, should adopt more than one denomination, or assume any rank or privileges different from those of his order.'[53] Similarly, in his chapter on the relationships between physicians and apothecaries, he suggests that physicians should refuse a request to visit the patients of an apothecary in the latter's absence: 'Physicians are the only proper substitutes for physicians; surgeons for surgeons; and apothecaries for apothecaries.'[54] Thus Percival tried to present clear guidelines which would prevent the continual disputes over the division of labour within the profession; his solution, as we have seen, was to call for the maintenance of the traditional divisions within the profession.

While most practitioners seem to have agreed that the breakdown of the traditional tripartite division of labour was a major cause of the jealousies and tensions within the profession, few were willing to accept Percival's conservative remedy. The radical position was most clearly set out in a long paper on medical ethics by Thomas Laycock, which was published anonymously in the *British and Foreign Medico-Chirurgical Review* in 1848. Laycock pointed out that the profession 'seems little better than a chaos; the whole mass is upheaving; decomposition and recomposition are going on; but we can discern no great principles by which coherence and strength may be given to the discordant elements. It is quite impossible that the intelligent lay public will notice the professional desire for organisation and legislation, so long as the impelling motives are nothing more dignified than sectional interests, grade prejudices, or interested clamours in a pecuniary sense.'[55] 'How,' he added, 'can members of Parliament and the educated classes esteem a profession, the members of which mutually disparage each other?'[56] Laycock then went on to examine the squabbles over the division of labour within the profession.

All bodies of men are intolerant of any departure from principles and practices that have become conventional. Although such departure may have nothing whatever in it morally wrong, yet it is visited 'with the utmost rigour of the law' — that may have been conventionally established. Thus physicians fully engaged in practice will bitterly regard the young physician who, feeling the pressure of the *res augusta domi,* may exercise any surgical talent he may possess, or who, suspecting that his medicamina are not well compounded, or of a spurious quality, may look to the manufacture of his powder, or point his own guns.[57]

He pointed out that even though all types of practitioners cooperated harmoniously in voluntary organisations like the Royal Medico-Chirurgical Society, the medical corporations continued to 'raise their Shibboleth before the public, before Parliament, and in the profession, and establish their differences where there is hardly any distinction'. Many surgeons treated medical cases as frequently as surgical ones. 'To all purposes, and in every way, the surgeon is a physician, with the ability to operate chirurgically superadded to his medical acquirements, and is conventionally permitted to operate, prescribe, and receive his fee, so long as he calls himself "surgeon". But let him add MD to his name, and conventionalism forthwith binds up his right hand, severs him from his College, and circumscribes the sphere of his usefulness.' Laycock added that 'if it could be proved that this line of demarcation, already obliterated in the voluntary associations, is of any use whatever to either the profession or the public when drawn between two classes of practitioners, in which the difference of education and attainments is *now* at least really but nominal, we would acquiesce at once in the arrangement. But it has yet to be shown that a union of these two educational institutions, and a reorganisation on a broad base of ethical principles, would either render the surgeon less skillful, or the physician less educated or intellectual. The whole matter is indeed hardly capable of serious argument.' Laycock thus called for the abolition of those professional divisions which Percival had defended in 1803. Only by taking such a step, argued Laycock, could the intra-professional squabbling and bickering be ended. Thus he concluded his paper by calling on enlightened practitioners to place the organisation of the profession on 'its proper basis', or else the profession would remain 'as it is — a chaos of conflicting elements'.[58]

Shortly afterwards, the *Lancet* gave Laycock's paper its 'warmest approbation'. Quoting extensively from the article, the *Lancet* said 'there are no passages in the article . . . with which we more cordially agree than those which describe the unworthy jealousies which rise between some among the different classes of the profession, when any man dares step out of his proper line; when the physician or surgeon, for instance, trenches upon the province of the general practitioner; when the general practitioner aspires to the work of the surgeon or physician; or when the physician and surgeon dare to defy artificial distinctions, and pass from one department to the other'. The *Lancet* added 'how constantly have we dealt on the meretricious separation, the unworthy caste-division, which seeks to make the highest surgeon lower than the physician, and the highest general practitioner lower than both'.[59] Since its foundation in 1823 the *Lancet* had, of course, campaigned consistently for the abolition of the tripartite professional structure, and by the middle of the nineteenth century there was widespread agreement amongst doctors that there could be no end to the disharmony and tensions within the profession as long as the tripartite structure remained. It is hardly surprising that this issue should have figured prominently in the literature on medical ethics.

These tensions, which were associated with structural

changes within the profession, were further exacerbated by the fact that, at least for much of the first half of the nineteenth century, medical men were involved in intensely competitive relationships with their fellow practitioners. In the early part of the century, this high level of competition between practitioners appears to have been associated with the fact that there was a rapid increase in the number of practitioners qualifying in the 1820s and 1830s, and, as we have seen, this may well have resulted in an overcrowded profession. This overcrowding, in turn, gave rise to a situation in which cut-throat competition between rival practitioners, particularly in the form of poaching of each other's patients, was common. Indeed, competition between local practitioners was so intense that many practitioners 'feared, and rightly, that they would lose patients to their competitors if they left town for a holiday'; as a result, some medical men never went away for more than a weekend during much of their professional lives.[60]

Highly competitive relationships of this kind not infrequently gave rise to disputes between practitioners serving similar or overlapping neighbourhoods. Such disputes, especially those involving allegations relating to the poaching of patients, were particularly likely to occur in situations where two practitioners were involved in treating the same patient; for example, in situations where one practitioner was called to attend the patient of another practitioner in the latter's absence, or where a second practitioner was called in for a consultation at the patient's bedside. As we shall see, the attempt to establish a set of guidelines which would have the effect of reducing the potential level of conflict between practitioners in such delicate situations constituted a second major concern of those writing on medical ethics at this time.

Before, however, we examine the relevant guidelines laid down by Percival and others, it is important to note that this high level of competition between practitioners cannot be wholly explained simply in terms of overcrowding within the profession for, important though this was — at least in the first half of the nineteenth century — there was a second aspect to this problem of competition between practitioners.

This arose from the fact that the two major roles within the profession — that of the general practitioner and of the consultant — were both, in a real sense, new roles; and as such they had not yet become as clearly differentiated and institutionalised as they are today. In particular, there was one critical area of overlap between the role of the consultant and the role of the general practitioner, an area of overlap which not only differentiates the nineteenth-century consultant from the present-day consultant, but which was also at the root of much of the conflict and competition which characterised consultations between practitioners in the nineteenth century.

This critical area of overlap arose because consultants did not then — as they do now — confine their practice to consulting work but, as we indicated earlier, they also normally acted as general practitioners to small numbers of wealthy clients. In addition, there was a considerable number of practitioners — particularly in the provinces, where consulting work was normally less readily available — who derived the major part of their income from general practice, but who also occasionally acted as consultants within their own locality. The result was that consultations were normally held between two practitioners, both of whom to some extent were in general practice; there was thus a real element of competition involved, particularly for wealthier clients. Within this situation, mutual suspicion and hostility between consultants and general practitioners were common. Allegations by general practitioners that consultants were trying to steal their patients either by calling on the patient a second time without the knowledge of the regular attendant, or by implicitly or explicitly criticising the treatment prescribed by the latter, were common. From the 1830s onwards, the *Lancet* published numerous letters from practitioners alleging unprofessional conduct on the part of other practitioners, the most common complaints being those which related to the conduct of consultations and the poaching of patients. In a paper on medical ethics published in 1849, W B Kesteven referred to the 'censurable condemnation of a professional brother, whether of a higher or lower grade, by looks, gestures, innuendos, etc. For example, a physician called in consultation takes occasion in the absence of the general practitioner to hint that a different treatment should have been adopted; or by indirect means, such as *friendly* visits, etc., supplants the ordinary attendant, or destroys his patient's confidence'.[61] In 1854, the *Association Medical Journal*, in reply to a correspondent who complained of the conduct of a consultant, agreed that it was easy for a consultant to:

> Convey a censure in a frown,
> And wink a reputation down.

The *Association Medical Journal* went on to point out that 'extreme watchfulness and honesty of act and feeling are essential requisites in this class of practitioners'.[62]

Given the potentiality for conflict inherent in the structure of consultations at this time, it is not surprising that a number of writers, from Percival onwards, should have seen the conduct of consultations and the poaching of patients as particularly problematic areas requiring regulation by a code of medical ethics. Percival's advice on these matters is quite detailed. Thus he recommends that punctuality should be observed by both parties to the consultation, and that 'No visits should be made but in concert, or by mutual agreement'.[63] When consultations are held, 'no rivalship or jealousy should be indulged. Candour, probity and all due respect should be exercised towards the physician or surgeon first engaged.'[64] 'Officious interference, in a case under the charge of another, should be carefully avoided.'[65] If a practitioner is called to a patient under the care of another practitioner, he should always observe 'the utmost delicacy towards the interest and character of the professional gentleman, previously connected with the family'.[66] The practitioner should 'interfere no farther than is absolutely necessary with the general plan of the treatment; to assume no further direction, unless it be expressly desired; and, in this case, to request an immediate consultation with the practitioner antecedently employed'.[67] Abraham Banks deals with many similar problems, advising consultants not to call on patients in the absence of the general practitioner,[68] giving advice on how to divide the fee when a consultation is held,[69] on how to act when a second party is called in to decide upon the treatment of another practitioner,[70] and on what to do in a situation in which one practitioner is called to attend the patient of another practitioner.[71] The fact that such situations were regarded as particularly delicate is further indicated by the fact that in W Fraser's 'Queries in medical ethics', a series of questions and answers on ethical problems published in the *London Medical Gazette* in 1849, no less than fourteen of the twenty-seven queries related specifically to problems which were associated either with consultations, or with taking over the management of a case from another practitioner.[72]

In summarising the argument thus far, we may say that the development of a code of medical ethics did not represent the outcome of any special interest on the part of medical men in the formulation of abstract philosophical principles; indeed, the probability is that medical men were no more given to abstract philosophical speculation than was any other section of the educated classes. Rather, the growing concern of medical men with ethical problems has to be seen as a practical concern which arose from and represented an attempt to resolve certain recurrent problems with which they were faced in the day-to-day practice of their profession. Moreover, the foregoing analysis has suggested that these practical problems arose primarily within the context of relationships *between* practitioners, partly as a result of the highly competitive nature of these relationships, and partly as a result of other structural tensions within the profession.

It is clear that this analysis of the development of medical ethics stands in sharp contrast to the commonly held view that medical ethics developed primarily in order to regulate relationships between practitioners and their patients; as we have seen, such a view finds little support from an analysis of nineteenth-century writings on medical ethics, in which ethical problems within the doctor-patient relationship occupy only a minor place. This is not to suggest, of course, that an understanding of practitioner-patient relationships is irrelevant to an understanding of the development of medical ethics, for there are some passages in the work of Percival and other writers which do relate to the doctor-patient relationship. What is suggested is that the significance of the doctor-patient relationship for an understanding of medical ethics has hitherto been considerably overemphasised, and that the development of medical ethics may be much more closely related to the need — widely perceived amongst nineteenth-century medical men — to regulate relationships between practitioners in such a way as to reduce what was felt to be the excessive and potentially damaging level of intra-professional conflict and competition.

The above argument — that the development of a code of medical ethics may be seen as a response to the perceived need to control intra-professional conflict and competition — may be taken as providing partial support for Berlant's view, mentioned in the previous chapter, that a code of ethics functions as an anti-competitive device which is consistent with a broader strategy of monopolisation on the part of the medical profession. It should be emphasised, however, that the argument in this chapter provides only limited support for Berlant's view. Thus whilst it has been argued that the development of medical ethics was indeed associated with a perceived need to restrict competition amongst medical men, it has been argued this development was also a response to other tensions within the profession which reflected other much deeper and more far-reaching changes within the structure of the profession, and that these other changes, which involved a radical redefinition of the roles and statuses of medical men, cannot be adequately conceptualised simply in terms of an increase in the level of competition within the profession. While the analysis in this chapter is consistent with Berlant's analysis, it also suggests that Berlant's exclusive concentration on the anti-competitive functions of medical ethics can provide only a partial and one-sided understanding of the development of medical ethics.

Moreover, it is also important to remember that, while nineteenth-century codes of ethics did indeed contain many statements of an anti-competitive kind, it should not be assumed that the development of a code of ethics automatically has an immediate or dramatic impact in terms of restricting the actual level of competition between practitioners and, indeed, such an assumption would not appear to be justified at least for the first half of the nineteenth century. Thus what is of importance is not simply the degree to which a code of ethics is elaborated, but also the extent to which that code is respected by, and enforced within, the profession as a whole. In this context, one might note that the frequency with which medico-ethical problems were raised in the medical literature of the early nineteenth century is not only an expression of the growing awareness of ethical problems on the part of many practitioners, but it is also an expression of the fact that what some practitioners were coming to regard as the rules governing 'proper' professional conduct continued to be disregarded by many practitioners.

In this respect, those who sought to impose what they saw as 'higher' standards of professional conduct were faced with two major problems. The first of these problems related to the difficulty of persuading medical men to act 'ethically' in a situation in which, as a result of overcrowding within the profession, they were constrained to compete with their fellow practitioners, sometimes in a quite ruthless fashion, simply in order to secure an adequate income for themselves and their families. In this sense, Peterson is undoubtedly correct, at least in relation to the first half of the nineteenth century, when she suggests that 'too many medical men in an overcrowded profession had to choose economic survival above loyalty to their peer group'.[73] Thus it is suggested that one reason why these developing codes of ethics appear to have had only a limited influence on the behaviour of medical men in the first half of the century was that other structural constraints led them to act in a highly competitive manner towards neighbouring practitioners. Indeed, it may be argued that, rather than the development of a code of ethics leading to a dramatic reduction in the level of competition between practitioners, it was a reduction in the actual level of competition between practitioners in the second half of the century which facilitated the more general acceptance of certain principles of 'ethical' behaviour within the profession; for within the context of a less competitive market for their services, medical men were no longer constrained to outbid or to undercut their colleagues in the way in which they had formerly been. As we saw in the previous chapter, following the 1858 Medical Act the profession was able very effectively to restrict entry to the profession, and there is little doubt that this had the effect of greatly reducing the level of competition between practitioners. The 1858 Act must thus be regarded as a development of major significance in helping to bring about those conditions which were conducive to the much more widespread acceptance of an agreed code of 'ethical' behaviour amongst all sections of the profession in the second half of the nineteenth century.

The second problem which faced these practitioners who sought to develop a code of medical ethics was the fact that, throughout this period, the only sanctions which they could use against those who broke the rules of this code were moral sanctions; for there was, of course, no single body which had any effective power to discipline practitioners for 'unprofessional' conduct. Again, this situation changed dramatically following the passage of the 1858 Medical Act, for the Act gave the General Medical Council formal powers to discipline practitioners and, as a final resort, to remove from the Medical Register the name of any practitioner who was judged by the Council to have been guilty of 'infamous Conduct in any professional Respect'. After 1858, therefore, the adherence to certain basic principles in the conduct of one's practice was no longer something which was dependent on the voluntary acceptance of those principles by each individual practitioner, for increasingly minimum standards of professional behaviour were not only defined, but also enforced, by a central body which had legally defined powers to discipline those practitioners whose behaviour, in its view, fell below those minimum standards.

In conclusion, it would be wrong to suggest that the work of writers such as Percival had an immediate impact on the behaviour of most practitioners, for the process of developing and enforcing a code of ethics was long and gradual and required, amongst other things, the development of a less competitive structure of relationships between practitioners and a new professional institution with the power to enforce those rules. If these conditions were not met in the first half of the nineteenth century, they were increasingly met in the second half, so that by the end of the century one could speak in meaningful terms about the way in which the behaviour of medical men was limited and controlled by a code of ethics. The medical profession, in other words, was finally beginning to develop an effective system of self-discipline.

9.

Professionalisation and the Development of Medical Autonomy

THROUGHOUT this book, the term 'medical profession' has been used to describe all those persons who held a formal qualification of whatever kind to practise medicine. This use of the term 'profession' is, of course, both convenient and conventional, but it does tend to mask the significance of the major changes which occurred in the organisation of medical practice in the course of the nineteenth century. For this reason, it is important to remind ourselves that, in the early nineteenth century, those who made a living by the provision of medical care — even those who were qualified — not only exhibited few of the characteristics which we have come to associate with modern professions but, equally importantly, they did not even constitute a single occupational group. In 1800, as we have seen, qualified medical care was available from members of three quite distinct and separately organised occupational groups, each of these occupational groups being sharply differentiated from the others in terms of the legal status of its members and in terms of the education and training which they had received. By 1900, however, these traditional divisions within the profession had lost most of their former relevance, and the medical profession had emerged as a single, relatively united, relatively homogeneous occupational group, at least in terms of the common pattern of basic medical education which had been prescribed for all practitioners by the 1886 Medical Act and of a common legal status for all registered practitioners. Moreover, during the same period in which medical practitioners were beginning to form a single, clearly differentiated occupational group, many other changes — some of the more important of which have been described in previous chapters —

were also taking place within medicine. As a result of these changes, the medical profession had, by the end of the nineteenth century, begun to emerge in something like the form in which we know it today, at least in terms of the institutional structure of the profession. In this sense, it may be argued that it was in the nineteenth century — and more particularly in the second half of the nineteenth century — that medicine emerged as a modern profession.

But in what precisely did this process of professionalisation consist? Amongst the many changes which occurred within the medical profession in the nineteenth century, is it possible to identify some more general process under which many of these particular changes may be subsumed? What, in other words, do we mean when we refer to the emergence of medicine as a modern profession?

In the last decade or so, sociologists have come increasingly to focus their attention on the fact that professional occupations are characterised by a high degree of autonomy from lay control. This emphasis derived initially from the work of Eliot Freidson, whose Sorokin Award winning book *Profession of Medicine* has since come to be widely regarded as the standard work on the sociology of the medical profession. In his work, Freidson argued that it is precisely this high degree of professional autonomy or self-regulation — or what, in a different context, he calls 'professional dominance' — which is the distinguishing characteristic of modern professional occupations.[1] Thus the strategic distinction between the professions and other occupations is held to lie in 'legitimate, organized autonomy — that a profession is distinct from other occupations in that it has been given the right to control its own work'.[2] In terms of this perspective, it is clear that any analysis of the development of medicine as a modern profession must include, as a major part of that analysis, an examination of the development of medical autonomy or, to put it slightly differently, it must include an analysis of the development of medical men's authority and control over their work, their patients, and the organisation of their professional lives.

Bearing these comments in mind, the significance of many of the developments examined in previous chapters becomes immediately apparent. Thus, in terms of the professionalisation of medicine, the significance of the establishment of the General Medical Council lay not merely in the fact that the Council was given certain powers to regulate medical practice throughout Britain but, more particularly, in the fact that the membership of the Council was itself dominated by the medical profession. Thus in effect it was the profession itself, acting through the General Medical Council, which was entrusted with the task of maintaining a medical register, just as it was the profession itself which was given the power to stipulate the minimum requirements, in terms of training and education, for admission to the register.

Similarly, the attempts to define a code of medical ethics in the first half of the nineteenth century represented the first tentative steps towards the establishment of a system of social control in which the professional activities of medical men would be regulated by the actions and sentiments of their professional colleagues. As we have seen, in the first half of the century, these efforts met with what one can only describe as, at best, very limited success. However, in the second half of the century, the enforcement of a code of ethics became increasingly effective, partly because relationships between practitioners during this period became less competitive as a consequence of the restriction of entry to the profession, and partly because the General Medical Council, under the 1858 Act, was given formal powers to discipline those members of the profession who were found guilty of unprofessional conduct.

All of these developments — the establishment of the General Medical Council and of a medical register, the stipulation of minimum standards of education and training, the restriction of entry to the profession, and the elaboration and enforcement of codes of medical ethics — may thus be seen as important parts of that process through which all major aspects of the practice of medicine came increasingly to be regulated by the profession itself. The establishment of a system of self-regulation of this kind, relatively free from lay control, lies at the very heart of the professionalisation process.

The analysis contained in previous chapters indicates quite

clearly that this process of professionalisation cannot be adequately understood without reference to the conscious efforts of medical men themselves to create new professional institutions and to raise the status of their occupation. As Norbert Elias has observed, if we examine processes of professional development, we come face to face 'with people struggling ... to adjust their inherited institutional framework with all its incongruities to what they feel to be their own needs'.[3] In medicine as in other professions, these struggles for institutional reform were of major importance for the development of the profession, for it was within this context of struggle that the modern medical profession began to emerge.

It would nevertheless be quite wrong to suggest that the development of the modern medical profession can be understood simply in terms of changes within the profession itself, for, to a considerable extent, the rise of the medical profession was also dependent on changes within the wider structure of society — changes over which medical men themselves had little or no control — which provided the social structural conditions favourable to the emergence not only of medicine, but also of many other occupations, as modern professions.[4] In order to understand the process of professionalisation more fully, therefore, it is necessary to examine in a little more detail the relationship between processes of change in the wider structure of society and changes within the structure of the profession itself. The object of this final chapter is to examine the interrelationship between two such processes which, it is held, were central to the development of the modern medical profession. The two processes with which we shall be concerned are, firstly, the development of a relatively high level of professional autonomy on the part of medical men and, secondly, the growth of the market for medical care in the nineteenth century. The latter process, it will be argued, had important implications for the development of the medical profession, particularly in so far as it helped to bring about conditions which were conducive to the emancipation of medical men from a variety of forms of lay control of medical practice.

Thus it will be suggested that the development of medical

authority and control cannot be adequately understood without reference to the changing structure of the market for medical care in the late eighteenth and nineteenth centuries; indeed, it will be argued that the growth of the market for medical care was, as Paul Starr has put it, 'one of the main currents deep beneath the changing structure of medical institutions'.[5] In this final chapter we shall, therefore, take a fairly long term view of the professionalisation process, and we shall be concerned specifically with an analysis of some of the major changes in the structure of the market for medical care from the late eighteenth century, and with some of the ways in which these changes within the market for medical care facilitated the development of a high level of professional autonomy.

On a general level, it is reasonable to suggest that one of the major constraints operating on the producers of any product is the structure of the market for that product. In view of this, it is perhaps somewhat surprising that so little work has been done on the structure of the market for medical care during the late eighteenth and nineteenth centuries, for as Starr has pointed out, 'the economic history of medicine, especially before the twentieth century, remains almost entirely to be written'.[6] Unfortunately, information on the structure of the market for medical care in the late eighteenth century is relatively scarce, but nevertheless a number of general points can be made with a reasonable degree of certainty. The first of these is that, throughout the eighteenth century, the provision of qualified medical care was relatively unimportant as an economic activity, for medicine did not then constitute the major industry which it has subsequently become in all industrialised societies. Thus Elliott has pointed out that the 'pre-industrial professions handled areas of life involving potential social problems and conflicts but their specific contributions to the economy . . . were marginal';[7] whilst Freidson has drawn attention to the fact that prior to the nineteenth century the services of qualified medical men were used by only a relatively small section of the population, for a variety of alternative sources of care were not only freely available, but in many cases were probably also more consistent with the indigenous belief systems of most ordinary people. Thus at the time when John Heysham was apprenticed to a country doctor in the latter half of the eighteenth century, the regular practitioner had 'much less of the confidence of the public than the itinerant quack. At all times he had to compete with the village blacksmith, the barber, and the herbalist, whose "culling of simples" . . . impressed the vulgar mind with uncommon faith'.[8] Freidson is almost certainly correct when he notes that 'Official medicine . . . had only a loose, variable connection with the general cultural beliefs of the population. . . . The bulk of everyday consultation of healers by the general population was not controlled by the organised medical occupation.'[9] Indeed, it is important to bear in mind that most care of the sick was not even part of the market economy, for it took place within the context of familial and neighbourhood relationships which were outside the realm of market exchange.

Although it is difficult to make any very precise estimate of the size and structure of the market for qualified health care in the eighteenth century, it is clear that that market — like the market for other specialised professional services[10] — was a relatively small one, and also that the demand for qualified medical care tended to be relatively highly concentrated amongst the wealthier sections of the community. Thus Reader has pointed out that, in the eighteenth century, most of the population simply could not afford qualified medical care,[11] whilst Franklin has similarly noted that most people in the predominantly rural society of eighteenth-century England were 'not in the habit of calling in a doctor in times of illness. A few medical men settled in the local country and market towns and visited the richer inhabitants of the neighbourhood but the ordinary villager and agricultural worker could not afford to employ them. Old wives' tales, traditional herbal recipes, or charms, were the mainstay of the sick.'[12]

Moreover, it should not be assumed that even those who could afford to pay for the services of qualified practitioners necessarily chose to use those services on a regular basis, for throughout the eighteenth century the traditions of domestic and folk medicine remained very strong, whilst the use of unqualified practitioners was also very common, and, as Turner has pointed out, even the highest status groups regularly patronised unqualified healers.[13] Evidence from eighteenth-century diaries also suggests that, even amongst relatively affluent and well educated groups, the services of unqualified practitioners or the use of domestic or folk remedies were frequently preferred to the services of qualified medical men.[14] Thus it seems that qualified medical men were by no means assured of a very stable or secure market for their services, even amongst those sections of the population which could afford qualified care.

It is important to emphasise, however, that in pre-industrial England — as in virtually all other pre-industrial societies — very many people were simply unable to afford the services of qualified practitioners. For those in the poorer sections of society, domestic care and folk medicine, perhaps supplemented by the help and advice of friends, neighbours or local lay healers, represented the only realistically available forms of health care. Thus it may be suggested that throughout the eighteenth century the market for qualified medical care was limited both by the inability of large sections of the population to pay for qualified medical care, and also by the persistence of traditional attitudes towards health and health care which continued to emphasise the importance of alternative sources of care over that provided by qualified practitioners.

It is of some interest to note, if only in passing, that the structure of the market for medical care outlined above was by no means unique to pre-industrial England, for it would seem that a relatively low level of effective demand for qualified medical care was — and indeed still is — a characteristic of pre-industrial societies generally, including the pre-industrial societies of eighteenth-century Europe and North America. It is significant, for example, that in describing the situation in late-eighteenth and early-nineteenth-century America, Starr has drawn attention to the relatively small size of the market for medical care, and has argued that the 'fundamental constraint on medicine in early American society was the relatively low level of demand for medical services, rather than any institutionalised restrictions on supply'.[15] Claudine Herzlich has similarly drawn attention to the 'absence of a real medical market' in France in the late-eighteenth and early-nineteenth centuries;[16] whilst Jean-Pierre Goubert, in a careful analysis of medical practice in France around 1780, emphasises not only the relatively small size of the market for qualified health care, but also the extent to which this demand was concentrated in what he calls 'the social elite'.[17]

It may be argued that there was a third major characteristic of the market for medical care during this period. This related to the fact that, throughout the eighteenth century, there was no real *national* market for medical care, but rather a series of loosely connected, more or less independent, *local* markets; again, this would seem to be a common characteristic of pre-industrial societies, in which the centralisation of government and administration and the integration of the society on a national level are — at least by modern standards — still relatively undeveloped. In England, the extent to which the organisation of medical practice continued to reflect the traditional orientation towards local markets rather than a national market may be seen in the purely local, guild-like structure of the medical corporations, for throughout the eighteenth century, there was no genuinely *national* organisation with either the inclination or the ability to control entry to the profession or, indeed, to regulate medical practice in any way. Instead, there was a large number of purely local licensing bodies, each of which was concerned only with the regulation of one particular branch of practice in its own locality.

Thus even the most prestigious of the licensing bodies in England, the Royal College of Physicians, was originally founded simply to control the practice of medicine in London and an area of seven miles around the capital. It is true, of course, that shortly afterwards the formal powers of the College were extended to cover the whole of England, but the College showed virtually no interest in exercising these broader powers and, instead, continued to concern itself almost entirely with maintaining the exclusive status of a small group of elite practitioners in London. Thus, as the official historian of the College has pointed out, throughout the eighteenth century the College 'showed no interest whatever' in regulating medical practice outside of the capital.[18] One indication of the extent to which the College was concerned almost exclusively with the London market is provided by the fact that, until 1783, the College's *Catalogue*, containing the names of those who held a licence from the College, listed only those who held a licence to practise in London; the names of those who held a licence to practise outside of London were simply omitted from the list. It is equally significant that, as late as 1800, the College listed 153 practitioners whom it had licensed to practise in London, whilst it listed only twenty-six physicians who were licensed to practise in the whole of the rest of the country. Indeed, it was not until the 1840s that the number of extra-licentiates — that is, those who held a licence to practise outside of London — began to show any significant increase, and it is not until the middle decades of the nineteenth century at the very earliest that the College can be regarded as having made any real contribution to the provision of medical care outside of London.[19]

Like the physicians, the surgeons and apothecaries also continued to be organised, throughout the eighteenth century, in local guild-like organisations. Thus until 1745 the surgeons were united with the barbers in the Company of Barber-Surgeons, which was one of the City of London Livery Companies and it was not until the Royal College of Surgeons was founded in 1800 that all connections between the surgeons and the City of London were formally severed.[20] Even then it was significant that the full title of the new College was the Royal College of Surgeons of London; it was not until the College received a new Charter in the mid-1840s that the 'London' was changed to 'England' in a belated recognition of the fact that the College, by this time, had become involved in supplying practitioners for a national market rather than a purely local one.

The third group of practitioners — the apothecaries — were similarly organised in what was a local society, for throughout the eighteenth century, the Society of Apothecaries merely had the power to regulate its members resident in London. It was only with the passing of the

Apothecaries' Act of 1815 that the Society assumed the responsibility for licensing practitioners on a national level.

Outside the capital, medical practice was very partially regulated through a variety of local institutions which included the final remnants of ecclesiastical control through bishops' licences, to the local Barber-Surgeons' Companies which persisted into the eighteenth century in some of the more important urban centres, including Bristol, Norwich, Chester, Newcastle and York.[21] In Scotland the situation was broadly similar, for here too there were no national licensing bodies, but rather a variety of institutions each of which exercised limited powers within its locality. Thus it may be suggested that insofar as the medical profession was organised at all during this period, its organisation reflected an orientation towards local markets rather than an orientation towards a single, national market.

Perhaps the clearest single indication of this fact is that, for the greater part of the eighteenth century, there was no national register of medical practitioners, the first such register being *The Medical Register for the Year 1779* published anonymously by Dr Samuel Foart Simmons. Moreover, this register was a 'purely private and unofficial venture', and doubtless it was also very incomplete.[22] Nevertheless, the publication of Simmons' register was a significant development, for the register made available for the first time relatively reliable information relating to the total number of practitioners and their distribution on a *national* level. As Sir George Clarke has put it, 'at long last in medical affairs the discovery of England was completed. It had become possible to know approximately how many members of each professional branch were in practice, and where. Vague speculations as to whether they were too few or too many in the country generally or in any particular region could now give way to calculations based on facts.'[23] In this case, Clark is quite correct to describe Simmons' register as 'a landmark in the history of the profession', for the publication of a national register — even a very imperfect one — may be taken as an early indication of a growing awareness of the fact that the focus of the medical market was steadily shifting from the local to the national level.

In summarising the argument thus far, we may say that throughout the eighteenth century the major characteristics of the market — or more precisely the markets — for medical care were that the level of effective demand for qualified care was both relatively low and relatively highly concentrated in the higher social strata, and also that these markets were local rather than national in character. We must now examine some of the implications of this market structure for the development of medicine as an occupation.

As we noted earlier, Starr has suggested that the 'fundamental constraint on medicine' in pre-industrial America was the relatively low level of demand for qualified medical care, and he goes on to note that 'Whether it was because of popular preference for domestic care and disbelief in the value of professional medicine, or the difficulty of obtaining and affording treatment, or the ease with which competitors entered the field, many physicians found it extremely difficult to support themselves solely from medical practice . . . Starting out in practice frequently meant protracted underemployment and hardship.'[24]   Starr's comments are, of course, made specifically in relation to the situation in pre-industrial America, but they could with equal accuracy be applied to the situation in eighteenth century England; for here, too, the low level of demand for qualified health care meant that for many practitioners medical practice on its own did not offer a stable, permanent or indeed full-time career. Thus a number of eighteenth-century practitioners are known to have left the profession after failing to secure an adequate income from medical practice,[25] whilst many more practitioners — probably a majority — were forced to supplement their income from medical practice with a second source of income.

A few practitioners, of course, were fortunate enough to have benefactors who were prepared to supplement their modest income from medical practice. One such practitioner was Mark Akenside, a friend of Doctor Samuel Johnson who, according to Dr Johnson, 'never attained any great extent of practice' despite the fact that he 'placed himself in view by all the common methods'. Johnson further tells us that, particularly in his early years of practice, Akenside

'would perhaps have been reduced to great exigencies' had
he been forced to live on his medical income alone. Fortun-
ately for Akenside, however, he was saved from such
exigencies by the generosity of an old friend, one Mr Dyson,
who allowed him three hundred pounds a year.[26]

Those practitioners whose medical incomes were inadequate
and who could not rely on such help from family or friends
were forced to find a different method of supplementing
their medical earnings, and the practice of having a second
occupation in addition to medicine seems to have been a
common one throughout the eighteenth century. Thus,
during the period in which they tried, without success, to
establish themselves in medical practice, both Oliver
Goldsmith and Tobias Smollett accepted literary commissions
in order to increase their total incomes.[27] Goldsmith, for
example, found that he was able to make only 'a threadbare
existence'[28] from medical practice, and it was during this
period that he accepted a number of literary commissions,
for 'though writing might not provide a respectable income
of itself, it could serve to supplement the slender living which
Goldsmith was making as a physician'.[29] Smollett made not
one, but two, equally unsuccessful attempts to establish
himself as a medical man. Though Smollett, like Goldsmith,
eventually achieved fame as a novelist, it is important to
note that originally Smollett 'did not aspire to write novels
but to practise medicine', and it was only as it became clear
that he could not support himself from his medical earnings
that he gradually resorted to writing for a living.[30] The
practitioner to whom George Crabbe was apprenticed in
1768 similarly 'had more occupations than one', for in
addition to his practice as a country surgeon, he also ran
a farm.[31]

There is little doubt, however, that the most usual method
of supplementing a purely medical income was that which
involved combining the role of a medical practitioner with
that of a retail trader. Thus throughout the eighteenth
century, many medical men continued to adopt a very
traditional and very broad conception of the doctor's role
which included not merely the dispensing and the sale of
drugs, but also the keeping of an open shop in which was

sold a whole variety of goods, some of which were more closely related to the role of a retail trader than to that of a medical practitioner. The lower branches of the profession, of course, had very strong historical links with certain aspects of the retail trade, and it is clear that those links remained strong throughout the eighteenth century. Thus in 1753, an advertisement announcing the sale of an apothecary's shop in Hampshire listed, along with the medical utensils, 'some good Tobacco and a Tobacco Engine'.[32] Similarly, the stock of James Shergold, an apothecary who practised at Salisbury in Wiltshire, included tea, chocolate, spirituous liquors and tobacco.[33] This involvement in the retail trade was particularly common — indeed, it was almost certainly normal practice — amongst the lower branches of the profession, but it was by no means unknown even amongst the elevated ranks of the physicians. Claver Morris, a physician who practised at Wells in Somerset in the eighteenth century, made his own cosmetics which he sold to his patients, including 'hair butter' and face and eye lotion, whilst in addition he also supplied one client regularly with scented snuff.[34]

It seems probable that these secondary sources of income slowly became less important towards the turn of the nineteenth century. In his analysis of provincial medical practice in England during this period, Kett has suggested that a growing number of apothecaries were 'leaving their shops and acquiring . . . a view of themselves as distinctly medical practitioners'.[35] Elsewhere in the same paper he has noted that the surgeon-apothecary was beginning to develop 'an idea of the requirements he would have to fulfill as a full-time medical practitioner'.[36] The emergence of medicine as a full-time occupation was, however, a very gradual process; as Thackeray's portrait of John Pendennis suggests, and as other evidence confirms,[37] the combination of medical practice and retail trade persisted until well into the nineteenth century.

From what has been said, it is clear that throughout the eighteenth century medical practice on its own frequently provided only a very unstable and insecure method of earning a living. This point is of considerable importance. As long as medical men were unable to support themselves from medical practice alone and therefore had to have a second source of income, medicine was severely limited not merely in terms of its development as a profession but at a much more basic level in terms of its development as a full-time, specialised occupation. During the nineteenth century, of course, medicine did emerge as a highly specialised, full-time occupation: medical men lost not only their shopkeeping functions and their other secondary occupations but also, with the development of new specialised occupational groups such as pharmacists,[38] those functions, such as the dispensing of drugs, which were ancillary to medical practice. However, this process of occupational specialisation — a process which is, of course, the basic prerequisite for the emergence of modern professional occupations — could only develop within the context of a large and growing market for health care which made it possible for medical practitioners to support themselves and their families on the basis of medical practice alone, without the necessity to supplement a medical income by engaging in other, non-medical activities. Thus it may be argued that, for as long as the level of demand for qualified care was relatively low (as was the case throughout the eighteenth century), medicine was severely limited in terms of its development into the relatively secure, specialised and full-time occupation which it was later to become.

It is important to remind ourselves, therefore, that throughout the eighteenth century, medicine not only had few of the characteristics which we associate with modern professions but that, even more basically, it was frequently not even a full-time occupation. Moreover, it is interesting to note that this was by no means a peculiar characteristic of medical practice in England, for a similar situation existed in other societies in the eighteenth and early-nineteenth centuries. Thus, in describing the situation in New England in the early-nineteenth century, Riznik has pointed out that 'most physicians were involved in a self-sufficient economy which was generally unable to support professional men ... at anything more than a low standard of living';[39] as a consequence, 'perhaps the majority of New England physicians ... made up income deficiences by farming and supplying their own needs'.[40] Similarly, Claudine Herzlich has argued that in late-eighteenth and early-nineteenth century France, the low level of demand for medical care meant that many practitioners had only a small clientele, whilst the fees they were able to charge 'were often very low and insufficient for earning a living'.[41] That this was certainly the case for at least some French practitioners is confirmed by the recently discovered account book and journal of Thomas Hérier, which provide unusually detailed information about the practice and finances of a country surgeon at the end of the eighteenth century. Lemay's analysis of Hérier's income from medical practice throughout the whole of his thirty-two year career as a medical man suggests that 'no matter how devoted to his profession he was, Hérier could not support a family on these earnings'.[42] Indeed it is significant that when, after seventeen years in practice, Hérier went to register the death of one of his children, his occupation was listed as 'cultivateur' or farmer, a fact which, as Lemay notes, 'shows the importance of what appeared to be his chief livelihood in the eyes of the parish priest'.[43]

In the Netherlands in the eighteenth century, it was also a common practice for medical men to supplement their earnings from medical practice by engaging in a variety of second occupations, including those of barber, innkeeper, fisherman, bailiff, schoolmaster and secretary in local government, whilst other practitioners were employed in the law courts and in the beer trade.[44] Thus not only in England, but probably in most societies in the eighteenth century, the relatively small size of the market for health care may be seen as a major constraint on the development of medicine as a full-time, specialised occupation.

Thus far it has been argued that the relatively low level of demand for qualified health care throughout the eighteenth century made it difficult for many practitioners to make a reasonable living from medical practice on its own. It would, however, be quite wrong to convey the impression that all practitioners faced similar difficulties in this respect. Thus we have already noted that during this period there was a marked tendency for the demand for health care to be concentrated amongst the highest social strata, and those practitioners who were fortunate enough to find favour amongst the aristocracy and gentry themselves enjoyed relatively high status and incomes as a result of their association with a high status clientele. However, whilst this group of practitioners was able to enjoy the lifestyle appropriate to eighteenth-century gentlemen, their involvement in the network of face-to-face relationships which constituted the patronage system also placed severe constraints on the development of professional autonomy. Thus, as a number of writers have noted, the patronage relationship was typically associated not with a structure of colleague control, but with a structure of client control, for within the patronage system the aristocratic and wealthy client was the dominant figure in the doctor-patient relationship. This point has, perhaps, been most forcefully made by Holloway, who noted that, by virtue of the wider social bases of his power, the client was in a position to define both his own needs and the manner in which those needs were to be met. As a consequence, 'the patient, not the doctor, determined the conditions on which service was rendered', whilst the doctor, 'faced by powerful, wealthy, critical, demanding, and ill-informed patients was forced into the role of lackey and mere comforter'.[45]

Elements of Holloway's analysis may be found in the work of a number of writers, but perhaps the most detailed and systematic analysis of the significance of the patronage system in eighteenth-century medicine is contained in the work of Jewson. Jewson points out that throughout the eighteenth century medical men were dependent upon the favour of a small group of upper class patients who had the ability to make or break the career of any individual practitioner. Aristocratic patients, he points out, 'were in a position to choose for themselves the most satisfactory or amusing practitioners from among the host of medical men who clamoured for their favours. It was the patient who judged the competence of the physician and the suitability of the therapy. The wealthy and influential threw their support behind whichever practitioner pleased them and withdrew it from those in whom they were disappointed. Thus it was the client who held ultimate control in the consultative relationship.'[46]

Jewson goes on to argue that this dependence of medical men on their lay patrons had important implications for the form and content of medical knowledge in the eighteenth century. He suggests that, in a situation in which the client held ultimate power in the consultative relationship, physicians 'had no choice but to tailor their theories and remedies to meet the expectations and requirements of their genteel patients' whilst 'upper class patients were able ... to direct the development of medical knowledge by shifting their patronage from one group of innovators to another'.[47] More specifically, Jewson suggests that what are generally recognised as the distinctive characteristics of eighteenth-century medical knowledge — an orientation towards symptoms rather than aetiology, a monistic pathology, and an absence of any sharp differentiation between afflictions of the body and of the mind — may be related to the constraints placed upon practitioners in a situation in which the careers of medical men were under lay rather than professional control, and in which practitioners were forced to compete with each other for the favours of a small group of wealthy and influential patients. Thus, in relation to the first of these characteristics — the orientation towards symptoms rather than aetiological processes — he suggests that

> One of the most important manifestations of the patient's power over the practitioner was his ability to dictate the very definition of illness itself. In particular, the patient's understandable desire to be cured of his symptoms, rather than diagnosed of his disease, had an indelible impact on contemporary theories of nosology and pathology. Medical knowledge revolved around the problems of the prognosis and therapy of symptoms, rather than the diagnosis and analysis of diseases. Symptoms were not regarded as the secondary signs of internal pathological events, but rather as the disease itself.

The attention paid by medical practitioners to psychosomatic conditions such as hypochondriasis illustrates the point: 'When the wealthy and powerful chose to identify emotional stress with disease, practitioners accepted their definition of the situation and acted as if such maladies were real pathological entities. The symptom based nosology of the eighteenth century was thus a reflection of a patient dominated medical system.'[48] On a more general level, it may be suggested that the development of professional autonomy was severely restricted under the patronage system, for both the problems requiring solution and the terms in which an acceptable solution was defined were determined by criteria established not by the profession, but by the patient.[49] The picture which emerges of medicine during this period is not, then, a picture of medicine as a highly autonomous profession, but rather that of an occupational group whose members were highly dependent on their lay patrons. As we shall see later, it was only with the structural changes in medical practice which occurred during the nineteenth century that doctors finally achieved a position of dominance within the consultative relationship, and it was only then that the emphasis in medical research began to move away from those problems of prime concern to the patient — that is, problems of therapy — towards the more basic scientific problems involved in the diagnosis and analysis of disease. The relatively high level of intellectual detachment of the nineteenth-century medical scientist was thus, at least in part, a function of his growing social detachment from the patient.[50]

Jewson's analysis brings out very clearly the fact that the patronage system was typically associated with a network of highly particularistic relationships between medical practitioners and their upper class patients. Thus wealthy and influential clients were in a position to demand *personal* attention and the practitioner — if he wished to make a success of his career — was constrained to orientate his behaviour towards the particular needs of each individual patient. A similar point has also been made by a number of other writers. Thus, in their classic study of the professions, Carr-Saunders and Wilson pointed out that the ties which bound the practitioner to his patron or patrons were those of loyalty and personal subservience, and they went on to note that such ties of personal dependence severely limit the development of professional consciousness and professional autonomy.[51] More recently, Johnson has also drawn attention to the fact that patronage is associated with a fragmented, locally oriented occupational group, where the individual practitioner defers to and identifies with his patron or patrons rather than with his professional colleagues. Under these conditions, he notes, the sense of occupational community remains relatively undeveloped, whilst the authority of the patron reduces the possibility of developing professionally imposed forms of social control, such as those which are involved in the development and enforcement of codes of professional ethics.[52]

Johnson's contribution, in particular, draws attention to the way in which an orientation towards local markets tends to fragment an occupational group by cutting practitioners off from their colleagues practising in other localities. Thus the patronage system has the effect of integrating practitioners into a network of relationships with clients at the local level and at the same time inhibiting the development of a network of relationships with colleagues at the national level. It is reasonable to suggest that this fragmentation of the profession into a large number of small, relatively isolated groups of practitioners was one of the processes which inhibited the development of a common professional consciousness or any real sense of professional 'community' in the eighteenth century. Quite clearly, a fragmented occupational group of this kind is unlikely to be able to develop its own internally imposed controls on the behaviour of its members and, indeed, under these conditions, the members of an occupational group are much more likely to orientate their behaviour towards the expectations of their clients rather than those of their colleagues. Thus as Freidson has pointed out, the more the everyday work setting of a practitioner integrates him into a network of relationships with professional colleagues, and the more the career structure of the individual is determined by the evaluation of his colleagues, the greater are the constraints on the practitioner to orientate his behaviour towards the expectations of his professional peers. In contrast, the practitioner whose work situation isolates him from his colleagues is much less subject to any form of intra-professional control. However, as Freidson goes on to point out, to the extent that a practitioner becomes less dependent on his professional colleagues, he also becomes more dependent on his clients, for it is they, rather than his colleagues, who are able to determine the practitioner's occupational success or failure.[53]

Freidson's framework is an extremely useful one in the sense that the structure of medical practice in the eighteenth century provides a particularly clear-cut example of what he calls 'client-dependent' as opposed to 'colleague-dependent' medical practice.[54] Thus, as we have hinted above, throughout the eighteenth century there was nothing resembling a 'professional community' of medical men in any real sense, not even — except in very rare cases — at the local level. There was, for example, no regular medical press on a secure footing until the *Lancet* began publication in 1823, whilst, as we have seen, a code of medical ethics governing professional behaviour was not highly elaborated, and certainly not effectively enforced, until considerably later. At the local level there were few medical societies prior to the end of the eighteenth century,[55] while the fact that medical men were involved in a highly competitive market in which there was a limited demand for their services meant that relationships between practitioners were all too frequently characterised not by cooperation, but by intense rivalry and mutual hostility. As Porter has pointed out, in the eighteenth century the structure of professional practice was such that it 'did not tend to breed binding corporate professionalism . . . Upward mobility was individual rather than collective. It was no-holds-barred in the clamour for advancement.'[56]

It is clear that in such a situation it was impossible for the profession to develop centralised, universalistic standards of either clinical or ethical behaviour independent of the particularistic customs and traditions of the local community; that this was so is clearly indicated by what, to a modern observer, appears to be the very 'low' standard of professional behaviour characteristic of many eighteenth-century medical men. Thus the intensely competitive relationships, the frequent public disputes and the patented inventions, and the many forms of conspicuous self-advertisement which were characteristic of medical life during this period would all, by today's standards, be regarded as highly improper and unprofessional forms of behaviour. It would, however, be quite inappropriate to judge these forms of behaviour by today's standards, for they simply reflect the fact that the eighteenth century practitioner perceived — quite accurately — that, in terms of his own career, it was more important to please his clients than to please his colleagues. Moreover, such forms of 'unprofessional' behaviour could only be eliminated as medical men became increasingly emancipated from lay control, and as medical career structures came increasingly under the control of the profession itself. This process, as we shall see, was associated with the growth of the market for medical care in the nineteenth century, and with the development of professional control of this enlarged market. It is to these issues that we must now turn.

In England, the growth of demand for qualified health care in the nineteenth century appears to have been closely associated with the development of an increasingly complex, urban industrial society. As the College of Physicians itself noted, 'The enlarged and improved state of society . . . has . . . much extended the demand for medical advice. Families which in a former condition of the Kingdom were either necessitated or content to apply for the relief of their indispositions to domestic medicine have recourse in these days of refinement and opulence to practitioners of physic.'[57] In particular, it was the growth of a sizeable middle class which provided the basis for the rapid development of the medical profession in the nineteenth century, for as Holloway has noted, 'the rise of the middle classes produced a prosperous, numerous and expanding clientele', especially for those practitioners who were willing to provide their services at more moderate rates than those traditionally charged by the 'consultant' physician and surgeon.[58] That it was possible for practitioners to offer their services at moderate rates was, at least in part, a function of the process of urbanisation which concentrated the clientele of the medical practitioner within a comparatively small area and thus facilitated a reduction in both travelling time and in the working expenses of the doctor's practice. In addition, certain innovations within the profession — notably the sliding scale of fees, which was increasingly adopted in the nineteenth century — also helped to reduce the cost of medical care to families living on relatively modest incomes, and thus had the effect of further widening the market for the services of the qualified practitioner.

Before we examine some of the more important implications of this changing market structure for the development of the medical profession, it may be appropriate to examine, if only briefly, some of the processes which lay behind this growth of demand. Anyone who is familiar with the history of medicine in the nineteenth century will not have failed to notice that this growth in the demand for medical care coincided with the development of an increasingly scientific basis for medical practice, and it is therefore tempting to suggest that this higher level of demand may have been a reflection of the improved effectiveness of scientific medicine. To assert the existence of such a simple relationship would, however, be extremely misleading; as numerous writers have pointed out, these improvements in medical science, whilst very real, did not immediately translate into significant therapeutic advances in medical practice;[59] indeed, there is little evidence to suggest any dramatic improvements in the effectiveness of medical care until the early part of the twentieth century. It is therefore important to note that, as Starr has pointed out, the 'increased demand for medical services seems to have preceded significant improvements in the effectiveness of physicians'.[60] If, therefore, we wish to understand those processes which led to the growth in demand for medical care, we must look elsewhere.

In part, of course, the expansion of demand for health care may simply have reflected the fact that in an increasingly prosperous society, an increasing number of people were able to afford specialised professional services, such as those provided by medical practitioners. However, it is reasonable to suggest that the increased demand for health care may also have been associated with changing attitudes towards health and disease in the nineteenth century. Holloway, writing about Victorian England, has hypothesised that, at least amongst the middle classes, the widespread belief in progress and in the rational control of the world was extended to include the idea that man could control disease in much the same way that he was so busily controlling other natural forces. Similarly, he has suggested that the emphasis on individual achievement which was such a marked feature of Victorian middle-class belief systems necessarily placed a high premium on the maintenance of health, for good health came increasingly to be seen 'both as a prerequisite for success and as a necessary condition for the enjoyment and exploitation of success'.[61]

In addition it may be suggested that the increasingly close association between medicine and science was also of major importance for, as Larson has pointed out, during this period science was coming to be seen as the 'cardinal system of cognitive validation and legitimation'.[62] In other words, although the increasingly scientific basis of medical practice had no immediate or dramatic impact in terms of therapeutic effectiveness, nevertheless the cultural status of science almost certainly lent prestige and authority to medical men, and may well have been a significant process in increasing the level of demand for their services.

The immediately preceding arguments are, of course, somewhat speculative, for the processes which lay behind the expansion of demand for health care in the nineteenth century were extremely complex and by no means fully understood. However, although we may not yet fully understand these complex processes, it is clear that the development of a large and growing market for health care on a national level had important implications for the development of the medical profession.

In the first place, the growth in demand — in purely quantitative terms — meant that in the course of the nineteenth century, medicine came to offer an increasingly stable and rewarding long term career, and this in turn was probably important both in terms of attracting recruits of a higher social status, and in terms of building up a sense of commitment to the profession on the part of those who had chosen a medical career. As we saw in chapter seven, in the second half of the century — and particularly after the profession had secured a significant degree of market control by restricting entry to the profession — the increasingly secure market situation of medical men was reflected in a significant increase in medical incomes.

It should be noted, however, that it was not simply the

growth of the market in purely quantitative terms which was important; equally important was the fact that as the market grew, it altered both the total amount of demand and the pattern of demand, by bringing into the market for health care many clients whose socio-economic status was relatively modest. One consequence of this process was that patronage became an increasingly atypical form of the doctor-patient relationship as the demand for medical care ceased to be concentrated in the higher status groups. Thus, by the mid-nineteenth century, the doctor-patient relationship was typically no longer one in which the practitioner faced a wealthy and influential patron, but one in which the status of the patient was comparable to or lower than that of the doctor. Moreover, the fact that the doctor increasingly earned his living not by treating a small number of patients for relatively high fees, but by treating large numbers of patients for relatively modest fees, inevitably served to reduce the doctor's dependence on any particular patient. Under the patronage system, to incur the displeasure of an influential patient could, as Jewson has pointed out, have disastrous consequences for a practitioner's career; to incur the displeasure of a ledger-clerk, who was just one of several hundred patients, would hardly be likely to have the same sort of consequences. As numerous studies have indicated, the relative status of doctor and patient within the wider society is always an important element in structuring the doctor-patient relationship, and there can be little doubt that the change in their relative statuses in the nineteenth century was an important part of that process whereby the balance of power shifted away from the patient and towards the doctor.

The most dramatic illustration of the consequences of a change in the relative statuses of doctor and patient is undoubtedly to be seen in the context of the development of charitable hospitals for meeting the medical needs of the poor in the late eighteenth and early nineteenth centuries. Hospitals of this kind were, of course, developed in many Western societies during this period, and wherever such hospitals were developed — in Britain, in France, in Vienna and in the United States — the fact that relatively high status practitioners were treating low status patients resulted in a dramatic reversal of the balance of power within the doctor-patient relationship.[63] Thus doctors were — perhaps for the first time — in a position to ignore the wishes of individual patients, and to treat them according to criteria which were now defined not by the patient, but by the profession. The relatively powerless position of the hospital patient who was both sick and poor, as well as the patient's inability to control what happened to his body are, perhaps, most poignantly captured in the words of Entralgo who, in describing the situation in Vienna, has said that the patient had a 'resigned and submissive attitude'; 'he handed himself over with a wordless "Here is my body, do what you like with it"'.[64] It is not perhaps surprising that, both in Europe and in the United States, hospital positions became very highly prized within the profession, partly because they gave access to a large amount of 'clinical material', as patients came to be called,[65] in the form of a dependent and highly vulnerable hospital population. It was, of course, no accident that the hospital emerged as the centre of both medical research and teaching in the nineteenth century. Equally, it was no accident that it was within the hospital that one first sees the shift from what Jewson has called a 'person orientated' to an 'object orientated' form of medical practice,[66] for the treatment of large numbers of patients of low status was associated with a process in which the patient was becoming increasingly depersonalised.

It is not suggested, of course, that this radical reversal of the balance of power between doctor and patient occurred in the same sudden and dramatic way in the situation of private practice; nevertheless, a similar process, associated with a decline in the status of the patient, was occurring in private practice throughout the nineteenth century. In the context of a comparative analysis of the degree of authority which physicians have over their patients, Marie Haug has correctly pointed out that the medical practitioner's 'degree of authority over clients depends in part on *client* characteristics rather than occupational characteristics alone',[67] and it is important to bear in mind that the rise of medical dominance in the nineteenth century was a process which was associated as much with a lowering of the status of the patient as it was with the raising of the status of the profession.

As we have already noted, within the hospitals medical dominance emerged in its most highly developed form; indeed, it may be said that the hospital was the institutional base for the early development of the modern pattern of medical dominance. This point is of considerable significance, for one aspect of the development of a national market for medical care was that, in relation to the supply of medical men, the process of producing medical practitioners increasingly moved away from the local level, and became centralised in a limited number of hospital medical schools, many of which came to enjoy not merely a local, but also a national — in some cases international — reputation for the quality of both their teaching and research. In order to appreciate the significance of this process of centralisation, it is necessary to bear in mind that, throughout the eighteenth century, the great majority of practitioners — indeed virtually all practitioners — had received their professional education through the apprenticeship system, and this had a number of important consequences. Amongst the more important of these consequences we might note that a highly decentralised, locally-based system of education of this kind made it impossible to control entry to the profession at a national level; perhaps of even greater importance, it also made it quite impossible to enforce any standardised system of education and training. Thus training through the apprenticeship system was likely to be both haphazard and unsystematic; since the apprentice was bound in a personal relationship to his master, the quality of training and education which the apprentice received was largely dependent on the character and the ability of the master to whom he was attached. Thus the country surgeon to whom George Crabbe was apprenticed in 1768 ran a farm in addition to his medical practice with the result that Crabbe found that he 'was often employed in the drudgery of the farm ... and was made the bedfellow and companion of the ploughboy'.[68] It is not suggested, of course, that an apprentice could not receive an adequate medical education if he was fortunate enough to be placed with an able and conscientious master; what is suggested is that the sort of education which the apprentice received almost certainly varied considerably from place to place, and from master to master. Thus not only the clinical training which an apprentice received, but also his socialisation into what may be called the 'jobways' of the profession, including acceptable standards of professional behaviour, were likely to reflect the particular demands of the local community within which his master's practice was situated. The particularistic relationship between doctor and patient in the eighteenth century was thus paralleled, in the sphere of medical education, by an equally particularistic relationship between teacher and pupil.

This traditional system of medical education began to change in the nineteenth century as the apprenticeship system steadily lost ground with the development of an increasingly centralised system of education, at first in the hospital medical schools and subsequently in the universities. Thus, with the growth of the hospital schools, the terms of apprenticeship agreements came to be interpreted very loosely in order to allow apprentices to spend an increasing amount of their time in hospitals; although apprenticeship was never formally abolished, it continued to decline as a means of medical education throughout the second half of the nineteenth century. One consequence of this change in the structure of medical education was that, in place of a particularistic relationship with his master, the medical student in the nineteenth century came increasingly to receive his professional education within a formal institutional context which encouraged shared experiences with other students and, by so doing, facilitated the development of a common professional identity and sense of professional community. As medical students came from all parts of the country to these emerging national and regional centres of medical education, and as large numbers of students passed through the hands of a relatively small number of teachers, the process of medical education became a relatively standardised one in which all students were subjected to broadly similar influences. Moreover, the dominant values within these institutions, well insulated as they were from the world of lay culture and lay values, were the values of the senior members of the profession. It thus became increasingly possible for this elite group of medical school teachers to define and to some extent to impose on all students their own definition of what constituted minimally acceptable standards of both clinical and ethical behaviour. As a result of these changes in the structure of medical education, medical students underwent a new and more intensive process of professional socialisation which both fostered a sense of professional community and asserted the primacy of professional rather than lay values. The centralisation and standardisation of medical education must therefore be seen as processes of major importance for the development of the modern medical profession, and the control which they came to exercise over the education and professional socialisation of the next generation of medical practitioners was to enable the elite group of medical school teachers to play a major part in shaping this process of professional development.

In this final section, we have examined some of the more important processes associated with the development of medicine as a modern profession. Within the present chapter, it has been argued that the market situation of medical men changed quite radically in the course of the nineteenth century and that, as a consequence, what had formerly been a relatively insecure and often only part-time occupation had, by the end of the century, developed into a relatively stable and secure full-time career. This process of occupational specialisation – the most basic of all processes involved in the development of modern professional occupations – was associated with a significant expansion of the market for medical care, as a result of which medical men were increasingly able to support themselves on the basis of full-time medical practice, without the necessity to engage in other, non-medical activities. In addition, the market situation of medical practitioners was further substantially improved by the effective restriction of entry to the profession, which we examined in a previous chapter. Whereas in the late-eighteenth and early-nineteenth centuries, medical men were involved in a relatively small and very competitive market for their services, by the latter part of the nineteenth century they were working within a much expanded market, one over which they themselves had a significant degree of control as a result of their ability to restrict the supply of medical practitioners. It is, of course, not surprising that these changes within the structure of the market for medical care resulted, as we saw previously, in a significant improvement in medical incomes in the latter part of the nineteenth century.

Changes in the structure of the medical profession were not, however, limited to changes in the market situation of medical practitioners considered in purely economic terms, though the importance of these changes should not, of course, be underestimated. However, it has been argued that both the growth in the size of the market for medical care, and changes in the structure of that market, were also associated with a weakening of a variety of locally-based forms of client control, such as that involved in the patronage system. Within this context medical men were, albeit very gradually, able to develop a network of new institutions which increasingly had the effect of centralising the control of more and more aspects of medical practice within the profession itself. In previous chapters, we have examined some major aspects of this movement towards professional self-regulation, including the early development and subsequently the more effective enforcement of codes of medical ethics and, closely associated with this, the development of the General Medical Council as the central controlling body within the profession. These developments, as we have seen, took place within a context of struggle and conflict within the profession, but out of these struggles there gradually developed, in the second half of the century, new institutions which provided the basis for a more united profession, characterised by a growing sense of professional community and professional identity. This growing professional consciousness was further enhanced by changes in the structure of medical education, as the process of producing the next generation of practitioners increasingly moved away from the local level and became centralised in a limited number of specialist institutions. As a result of this development, the process of professional socialisation became one in which all students were exposed to broadly similar influences under the tutelage of senior medical school teachers who were themselves increasingly able to assert the primacy of professional values over those of the lay world. As a consequence of this whole complex of interrelated processes, medical men in the second half of the nineteenth century came to enjoy a relatively secure and steadily improving market situation and, equally importantly, a steadily increasing degree of control over their work, their patients, and their own careers. Medicine, in other words, was beginning to emerge as a modern profession.

Notes

Chapter One

1. J W Willcock, *The Laws Relating to the Medical Profession*, London, 1830, 30.

2. A M Carr-Saunders and P A Wilson, *The Professions*, 2nd impression, London, 1964, 68.

3. C Singer and S W F Holloway, 'Early Medical Education in England in Relation to the Pre-History of London University', *Medical History*, IV/1 (January 1960), 6. For an analysis of the relationship between the fellows and licentiates in the eighteenth century, see I Waddington, 'The Struggle to Reform the Royal College of Physicians, 1767-1771: A Sociological Analysis', *Medical History*, XVII/2 (April 1973), 107-126.

4. Sir George Clark, *A History of the Royal College of Physicians of London*, Oxford, 1966, Vol II, Appendix II, 738.

5. Despite a growth in the number of physicians in the first half of the nineteenth century, the College of Physicians still represented less than five per cent of all medical practitioners in England in the middle of the nineteenth century. See M Jeanne Peterson, *The Medical Profession in Mid-Victorian London*, Berkeley, Los Angeles and London, 1978, 8.

6. Peterson, *The Medical Profession*, 8-9.

7. Quoted in B Hamilton, 'The Medical Professions in the Eighteenth Century', *Economic History Review*, 2nd series, IV/2 (1951), 147.

8. *Gentleman's Magazine*, new series, 1 (March 1834), 334.

9. C Newman, *The Evolution of Medical Education in the Nineteenth Century*, London, 1957, 5.

10. *Select Committee on Medical Education*, 1834 (602-1) Part I, Q 511. Hereafter, this Select Committee will be referred to as SCME.

11. SCME, 1834, Part I, Q 3014.

12. As Singer and Holloway have noted, 'the medical departments at Oxford and Cambridge were merely nominal until after the middle of the nineteenth century'. See Singer and Holloway, 'Early Medical Education in England', *Medical History*, IV/1, 2.

13. Newman, *The Evolution of Medical Education*, 17.

14. Z Cope, *The Royal College of Surgeons of England: A History*, London, 1959, 13.

15. Cope, *The Royal College of Surgeons*, 7, 21.
16. R E Franklin, 'Medical Education and the Rise of the General Practitioner', (PhD thesis, University of Birmingham 1950), 112.
17. *Lancet*, 1827-28, i, 3.
18. Willcock, *The Laws Relating to the Medical Profession*, 30.
19. Willcock, *The Laws*, 30-31.
20. Willcock, *The Laws*, 56.
21. Willcock, *The Laws*, 56.
22. Willcock, *The Laws*, ccxx.
23. Clark, *A History of the Royal College of Physicians*, vol II, 476-9.
24. Willcock, *The Laws*, 67.
25. Peterson, *The Medical Profession*, 12.

Chapter Two

1. S W F Holloway, 'Medical Education in England, 1830-1858: A Sociological Analysis', *History*, XLIX (1964), 299-324.
2. Newman, *The Evolution of Medical Education*, 1.
3. SCME, 1834, Part I, Q 2257.
4. *Third Report from the Select Committee on Medical Registration and Medical Law Amendment*, 1847-48, (702), Q 1969, 1975.
5. Holloway, 'Medical Education in England', 307-8.
6. *First and Second Reports from the Select Committee on Medical Registration and Medical Law Amendment*, 1847-48, (210), Q 1215.
7. A Trollope, *Doctor Thorne*, London, 1967, 25-6.
8. I. Waddington, 'The Struggle to Reform the Royal College of Physicians', *Medical History*, XVII, 1973, 107-126.
9. SCME, 1834, Part II, Q 5980.
10. *Third Report from the Select Committee*, 1847-48, Q 1977.
11. SCME, 1834, Part I, Q 2470.
12. Hamilton, 'The Medical Professions in the Eighteenth Century', 150.
13. SCME, 1834, Part II, Q 5679-83.
14. *Ibid*, Q 5980-1.   15. *Ibid*, Q 6384.   16. *Ibid*, Q 6257.
17. *First and Second Reports*, 1847-48, Q 268-9.
18. J F Clarke, *Autobiographical Recollections of the Medical Profession*, London, 1874, 113.
19. B B Cooper, *The Life of Sir Astley Cooper*, London, 1843, vol I, 235.
20. *First and Second Reports*, 1847-48, Q 1227.
21. SCME, 1834, Part II, Appendix 44, 87.
22. *Ibid*, Q 4791, 5372.   23. *Ibid*, Q 6299.
24. *First and Second Reports*, 1847-48, Q 495.
25. *Ibid*, Q 1124.   26. *Ibid*, Q 136.
27. *Lancet*, 1841-42, *i*, 422.
28. In 1856, the *Association Medical Journal* estimated that 'there are 2,603 gentlemen practising medicine and surgery with only one qualification', of whom 879 held only the licence of the Apothe-

caries' Society. See *Association Medical Journal*, 4, 1856, 254. In his detailed study of medical practitioners in mid-nineteenth century Bristol, Brown found that two-thirds of those holding only the licence of the Apothecaries' Society described themselves as general practitioners. See P S Brown, 'The Providers of Medical Treatment in Mid-Nineteenth Century Bristol', *Medical History*, XXIV, 1980, 302.

29. SCME, 1834, Part II, Appendix 44, 87.

30. *First and Second Reports*, 1847-48, Q 1061-4.

31. *Ibid*, Q 934.   32. *Ibid*, Appendix, 133.

33. Holloway, 'Medical Education in England', 314.

34. *London and Provincial Medical Directory*, 1847, xv-xvi.

35. W J Bishop, 'The Evolution of the General Practitioner in England', in *Science, Medicine and History: Essays in Honour of Charles Singer*, ed E Ashworth Underwood, London, 1953, vol II, 355.

36. See, for example, Waddington, 'The Struggle to Reform', 107-26.

37. *London and Provincial Medical Directory*, 1847, xvi.

38. *Quarterly Review*, LXVII, (1840-41), 59.

39. *Lancet*, 1840-41, *i*, 272.

40. *London and Provincial Medical Directory*, 1847, xvi.

41. *Quarterly Review*, LXVII (1840-41), 58-9.

42. M Jeanne Peterson, *The Medical Profession in Mid-Victorian London*, 6.

43. See, for example, T H Marshall, 'The Nature and Determinants of Social Class', in T H Marshall, *Sociology at the Crossroads*, London, 1963, 183-4, and F Toennies, 'Estates and Classes', in R Bendix and S M Lipset (eds), *Class, Status and Power*, 2nd edition, London, 1967, 12-21.

44. Peterson, *The Medical Profession*, 12.

45. Quoted in A M Carr-Saunders and P A Wilson, *The Professions*, Oxford, 1933, reprinted London, 1964, 75.

46. P Elliott, *The Sociology of the Professions*, London and Basingstoke, 1972, 21.

47. Carr-Saunders and Wilson, *The Professions*, 71.

48. Elliott, *The Sociology of the Professions*, 14.

49. Carr-Saunders and Wilson, *The Professions*, 71.

50. As numerous social historians have pointed out, in the eighteenth century high status was associated with the ownership of landed property rather than with the performance of occupational tasks. In addition, a particularly important cleavage within the social hierarchy was that which separated gentlemen from the 'common people', a division which, as Perkin has noted, 'could scarcely be defined in economic terms'. Rather, the distinction appears to have been made in terms of a combination of birth, manners, speech, deportment and social acceptance. By comparison with these attributes, work — no matter how skilled — was a very poor claim to high status; indeed, ideally a gentleman was expected to maintain a leisured lifestyle without actively working to support it.

In marked contrast of course, work — in the sense of full-time occupation — constitutes the very basis of the stratification system in modern industrial societies. For discussion of the system of rank and status in eighteenth century England, see G E Mingay, *English Landed Society in the Eighteenth Century*, London, 1963; D Marshall, *Eighteenth Century England*, London, 1963; and H J Perkin, *The Origins of Modern English Society 1770-1800*, London and Toronto, 1969.

51. *From Max Weber, Essays in Sociology*, trans and ed by H H Gerth and C W Mills, London, 1961, 191.
52. Elliott, *The Sociology of the Professions*, 32.
53. *Westminster Review*, XIII, (April 1858), 526.
54. *Lancet*, 1842-43, *i*, 721.
55. *Westminster Review*, XIII, (April 1858), 510.
56. *Ibid*, XIV, (July 1858), 134.   57. *Ibid*, XIV, (July 1858), 124.
58. *Gentleman's Magazine*, 100, 1830, 7.
59. Quoted in Hamilton, 'The Medical Professions in the Eighteenth Century', 141-2.
60. Holloway, 'Medical Education in England', 316.
61. R Franklin, *Medical Education and the Rise of the General Practitioner*, Ph.D. Thesis, University of Birmingham, 1950, 4.
62. SCME, 1834, Part I, Q 3534-5.
63. *Ibid*, Part II, Q 6257.   64. *Ibid*, Part I, Q 2267-2273.
65. Many working class people, like the unfortunate Bessy Higgins in Mrs Gaskell's *North and South*, probably suffered serious illness and death without being attended by a qualified practitioner. As William Lawrence pointed out in 1847, poor people 'cannot afford to employ a well qualified practitioner. For one-sixth of the expense, or even much less, they get what seems to them to answer the purpose equally well from the chemist and druggist.' See *Report from the Select Committee on Medical Registration*, 1847 (620), Q 1962.
66. See, for example, B Abel-Smith, *The Hospitals, 1800-1948*, London, 1964, and J Woodward, *To Do The Sick No Harm*, London, 1974.
67. Peterson, *The Medical Profession*, especially Chapter IV.
68. T. McKeown, 'A Sociological Approach to the History of Medicine', *Medical History*, XIV, (1970), 437.
69. Peterson, *The Medical Profession*, 16.

Chapter Three

1. Max Neuberger, 'C G Carus on the State of Medicine in Britain in 1844', in E Ashworth Underwood (ed), *Science, Medicine and History, Essays in Honour of Charles Singer*, London, 1953, vol II, 263-73.
2. Sir Samuel Squire Sprigge, *The Life and Times of Thomas Wakley*, London, 1899, 77.
3. B Abel-Smith, *The Hospitals 1800-1948*, London, 1964, 18.

4. Stephen Paget (ed), *Memoirs and Letters of Sir James Paget*, London, 1901, 82.
5. *Lancet*, 1917, *i*, 434.
6. R Franklin, *Medical Education and the Rise of the General Practitioner*, 60.
7. J Woodward, *To Do the Sick No Harm*, London, 1974, 26.
8. Paget, *Memoirs and Letters*, 186.
9. Abel-Smith, *The Hospitals*, 18-19.
10. *Quarterly Review*, LXVII (1840-41), 58-9.
11. B B Cooper, *The Life of Sir Astley Cooper*, London, 1843, vol II, 158-9.
12. *Ibid*, p. 193. See also M Jeanne Peterson, *The Medical Profession in Mid-Victorian London*, 207.
13. Cooper, *The Life of Sir Astley Cooper*, 157.
14. Peterson, *The Medical Profession*, 207-8.
15. Paget, *Memoirs and Letters*, 185.
16. J F Clarke, *Autobiographical Recollections of the Medical Profession*, London, 1874, 115-6.
17. *Munk's Roll*, vol II, 404.
18. Sir George Clark, *A History of the Royal College of Physicians of London*, Oxford, 1966, vol II, 655.
19. *Munk's Roll*, vol III, 197.
20. Peterson, *The Medical Profession*, 209.
21. Cope, *The Royal College of Surgeons*, 43.
22. *Lancet*, 1825-26, 725-43.
23. Cope, *The Royal College of Surgeons*, 43. See also Cope's essay on 'The Private Medical Schools of London (1746-1914)', in F N L Poynter (ed), *The Evolution of Medical Education in Britain*, London, 1966, 89-109.
24. *Lancet*, 1823-24, *ii*, 104-6.
25. *Lancet*, 1830-31, *i*, 597.
26. *Lancet*, 1823-24, *ii*, 105.
27. *Lancet*, 1823-24, *ii*, 199.
28. Walter Rivington, *The Medical Profession*, Dublin, 1879, 3-4. Differences in the provision of medical care ranged from one medical man to 210 persons in Buxton, to one to 6,295 in Aberdare.
29. W M Thackeray, *Pendennis*, London, 1906, 6-7.
30. *Ibid*, 6.
31. *Lancet*, 1840-41, *ii*, 107.
32. H N Hardy, *The State of the Medical Profession in Great Britain and Ireland in 1900*, Dublin, 1901, 70.
33. *Lancet*, 1875, *ii*, 512.
34. *Lancet*, 1875, *ii*, 580.
35. F B Smith, *The People's Health, 1830-1910*, London, 1979, 41.
36. *Census of England and Wales for the Year 1861*, vol III, General Report, Appendix to Report, 1863 (3221), 244.
37. *Lancet*, 1841-42, *ii*, 100.
38. Hardy, *The State of the Medical Profession*, 15.

39. H C Cameron, *Mr. Guy's Hospital, 1726-1948*, London, 1954, 83, note 14.
40. Cope, *The Royal College of Surgeons*, 8.
41. Clark, *A History of the Royal College of Physicians*, vol II, 621.
42. SCME, 1834, part I, Q 4306.
43. *Ibid*, part III, Q 335-6.
44. *Ibid*, part I, Q 239.   45. *Ibid*, Q 242.
46. Clark, *A History of the Royal College of Physicians*, vol II, 566.
47. *First and Second Reports*, 1847-48, Q 11.
48. *First and Second Reports*, Q 804.
49. SCME, 1834, part II, Q 4725.
50. *Ibid*, Q 4732-33.
51. *First and Second Reports*, 1847-48, Q 1393.
52. Clark, *A History of the Royal College of Physicians*, vol II, 664.
53. SCME, 1834, part I, Q 232.
54. *Ibid*, part I, Q 234.
55. Statement read by Wilson to the SCME, part I, 99, and Q 1598.
56. SCME, 1834, part II, Q 4801.
57. SCME, 1834, part II, Q 4801.
58. *Westminster Review*, xiv, 1858, 135.
59. Paget, *Memoirs and Letters*, 62.
60. *Lancet*, 1839-40, *ii*, 642.
61. *Lancet*, 1842-43, *ii*, 719-22.
62. See S W F Holloway, 'The Apothecaries' Act, 1815: a Reinterpretation', *Medical History*, 10, 1966, 107-29 and 221-35.
63. *First and Second Reports*, 1847-48, Q 1248-51.
64. *Ibid*, Q 1152.
65. *Lancet*, 1836-37, *i*, 305-6.
66. *Lancet*, 1842-43, *i*, 722.
67. *Lancet*, 1839-40, *ii*, 795-7.
68. Peterson, *The Medical Profession*, 22-3.
69. *Lancet*, 1825-6, 701.

Chapter Four
1. S Squire Sprigge, *The Life and Times of Thomas Wakley*, 102.
2. *Lancet*, 1823-24, *ii*, 105.
3. John Armstrong, *An address to the Members of the Royal College of Surgeons of London on the injurious conduct and defective state of that corporation, with reference to professional rights, medical science, and the public health*, London, 1825.
4. *Lancet*, 1825, 20, 88-89, 246-7, and 1825-26, 135-7 and 364-5.
5. Sprigge, *The Life and Times*, 185.
6. *Lancet*, 1825-26, 725-743.   7. *Ibid*, 740.
8. Sprigge, *The Life and Times*, 190.   9. *Ibid*, 198.
10. *BMJ*, 1857, *i*, 673-4.
11. *Lancet*, 1830-31, *i*, 864.
12. *Cobbett's Parliamentary Debates*, new series, XVII, June 20, 1827, col 1347.

13. *Ibid*, col 1348.   14. *Ibid*, col 1348.
15. Sprigge, *The Life and Times*, 209.
16. The conflict within the College was reported in *The Times*, June 22, 1827, and June 28, 1827, whilst on June 25, the *Morning Chronicle* published a letter from William Lawrence, who had taken an active part in the members' campaign.
17. *Lancet*, 1830-31, *i*, 598.
18. *Ibid*, 1830-31, *i*, 633.   19. *Ibid*, 1830-31, *i*, 667.
20. A detailed report of the meeting may be found in *Lancet*, 1830-31, *i*, 694-700.
21. Cope, *The Royal College of Surgeons*, 51.
22. *Lancet*, 1830-31, *i*, 766.
23. A full report of these events at the College may be found in *Lancet*, 1830-31, *i*, 785-797. The announcement that the order relating to naval surgeons had been withdrawn was made in *Lancet*, 1830-31, *i*, 832.
34. *Lancet*, 1830-31, *i*, 798.   25. *Ibid*, 1830-31, *i*, 797.
26. A short report of this meeting may be found in *Lancet*, 1830-31, *i*, 821-23, and a longer report in the same volume, 846-865.
27. *Lancet*, 1830-31, *ii*, 177-83.
28. *Ibid*, 1830-31, *i*, 857.   29. *Ibid*, 1830-31, *ii*, 181-2.
30. *Ibid*, 1830-31, *i*, 865-6.   31. *Ibid*, 1830-31, *ii*, 181.
32. *Ibid*, 1830-31, *ii*, 181.
33. Sprigge, *The Life and Times*, 221.
34. *Lancet*, 1830-31, *ii*, 381.   35. *Ibid*, 1830-31, *ii*, 822.
36. *Ibid*, 1831-32, *i*, 127.   37. *Ibid*, 1832-33, *i*, 62.
38. SCME, 1834, Part II, Appendix 7, and Part III, Appendix 7. In the five year period from 1829-33 the College of Surgeons examined 2324 candidates; in the similar period from 1829-30 to 1833-4, the Society of Apothecaries examined 2246.
39. Sprigge, *The Life and Times*, 224.
40. See, for example, the petitions presented to Parliament by the licentiates of the Royal College of Physicians, *Lancet*, 1840-41, *ii*, 668-70.
41. *Lancet*, 1836-37, *i*, 224.   42. *Ibid*, 1836-37, *i*, 227, 597.
43. *Ibid*, 1836-37, *i*, 226.   44. *Ibid*, 1836-37, *i*, 594-5.
45. *Ibid*, 1836-37, *i*, 596.   46. *Ibid*, 1836-37, *i*, 596.
47. *Ibid*, 1836-37, *i*, 576.   48. *Ibid*, 1836-37, *i*, 601-2
49. *Ibid*, 1836-37, *ii*, 939.   50. *Ibid*, 1836-37, *i*, 265.
51. *Ibid*, 1836-37, *i*, 304.   52. *Ibid*, 1836-37, *i*, 644-5.
53. *Ibid*, 1838-39, *i*, 77, and 1840-41, *i*, 117.
54. *Ibid*, 1837-38, *i*, 57-8; 1839-40, *i*, 542; 1839-40, *i*, 628-9; 1839-40, *ii*, 61.
55. *Ibid*, 1838-39, *ii*, 630-1.
56. *Ibid*, 1836-37, *i*, 265.   57. *Ibid*, 1839-40, *i*, 94.
58. W H McMenemy, *The Life and Times of Sir Charles Hastings*, Edinburgh and London, 1959, 207.
59. *Lancet*, 1840-41, *ii*, 57.   60. *Ibid*, 1804-41, *ii*, 136.
61. *Ibid*, 1840-41, *ii*, 91.   62. *Ibid*, 1840-41, *i*, 116.

Chapter Five

1. Much of the early work of both the BMA and the PMSA in relation to the system of poor law medical relief is documented in W F McMenemey, *The Life and Times of Charles Hastings*.
2. *Hansard*, 3rd series, LXIII, May 23, 1842, col 608-9.
3. *Ibid*, 3rd series, LXXVI, August 7, 1844, col 1896-1911.
4. Graham's Bill may be found in *British Sessional Papers*, House of Commons, 1844 (600), III, 235-246.
5. As Charles Newman has correctly noted, under Graham's Bill, 'the "orders" were ... not only maintained, but provided with progressively increasing requirements to correspond with their progressive status'. See Newman, *The Evolution of Medical Education*, 169-60. In this progressive hierarchy the general practitioners were, of course, to be at the bottom.
6. *Hansard*, 3rd series, LXXVI, August 7, 1844, col 1906-7.
7. *First and Second Reports*, 1847-48, Q 934.
8. *Ibid*, Q 935.   9. *Ibid*, Q 935.   10. *Ibid*, Q 1149-50, 1152.
11. *British Sessional Papers*, House of Commons, 1845 (67), IV, 485-498.
12. *Hansard*, 3rd series, LXXVII, February 25, 1845, col 1216-7.
13. *First and Second Reports*, 1847-48, Q 942-944.
14. *Ibid*, Q 946.
15. *Hansard*, 3rd series, LXXIX, April 25, 1845, col 1356-7.
16. *Ibid*, 3rd series, LXXX, May 7, 1845, col 250-2.
17. *British Sessional Papers*, House of Commons, 1845 (283), 499-516.
18. *Hansard*, 3rd series, LXXX, May 7, 1845, col 249, 257.
19. *Ibid*, LXXX, May 7, 1845, col 264.
20. *Lancet*, 1845, *8*, 561, 564.
21. The memorial from the College of Physicians was reprinted in the *Report from the Select Committee on Medical Registration*, 1847, Q 681.
22. *First and Second Reports*, 1847-48, Q 1167. See also Cope, *The Royal College of Surgeons*, 77-8.
23. *British Sessional Papers*, House of Commons, 1845 (579), IV, 517-530.
24. *First and Second Reports*, 1847-48, Q 745.
25. The statement of 'Principles' was reproduced as Appendix II to the *Third Report from the Select Committee*, 1848, pp 381-3.
26. *First and Second Reports*, 1847-48, Q 1008.
27. *Ibid*, Q 1164.   28. *Ibid*, Q 1166.
29. *Ibid*, Q 1167-8.   30. *Ibid*, Q 1420.
31. *Ibid*, Q 1433, 1435.   32. *Ibid*, Q 1375.
33. *Minutes of Council*, Royal College of Surgeons, 16 March 1849.
34. The last meeting between the medical corporations and the National Institute appears to have been on 9 February 1850. See Cope, *The Royal College of Surgeons*, 94-5.
35. *Lancet*, 1825-6, 733.
36. *Ibid*, 1830-31, *i*, 857.   37. *Ibid*, 1836-7, *i*, 594.
38. *First and Second Reports*, 1847-48, Q 1152.

39. *Report from the Select Committee on Medical Registration*, 1847, Q 87.
40. *Ibid*, Q 1186.   41. *Ibid*, Q 1576.   42. *Ibid*, Q 2031.
43. Wakley's Bill was printed in full in *Lancet*, 1847, 466-70.
44. Newman, *The Evolution of Medical Education*, 169.
45. *Minutes of Council*, Royal College of Surgeons, 3 May 1847.
46. *Ibid*, 10 June 1847.
47. *Report from the Select Committee on Medical Registration*, 1847, Q 62-3.
48. *Ibid*, Q 89.   49. *Ibid*, Q 1146.
50. *Ibid*, Q 1106.   51. *Ibid*, Q 1187.
52. *Ibid*, Q 1462-3.   53. *Ibid*, Q 104.
54. *Ibid*, Q 1650.   55. *Ibid*, Q 1695.
56. *Ibid*, Q 1577.   57. *Ibid*, Q 2010-2011.
58. *First and Second Reports*, 1847-48, Q 138.
59. *Ibid*, Q 305.

Chapter Six
1. Newman, *The Evolution of Medical Education*, 179.
2. The memorandum was entitled 'To the Right Hon W F Cowper, MP and the other Members of the Select Committee to which the Medical Bills have been referred' and dated 23 April 1856. In the library of the Royal College of Physicians in London there are two box files labelled 'Medical Reform' which contain a collection of apparently uncatalogued documents relating to the medical reform movement in the 1840s and 1850s; a copy of the College's memorandum to the Select Committee is contained in one of these boxes. In subsequent references, these boxes. In subsequent references, these boxes will be referred to as 'Medical reform boxes', RCP.
3. Newman, *The Evolution of Medical Education*, 179.
4. *Minutes of Council*, Royal College of Surgeons, 7 August 1856.
5. *Ibid*, 16 October 1856.
6. The minutes of this conference are contained in 'Medical reform boxes', RCP.
7. *Minutes of Council*, RCS, 30 October 1856.
8. *Minutes of Council*, RCS, 11 December 1856.
9. According to the minutes of the conference, it was agreed that seven clauses of Headlam's Bill of February 1856 should be incorporated in the Corporations' Bill.
10. This information is contained in a letter dated 27 January 1857 from John Simon to Francis Hawkins, the Registrar of the College. The original of this letter may be found in 'Medical reform boxes', RCP.
11. It was in December 1857 that Cowper announced his intention of bringing in a Bill; whether he was thinking along these lines in January 1857 one cannot, of course, say.
12. Letter from Simon to Hawkins, 27 January 1857.

13. *Minutes of Council*, RCS, 16 February 1857 and 13 May 1857.
14. A Bill to alter and amend the Laws regulating the Medical Profession, *British Sessional Papers*, House of Commons, 1857 (17 Session 2), III, 257ff.
15. *Report from the Select Committee on Medical Registration*, 1847, Q 104.
16. 'To the Right Hon. W. F. Cowper, M.P. and other Members of the Select Committee', 23 April 1856, 'Medical reform boxes', RCP.
17. This was stipulated in Clause XXI of the Corporations' Bill.
18. *Ibid*, Clause XXII.   19. *Ibid*, Clause XXII.
20. *Ibid*, Clause XXII.   21. *Ibid*, Clause XXIII.
22. *Hansard*, Third series, CXLV, 13 May 1857, col 245.
23. Newman, *The Evolution of Medical Education*, 183.
24. A copy of the College's petition to the Commons may be found in 'Medical reform boxes', RCP.
25. 'Medical reform boxes', RCP.
26. *Minutes of Council*, RCS, 10 June 1857.
27. *Hansard*, CXLVI, 1 July 1857, col 709-10.
28. *Ibid*, col 717-8.   29. *Ibid*, col 731.
30. *Ibid*, col 751.   31. *Ibid*, col 752.
32. The minutes of this meeting are recorded in a printed document simply headed *Royal College of Physicians*, in 'Medical reform boxes', RCP.
33. *Minutes of Council*, RCS, 15 March 1858.
34. Document headed *Royal College of Physicians*, in 'Medical reform boxes', RCP.
35. 'Memorandum prepared in 1858 by the Medical Officer of the then General Board of Health (Mr Simon), in explanation of the Medical Practitioners Bill of that year, as drawn for the Board under Mr Cowper's presidency', in *Special Report from the Select Committee on the Medical Act (1858) Amendment (No 3) Bill (Lords), British Sessional Papers*, 1878-79, xii, Appendix 1, 305-310.
36. *Ibid*, 305.   37. *Ibid*, 306-7.   38. *Ibid*, 307.
39. Cowper's Bill, as introduced into the Commons, may be found in *British Sessional Papers*, 1857-58, (37), III, 461-476.
40. 'Memorandum prepared in 1858', 307.
41. *Ibid*, 309.   42. *Ibid*, 308.
43. The Bill stipulated that those who sat on the General Medical Council as representatives of the medical corporations and universities must be qualified to register under the Act. This condition did not, however, apply to the six additional members of Council, thus implying the possibility that some lay persons could sit on the Council.
44. *Lancet*, 1858, i, 368.   45. *Ibid*, 390.   46. *Ibid*, 416.
47. *Ibid*, 368.   48. *Ibid*, 448-9.   49. *Ibid*, 440.
50. *Ibid*, 512.   51. *Ibid*, 512.   52. *Ibid*, 512.
53. *Ibid*, 617.
54 At its meeting on 8 April 1858, the Council of the College of

Surgeons decided that Cowper's Bill 'is not entitled to the support of this Council' and the other London corporations took a similar view at a conference held on 13 April, and reported in the *Minutes of Council*, RCS, 14 April 1858.

55. *Minutes of Council*, RCS, 22 April 1858.
56. *Ibid*, 13 May 1858.
57. *Hansard*, Third series, CL, 2 June 1858, col 1412.
58. *Lancet*, 1858, *i*, 416.
59. *Ibid*, 440.   60. *Ibid*, 416.   61. *Ibid*, 513.
62. The College of Physicians presented a single petition against all three Bills, that is, the Bills of Cowper, Elcho and Duncombe. The text of this petition may be found in the Royal College of Physicians' *Annals*, vol 25, 1852-58, 14 April 1858.
63. *Hansard*, Third series, CL, 2 June 1858, col 1408.
64. *Minutes of Council*, RCS, 10 June 1858.
65. *Hansard*, Third series, CL, 2 June 1858, col 1416-7.
66. *Ibid*, col 1420.   67. *Lancet*, 1858, *i*, 631.
68. *Ibid*, 619.   69. *Ibid*, 619.
70. The amended version of Cowper's Bill may be found in *British Sessional Papers*, House of Commons, 1857-58 (152), III, 477-92.
71. *Special Report from the Select Committee on the Medical Act (1858) Amendment (No. 3) Bill (Lords)*, *British Sessional Papers*, 1878-9, Q 558-9.
72. As we shall see, Simon was to denounce the corporations for their 'utter corruption' in a speech which he made in 1868.
73. *Hansard*, Third series, CLI, 6 July 1858, col 996.
74. *Ibid*, col 998, and *Lancet*, 1858, *ii*, 48.
75. *Lancet*, 1858, *ii*, 147.   76. *Ibid*, 175.
77. *Minutes of Council*, RCS, 14 October 1858.
78. *Lancet*, 1858, *ii*, 459.
79. *Minutes of Council*, RCS, 11 November 1858.
80. *Ibid*, 11 November 1858.
81. Newman, *The Evolution of Medical Education*, chapter V.
82. *Lancet*, 1858, *ii*, 175.   83. *Ibid*, 205.   84. *Ibid*, 458.
85. *Ibid*, 147.   86. *Ibid*, 205.   87. *Ibid*, 458.
88. *Special Report from the Select Committee on the Medical Act (1858)*, *British Sessional Papers*, 1878-9, Q 553, 561.
89. Memorandum prepared in 1873 by the then Medical Officer of the Privy Council (Mr Simon) on the Constitution of the General Medical Council, as fixed by the Medical Act, 1858, and on certain Proposals for changing that Constitution, *Special Report from the Select Committee on the Medical Act*, 1878-9, Appendix 2, 330.
90. Letter from Simon to C E Norton, 19 April 1870, cited in Royston Lambert, *Sir John Simon, 1816-1904*, London, 1963, 466.
91. *Ibid*, 468.
92. *Minutes of Council*, RCS, 12 August 1858.
93. *Lancet*, 1857, *i*, 15.   94. *Ibid*, 1858, *i*, 440.

Chapter Seven

1. N G Horner, *The Growth of the General Practitioner of Medicine in England*, London, 1922, 42-43.
2. F N L Poynter, 'Education and the General Medical Council', in Poynter (ed), *The Evolution of Medical Education in Britain*, London, 1966, 196.
3. A P Thomson, 'The Influence of the General Medical Council on Education', *British Medical Journal*, 1958, *ii*, 1249.
4. *Report of the Committee of Inquiry into the Regulation of the Medical Profession*, Cmnd 6018, 1975, 3.
5. Noel Parry and José Parry, *The Rise of the Medical Profession*, London, 1976, 79.
6. Noel and José Parry, 'Social Closure and Collective Social Mobility', in R Scase (ed), *Industrial Society: Class, Cleavage and Control*, London, 1977, 112.
7. J L Berlant, *Profession and Monopoly: A Study of Medicine in the United States and Britain*, Berkeley, 1975, especially chapters 3 and 4.
8. *Lancet*, 1831-32, *ii*, 88.   9. *Ibid*, 89.
10. 'Medical Reform', *Quarterly Review*, 1840-41, LXVII, 64.
11. *Hansard*, CL, 1858, col 1407.
12. F. Musgrove, 'Middle-class Education and Employment in the Nineteenth Century', *Economic History Review*, second series, 12, 1959-60, especially 108-110.
13. SCME, 1834, Part II, (602-II), Appendix 2.
14. SCME, 1834, Part III (602-III), Appendix 7.
15. Peterson, *The Medical Profession*, 116.
16. The letter, dated 20 September 1774, is to be found in J R McCulloch (ed), *The Wealth of Nations*, Edinburgh and London, 1838, Note XX, 582-5.
17. *Lancet*, 1842-43, *i*, 764.   18. *Lancet*, 1847, *i*, 135.
19. Musgrove, 'Middle-class Education', 106.
20. *Lancet*, 1842-43, *i*, 795-6.
21. *Ibid*, 1847, *i*, 600.   22. *Ibid*, 1841-42, *ii*, 650.   23. *Ibid*, 650.
24. Peterson, *The Medical Profession*, 130.
25. *Ibid*, 134.   26. *Ibid*, 36.
27. *Lancet*, 1841-42, *ii*, 781.
28. See, for example, *Hansard*, LXXVI 1844, col 1910, and *Lancet*, 1841-42, *ii*, 133, and *Lancet*, 1858, *ii*, 120.
29. *Hansard*, LXXVI, 1844, col 1905.
30. Newman, *The Evolution of Medical Education*, 161-2; Peterson, *The Medical Profession*, 32.
31. *Hansard*, LXXVI, 1844, col 1910.
32. Peterson, *The Medical Profession*, 31.
33. *Quarterly Review*, LXVII, 1840-41, 55-6.
34. *Ibid*, 57.   35. *Ibid*, 60.   36. *Ibid*, 56.
37. *Lancet*, 1841-42, *ii*, 513.
38. *Ibid*, 1847, *i*, 627.
39. David L Cowan, 'Liberty, Laissez-faire and Licensure in Nineteenth

century Britain', *Bulletin of the History of Medicine*, 43, 1969, 30-40.

40. These restrictions were set out in Clause 36 of the Act.

41. A M Carr-Saunders and P A Wilson, *The Professions*, 1933, reprinted London, 1964, 88.

42. Berlant, *Profession and Monopoly*, 156.

43. *Hansard*, LXXVI, 1844, col 1898.

44. Berlant, *Profession and Monopoly*, 167.

45. These census figures are taken from Musgrove, *op. cit.*, 105. It should be noted, however, that Musgrove's figure of 15,901 practitioners in 1881 is a mistake; this should read 15,091.

46. The percentage growth of the employed male population and of the total population has been calculated from the figures in H J Perkin, 'Middle-class Education and Employment in the Nineteenth Century: A Critical Note', *Economic History Review*, second series, 14, 1961-62, 128.

47. When Rivington calculated doctor-patient ratios in his Carmichael Prize essay of 1879, he used slightly different figures for the increase in the total population from those given in Perkin's article. However, those differences were too small to make any significant difference between his conclusions and those set out in this chapter. Thus Rivington calculated that the reduction in the provision of qualified medical care had been from 7.2 doctors per 10,000 population in England and Wales in 1861, to 6.4 per 10,000 in 1871. See Walter Rivington, *The Medical Profession*, Dublin, 1879, 2.

48. In 1861 there was one practitioner for every 1392 persons, and in 1911 one to every 1469.

49. Rivington, *The Medical Profession*, 2.

50. *Report of the Royal Commission Appointed to Inquire into the Medical Acts*, 1882 (C-3259-I), Q 1671.

51. *Ibid*, Q 1165.   52. *Ibid*, Q 1166.   53. *Ibid*, Q 1168.

54. *Report of the Committee appointed by the Secretary of State to enquire into the causes which tend to prevent sufficient eligible candidates from coming forward for the Army Medical Department*, 1878 (C-2200), 28-9.

55. *Ibid*, 49.   56. *Ibid*, 49.   57. *Ibid*, 29.   58. *Ibid*, 20.

Chapter Eight

1. Ludwig Edelstein, 'The Hippocratic Oath: Text, Translation and Interpretation', *Bulletin of the History of Medicine*, Supplement No. 1, Baltimore, 1943, 55.

2. Chauncey D Leake (ed), *Percival's Medical Ethics*, Baltimore, 1927, 36.

3. *Ibid*, 23-24.

4. R T Barton, 'Sources of Medical Morals', *Journal of the American Medical Association*, 1965, 193: 133-8.

5. R M S McConaghey, 'Medical Ethics in a Changing World', *Journal*

of the College of General Practitioners, 1965: 10: 3-17.

6. Robert Forbes, 'A Historical Survey of Medical Ethics', *St Bartholomew's Hospital Journal*, 1955, 59, 282-86, 316-19.

7. William Ogilvie Porter, *Medical Science and Ethicks: an Introductory Lecture*, Bristol, 1837.

8. Abraham Banks, *Medical Etiquette*, London, 1839.

9. The rules and bye-laws of the Manchester Medico-Ethical Association were published in 1848, and reviewed in an anonymous article entitled 'Medical ethics', *British and Foreign Medico-Chirurgical Review*, 1848, 2: 1-30.

10. Ernest Muirhead Little, *History of the British Medical Association 1832-1932*, London, n d, 288. In 1853 the Association was, of course, still called the Provincial Medical and Surgical Association.

11. Carr-Saunders and Wilson, *The Professions*, 302.

12. 'The Recent History of Professionalism in Relation to Social Structure and Social Policy', in T H Marshall, *Sociology at the Crossroads and Other Essays*, London, 1963, 150-170. This essay was originally published in the *Canadian Journal of Economics and Political Science*, 1939, 5: 325-34.

13. For a statement of this position see, for example, William J Goode, 'Community within a Community: the Professions', *American Sociological Review*, 1957, 22: 194-200, and Barrington Kaye, *The Development of the Architectural Profession in Britain*, London, 1960, 11-21.

14. Leake, *Percival's Medical Ethics*, 71.

15. *Ibid*, 90.   16. *Ibid*, 72.   17. *Ibid*, 73.

18. *Ibid*, 90.   19. *Ibid*, 80.   20. *Ibid*, 81.

21. *Ibid*, 96.   22. *Ibid*, 2.   23. *Ibid*, 1.

24. *Ibid*, 30-32.   25. *Ibid*, 37.

26. Lester S. King, 'Development of Medical Ethics', *New England Journal of Medicine*, 1958, 258: 480-86.

27. Banks, *Medical Etiquette*.

28. See, for example, *Lancet*, 1839-40, *ii*, 875; 1839-40, *ii*, 942; 1840-41, *i*, 68-9; 1841-2, *i*, 549; 1847, *ii*, 266-7; 1848, *ii*, 538; 1850, *ii*, 186-7; 1850, *ii*, 249; 1850, *ii*, 489-90; 1850, *ii*, 621.

29. Banks, *Medical Etiquette*, 1-4.

30. *Lancet*, 1845, *ii*, 492.

31. *Lancet*, 1837-38, *i*, 346-7.

32. *Lancet*, 1845, *i*, 657-8.

33. Banks, *Medical Etiquette*, 39.

34. Anthony Trollope, *Doctor Thorne*, 27-28.

35. George Eliot, *Middlemarch*, ed W J Harvey, Harmondsworth, 1965.

36. *Lancet*, 1831-32, *i*, 2.

37. Banks, *Medical Etiquette*, 57.

38. Porter, *Medical Science and Ethicks*, 29.

39. *Ibid*, 29.

40. *Lancet*, 1845, *ii*, 687.

41. W B Kesteven, 'Thoughts on medical ethics', *London Medical Gazette*, 1849, 9: 408-414.

42. *Ibid*, 414.
43. *Lancet*, 1841-42, *ii*, 728-31.
44. *Lancet*, 1840-41, *ii*, 107-8
45. Chauncey D Leake, 'Percival's Medical Ethics: promise and problems', *California Medicine*, 1971, 114: 68-70.
46. See Harvey's introduction to the Penguin edition of G Eliot, *Middlemarch*, 19.
47. *Ibid*, 19-20.
48. *Westminster Review*, 1858, *xiii*: 479.
49. *Westminster Review*, 1856, *ix*: 532.
50. F N L Poynter, 'The Centenary of the General Medical Council', *British Medical Journal*, 1958, 2: 1245.
51. Sir George Clark, *A History of the Royal College of Physicians*, Oxford, 1964-66, vol 2, 566.
52. Leake, *Percival's Medical Ethics*, 76.
53. *Ibid*, 93-94.   54. *Ibid*, 117-8.
55. 'Medical ethics', *British and Foreign Medico-Chirurgical Review*, 1848, 2: 1-30.
56. *Ibid*, 24.   57. *Ibid*, 27.
58. *Ibid*, 30.   59. *Lancet*, 1848, *ii*, 44-5
60. Peterson, *The Medical Profession*, 102.
61. Kesteven, 'Thoughts on Medical Ethics', 412.
62. *Association Medical Journal*, 1854, 2: 1085-6.
63. Leake, *Percival's Medical Ethics*, 97.
64. *Ibid*, 94.   65. *Ibid*, 92.
66. *Ibid*, 98.   67. *Ibid*, 106.
68. Banks, *Medical Etiquette*, 10.
69. *Ibid*., 5-9.   70. *Ibid*, 54-9.   71. *Ibid*, 43-47.
72. W Fraser, 'Queries in medical ethics', *London Medical Gazette*, 1849, 9: 181-7, 227-32.
73. Peterson, *The Medical Profession*, 118.

Chapter Nine
1. E Freidson, *Professional Dominance*, Chicago, 1970, esp 127-64.
2. E Freidson, *Profession of Medicine*, New York, 1972, 71.
3. Norbert Elias, 'Studies in the Genesis of the Naval Profession', *British Journal of Sociology*, 1950, 1: 293.
4. For a general overview of the development of modern professions in the nineteenth century see Carr-Saunders and Wilson, *The Professions* and W J Reader, *Professional Men*, London, 1966.
5. Paul Starr, 'Medicine, Economy and Society in Nineteenth Century America', in P Branca (ed), *The Medicine Show*, New York, 1977, 47.
6. *Ibid*, 47.
7. P Elliot, *The Sociology of the Professions*, London, 1972, 15.
8. H. Lonsdale, *The Life of John Heysham, MD*, London, 1870, 7-8.
9. Freidson, *Profession of Medicine*, 12.

10. In relation to legal services, for example, it has been pointed out that in the eighteenth century 'the vast bulk of the population had no demand for legal services'. See B Abel-Smith and R Stevens, *Lawyers and the Courts*, London, 1970, 14.

11. Reader, *Professional Men*, 32.

12. Franklin, 'Medical Education and the Rise of the General Practitioner', 2.

13. E S Turner, *Call the Doctor: A Social History of Medical Men*, London, 1958, 104-118.

14. See, for example, J J Bagley, *Lancashire Diarists*, London, 1975, 97-8, and N C Hultin, 'Medicine and Magic in the Eighteenth Century: the Diaries of James Woodforde', *Journal of the History of Medicine and Allied Sciences*, 1975, 30, 349-66.

15. Starr, 'Medicine, Economy and Society', 51.

16. Claudine Herzlich, 'The Evolution of Relations between French Physicians and the State from 1880-1980', *Sociology of Health and Illness*, 1982, 4, 241.

17. Jean-Pierre Goubert, 'The Extent of Medical Practice in France around 1780', in Branca (ed), *The Medicine Show*, 214, 217.

18. Sir George Clark, *A History of the Royal College of Physicians of London*, vol II, 538.

19. As late as 1840, there were still only seventy-six physicians who were licensed by the College to practise outside of London. In the middle 1840s this number began to increase more rapidly, and had reached 253 by 1847. See Clark, *A History of The Royal College of Physicians*, vol II, Appendix II, 739.

20. Cope, *The Royal College of Surgeons*, 18-21.

21. *Ibid*, 4.

22. Clark, *A History of the Royal College of Physicians*, vol II, 601-2.

23. *Ibid*, 602.

24. Starr, 'Medicine, Economy and Society', 51.

25. Amongst the more famous of those who left the medical profession after failing to secure an adequate income from medical practice were George Crabbe, Tobias Smollett and Oliver Goldsmith. The biographies of unsuccessful practitioners are as important as — indeed, perhaps more important than — those of successful practitioners in terms of what they tell us about the structure of medical careers. Unfortunately, the biographies of unsuccessful practitioners are, of course, rarely written, and we know of the cases cited above only because, having failed in medical practice, they subsequently achieved fame in the world of literature. How many unsuccessful practitioners there were who never achieved fame in another field, and whose biographies were therefore never written, we cannot know, but the number was probably considerable.

26. *The Works of Samuel Johnson*, London, 1823, vol 8, 360.

27. On Smollett's medical career, see David Hannay, *Life of Tobias George Smollett*, London, 1887; Lewis M Knapp, *Tobias Smollett*,

Princeton, 1949, and George M Kahrl, *Tobias Smollett*, Chicago, 1945. For a biography of Goldsmith, see Ralph M Wardle, *Oliver Goldsmith*, Lawrence, Kansas and London, 1957.

28. Wardle, *Oliver Goldsmith*, 73.
29. *Ibid*, 73.
30. Kahrl, *Tobias Smollett*, 12.
31. *The Life of George Crabbe by his Son*, London, 1947, 17.
32. Joseph F Kett, 'Provincial Medical Practice in England, 1730-1815', *Journal of the History of Medicine and Allied Sciences*, 1964, 19, 18.
33. *Ibid*, 18.
34. E Hobhouse (ed), *The Diary of a West Country Physician*, London, 1935, 27.
35. Kett, 'Provincial Medical Practice, 19.
36. *Ibid*, 23.
37. See for example, *Lancet*, 1840-41, *ii*, 107.
38. On the development of pharmacists as a specialised occupational group, see Carr-Saunders and Wilson, *The Professions*, 132-41.
39. Barnes Riznik, 'The Professional Lives of Early Nineteenth Century New England Doctors', *Journal of the History of Medicine and Allied Sciences*, 1964, 19, 6.
40. *Ibid*, 7.
41. Herzlich, 'The Evolution of Relations', 242.
42. Edna H Lemay, 'Thomas Hérier, a Country Surgeon outside Angoulême at the End of the XVIIIth Century: a Contribution to Social History', in Branca (ed), *The Medicine Show*, 233.
43. *Ibid*, 229.
44. Dirk Jan Baptist Ringoir, *Plattelandschirurgijns in De 17e en 18e Eeuw*, Bunnik, Uitgeverij Lebo, 1977, especially 86-92. I am grateful to Henk Heijnen of the Sociologisch Instituut, Universiteit van Amsterdam, for bringing this reference to my notice.
45. S W F Holloway, 'Medical Education in England, 1830-58: a Sociological Analysis', *History*, 1964, 49, 301-2.
46. N D Jewson, 'Medical Knowledge and the Patronage System in 18th century England', *Sociology*, 1974, 8, 375-6.
47. *Ibid*, 376.   48. *Ibid*, 376-7.
49. Holloway, 'Medical Education in England', 317.
50. The increasing intellectual detachment of the nineteenth-century medical scientist, and the concomitant growth of his social detachment from the patient is analysed in N D Jewson, 'The Disappearance of the Sick-man from Medical Cosmology, 1770-1870', *Sociology*, 1976, 10, 225-244.
51. Carr-Saunders and Wilson, *The Professions*, 300.
52. Terence J Johnson, *Professions and Power*, London, 1972, 68-9.
53. E Freidson, 'Client control and medical practice', *American Journal of Sociology*, 1960, 65, 374-82. See also Freidson, *Profession of Medicine*, especially chapter 5.
54. Freidson uses these terms primarily to highlight differences in the

work situation of those involved in 'neighbourhood practice' as opposed to hospital practice in modern American society. However, it may be argued that the work situation of many practitioners in eighteenth-century England provides a much more clear cut and extreme form of 'client-dependent' practice.

55. For a description of one of the earliest local medical societies in England, see Arthur Rook, 'General practice, 1793-1803: the Transactions of a Huntingdonshire Medical Society', *Medical History*, 1960, 4, 236-52. Other early medical societies were those at Warrington (1770), Colchester (1774), Plymouth (1794), and Leicester (1800).

56. Roy Porter, *English Society in the Eighteenth Century*, Harmondsworth, 1972, 92.

57. Quoted in Holloway, 'Medical Education in England', 318.

58. *Ibid*, 316.

59. See, for example, R H Shryock, *The Development of Modern Medicine*, London, 1948, 138, 158-9, 205-6; T McKeown, *Medicine in Modern Society*, London, 1965, 39-58; and J V Pickstone, 'The Professionalization of Medicine in England and Europe: the State, the Market and Industrial Society', *Japanese Journal of Medical History*, 1979, 25, 1-31.

60. Starr, 'Medicine, Economy and Society', 51.

61. Holloway, 'Medical Education in England', 320.

62. M S Larson, *The Rise of Professionalism*, Berkeley, Los Angeles and London, 1977, 34.

63. Some of the implications of this change in the balance of power between doctor and patient have been analysed in relation to the situation in France in I Waddington, 'The Role of the Hospital in the Development of Modern Medicine: a Sociological Analysis', *Sociology*, 1973, 7, 211-224. Information on the situation in American hospitals may be found in Morris J Vogel, 'Patrons, Practitioners and Patients: the Voluntary Hospital in Mid-Victorian Boston', in D W Howe (ed), *Victorian America*, Philadelphia, 1976, 121-138. A good deal of information relating to the treatment of hospital patients in Britain during this period may be found in F B Smith, *The People's Health, 1830-1910*, London, 1979, whilst some information on the situation in Viennese hospitals may be found in P Lain Entralgo, *Doctor and Patient*, New York and Toronto, 1969.

64. Entralgo, *Doctor and Patient*, 117.

65. The reference to patients as 'clinical material' is taken from Charles Bell Keatley's *The Student's and Junior Practitioner's Guide to the Medical Profession*, London, 1885, cited in Peterson, *The Medical Profession*, 174. Keatley praised the resources of a teaching hospital in the following terms: 'The clinical material is simply overflowing, especially in the surgical and gynaecological departments, and there is any amount of opportunity for men to work clinically at dresserships and clerkships, if they will only come and finger the material

for themselves. It is a perfect paradise for every kind of tumour known, and the accidents are numerous.' The whole tone of Keatley's comments provides a clear illustration of the extent to which medicine had become, in Jewson's words, 'object orientated' rather than 'person orientated'.

66. Jewson, 'The Disappearance of the Sick-Man', 225-244.
67. Marie R Haug, 'The Erosion of Professional Authority: A Cross-cultural Inquiry in the Case of the Physician', *Millbank Memorial Fund Quarterly*, 1976, 54, 101.
68. *The Life of George Crabbe*, 17.

Bibliography

1. OFFICIAL DOCUMENTS

Parliament

Cobbett's Parliamentary Debates
Hansard's Parliamentary Debates
Journals of the House of Commons

British Sessional Papers

Report from the Select Committee on Medical Education, 1834,
    Part I (602-I), Royal College of Physicians
    Part II (602-II), Royal College of Surgeons
    Part III (602-III), Society of Apothecaries
Report from the Select Committee on Medical Registration, 1847, (620)
First and Second Reports from the Select Committee on Medical Registration and Medical Law Amendment, 1848, (610)
Third Report from the Select Committee on Medical Registration and Medical Law Amendment, 1848, (702)
Return showing the Number of Practitioners in Medicine, According to the Census of 1851, for each County of England and Wales, According to the Registration Division, and for each County of Scotland, and of the Islands in the British Seas, 1854, (145), LXII, 627-36
Census of England and Wales for the Year 1861, vol. III, General Report, Appendix to Report, 1863, (3221)
'Memorandum prepared in 1858 by the Medical Officer of the then General Board of Health (Mr Simon), in explanation of the Medical Practitioners Bill of that year, as drawn for the Board under Mr Cowper's presidency', *Special Report from the Select Committee on the Medical Act (1858) Amendment (No. 3) Bill (Lords)* 1878-79, *xii* Appendix 1, 305-10
'Memorandum prepared in 1873 by the then Medical Officer of the Privy Council (Mr Simon) on the Constitution of the General Medical Council, as fixed by the Medical Act, 1858, and on certain proposals for changing the Constitution', *Special Report from the Select Committee on the Medical Act (1858) Amendment (No. 3) Bill (Lords)*, 1878-79, xii, Appendix 2, 330-34
Report of the Committee appointed by the Secretary of State to enquire into the causes which tend to prevent sufficient eligible candidates

from coming forward for the Army Medical Department, 1878-79,
(C-2200)

Report of the Royal Commission Appointed to Inquire into the Medical
   Acts, 1882, (C-3250-I)

Report of the Committee of Inquiry into the Regulation of the Medical
   Profession, Cmnd 6018, 1975

Royal College of Physicians of London

Annals of the College, vol. XXV, 1852-58, RCP Mss

The Roll of the Royal College of Physicians of London, 2nd ed, compiled by William Munk, 3 vols, London: Royal College of Physicians,
   1878 [Munk's Roll, I-III]

*To the Right Hon W F Cowper, MP, and the other Members of the
   Select Committee to which the Medical Bills have been referred*, 23
   April, 1856

In addition to the sources listed above, the library of the Royal College
   of Physicians contains two box files labelled "Medical Reform", in
   which may be found a collection of printed but apparently uncatalogued documents relating to the medical reform movement in the
   1840s and 1850s. Amongst the more important of these documents
   which have been consulted are the following:

Royal College of Physicians, minutes of meetings of the English Department of Conference, 10 March 1858 and 16 March 1858

At a Conference at the Royal College of Surgeons of England, 21 October
   — 24 October, 1856 (minutes of conference)

*Medical Reform Reasons, on Behalf of the Medical Incorporations, in
   Favour of Mr Headlam's Medical Bill, and Against that of Lord
   Elcho*, 1857

*Remarks on Mr Headlam's "Medical Profession Bill", and Lord Elcho's
   Opposition* (nd)

*A Short Statement of the Respective Merits of the Medical Bills now
   before Parliament* (nd)

*Brief Display of the Essential Points in Mr Headlam's Bill and in the
   Counter Bill of Lord Elcho* (nd)

The last three documents are not dated, but since they all relate to the
   Bills introduced by Mr Headlam and Lord Elcho in 1857 it may
   safely be presumed that they were printed in that year.

Royal College of Surgeons of England

Minutes of Council, vols VIII-X, 1846-59, RCS Mss

At a Conference at the Royal College of Surgeons of England, 21 October
   — 24 October, 1856 (minutes of conference). See under: Royal
   College of Physicians.

2. OTHER PRIMARY SOURCES

Anon, 'Medical Ethics', *British and Foreign Medico-Chirurgical Review*,
   1848, 2, 1-30

Armstrong, J, *An Address to the Members of the Royal College of*

Surgeons of London on the Injurious Conduct and Defective State of that Corporation, with Reference to Professional Rights, Medical Science and the Public Health, London, Baldwin and Co, 1825

Association Medical Journal [Organ of the Provincial Medical and Surgical Association] , London

Banks, Abraham, *Medical Etiquette*, London, Charles Fox, 1839

British Medical Journal: being the Journal of the British Medical Association, London

Churchill's Medical Directory: see *The London and Provincial Medical Directory*

Clarke, J F, *Autobiographical Recollections of the Medical Profession*, London, Churchill, 1874

Cooper, B B, *The Life of Sir Astley Cooper, Bart, Interspersed with Sketches from his Note-books of Distinguished Contemporary Characters*, 2 vols, London, John W Parker, 1843

Eliot, George, *Middlemarch* ed W J Harvey, Harmondsworth, Penguin, 1965

Everitt, G, *Doctors and Doctors: Some Curious Chapters in Medical History and Quackery*, London, Sonnenschein and Co, 1888

Fraser, W, 'Queries in Medical Ethics', *London Medical Gazette*, ns, *9* 1849, 181-7, 227-32

Gaskell, Elizabeth, *North and South*, Harmondsworth, Penguin 1970

Gaskell, Elizabeth, *Wives and Daughters*, Harmondsworth, Penguin, 1969

The Gentleman's Magazine, and Historical Chronicle, London

Glenn, R G, *A Manual of the Laws Affecting Medical Men*, London, Churchill, 1871

Hardy, H N, *The State of the Medical Profession in Great Britain and Northern Ireland in 1900*, Dublin, Fannin and Co, 1901

Huxley, T H, 'The State and the Medical Profession', *Nineteenth Century*, *15*, 1884, 228-38

Johnson, S, *The Works of Samuel Johnson, LL D*, London, FC and J Rivington, 1823

Kesteven, W B, 'Thoughts on Medical Ethics', *London Medical Gazette*, ns, *9*, 1849, 408-14

The Lancet, London

The London and Provincial Medical Directory, London, Churchill, 1847

Morris, C, *The Diary of a West Country Physician, AD 1684-1726*, ed E Hobhouse, London, Simpkin Marshall, 2nd ed, 1935

Munk's Roll: See section 1, under Royal College of Physicians of London

Paget, Sir James, *Memoirs and Letters of Sir James Paget*, ed Stephen Paget, London, Longmans, Green and Co, 1901

Percival, T, *Medical Ethics: or, a Code of Institutes and Precepts Adapted to the Professional Conduct of Physicians and Surgeons*, Manchester, 1803

Porter, William Ogilvie, *Medical Science and Ethicks: An Introductory Lecture*, Bristol, W Strong, 1837

The Quarterly Review, London

Rivington, W, *The Medical Profession*, Dublin: Fannin and Co, 1879

Simon, Sir John, *English Sanitary Institutions, Reviewed in their Course of Development, and in Some of their Political and Social Relations*, London, John Murray, 1897

Smith, A, *The Wealth of Nations*, ed J R McCulloch, Edinburgh, A and C Black, 1838

Thackeray, W M, *The History of Pendennis: His Fortunes and Misfortunes, His Friends and His Greatest Enemy*, London, Macmillan, 1905

Trollope, A, *Doctor Thorne*, London, Everyman's, 1967

The Westminster Review, London

Willcock, J W, *The Laws Relating to the Medical Profession; with an Account of the Rise and Progress of its Various Orders*, London, 1830

Winslow, Forbes, *Physic and Physicians: A Medical Sketch Book, Exhibiting the Public and Private Life of the Most Celebrated Medical Men of Former Days: With Memoirs of Eminent Living London Physicians and Surgeons*, 2 vols, London, Longman, Orme, Browne and Co, 1839

3. SECONDARY LITERATURE

Bagley, J J, *Lancashire Diarists: Three Centuries of Lancashire Lives*, London, Phillimore, 1975

Barton, R T, 'Sources of Medical Morals', *Journal of the American Medical Association*, 193, 1965, 133-8

Berlant, J L, *Profession and Monopoly: A Study of Medicine in the United States and Britain*, Berkeley, Los Angeles and London, University of California Press, 1975

Bishop, W J, 'The Evolution of the General Practitioner in England', in Underwood, E Ashworth (ed), *Science, Medicine and History: Essays on the Evolution of Scientific Thought and Medical Practice, Written in Honour of Charles Singer*, London, Oxford University Press, 1953, vol II, 351-57

Branca, P (ed), *The Medicine Show: Patients, Physicians and the Perplexities of the Health Revolution in Modern Society*, New York, Science History Publications, 1977

Brown, P S, 'The Providers of Medical Treatment in Mid-Nineteenth Century Bristol', *Medical History*, *XXIV*, 1980, 297-314

Cameron, H C, *Mr Guy's Hospital, 1726-1948*, London, New York and Toronto, Longman's, Green, 1954

Carr-Saunders, A M, and Wilson, P A, *The Professions*, Oxford University Press, 1933, reprinted London, Cass, 1964

Chaplin, A, *Medicine in England during the Reign of George III*, London, Henry Kimpton, 1919

Clark, Sir George, *A History of the Royal College of Physicians of London*, 2 vols, Clarendon Press, Oxford, for the Royal College of Physicians, 1966

Cope, Sir Zachary, *The Royal College of Surgeons of England: A History*, London, Anthony Blond, 1959

Cope, Sir Zachary, 'The Private Medical Schools of London (1746-1914)', in Poynter, F N L (ed), *The Evolution of Medical Education in Britain*, London, Pitman 1966, 89-109

Cowan, D L, 'Liberty, Laissez-faire and Licensure in Nineteenth Century Britain', *Bulletin of the History of Medicine, 43*, 1969, 30-40

Crabbe, G, *The Life of George Crabbe: By His Son*, with an introduction by Edmund Blunden, London, Cresset Press, 1947

Edelstein, L, 'The Hippocratic Oath: Text, Translation and Interpretation', *Bulletin of the History of Medicine*, Supplement no 1, Baltimore, Johns Hopkins Press, 1943

Elias, N, 'Studies in the Genesis of the Naval Profession', *British Journal of Sociology, 1*, 1950, 291-309

Elliot, P, *The Sociology of the Professions*, London and Basingstoke, Macmillan, 1972

Forbes, R, 'A Historical Survey of Medical Ethics', *St Bart's Hospital Journal, 59*, 1955, 282-6, 316-9

Franklin, R E, 'Medical Education and the Rise of the General Practitioner', PhD thesis, University of Birmingham, 1950

Freidson, E, 'Client Control and Medical Practice', *American Journal of Sociology, 65*, 1960, 374-82

Freidson, E, *Profession of Medicine: A Study of the Sociology of Applied Knowledge*, New York, Dodd, Mead, 1970

Freidson, E, *Professional Dominance: The Social Structure of Medical Care*, New York, Atherton Press, 1970

Goods, W J, 'Community within a Community: the Professions', *American Sociological Review, 22*, 1957, 194-200

Gordon, R, *The Sleep of Life*, Harmondsworth, Penguin 1976

Goubert, J-P, 'The Extent of Medical Practice in France around 1780', in Branca, P, (ed), *The Medicine Show*, New York, Science History Publications, 1977, 211-28

Hamilton, B, 'The Medical Professions in the Eighteenth Century', *Economic History Review*, 2nd series, *IV*, 1951, 141-69

Hannay, D, *Life of Tobias George Smollett*, London, Walter Scott, 1887

Haug, M R, 'The Erosion of Professional Authority: a Cross-cultural Inquiry in the Case of the Physician', *Millbank Memorial Fund Quarterly, 54*, 1976, 83-106

Herzlich, C, 'The Evolution of Relations between French Physicians and the State from 1880-1980', *Sociology of Health and Illness, 4*, 1982, 241-53

Holloway, S W F, 'Medical Education in England, 1830-1858: A Sociological Analysis', *History, XLIX*, 1964, 299-324

Holloway, S W F, 'The Apothecaries' Act, 1815: A Reinterpretation', *Medical History, X*, 1966, Part I, 107-29, Part II, 221-35

Horner, N G, *The Growth of the General Practitioner of Medicine in England*, London, Bridge and Co, 1922

Hultin, N C, 'Medicine and Magic in the Eighteenth Century: the Diaries of James Woodforde', *Journal of the History of Medicine and Allied Sciences, 30*, 1975, 349-66

Jewson, N, *Eighteenth Century Medical Theories: A Sociological Analysis*, Working Papers in Historical Sociology, no 1, University of Leicester, Department of Sociology, 1974

Jewson, N, 'Medical Knowledge and the Patronage System in Eighteenth Century England', *Sociology*, *8*, 1974, 369-85

Jewson, N, 'The Disappearance of the Sick-man from Medical Cosmology 1770-1870', *Sociology*, *10*, 1976, 225-44

Johnson, T J,*Professions and Power*, London and Basingstoke, Macmillan, 1972

Kahrl, G M, *Tobias Smollett, Traveller − Novelist*, Chicago, University Press, 1945

Kaye, B, *The Development of the Architectural Profession in Britain: A Sociological Study*, London, Allen and Unwin, 1960

Kett, J F, 'Provincial Medical Practice in England, 1730-1815', *Journal of the History of Medicine and Allied Sciences*, *19*, 1964, 17-29

King, L S, 'Development of Medical Ethics', *New England Journal of Medicine*, *258*, 1958, 480-6

Knapp, L M, *Tobias Smollett, Doctor of Men and Manners*, Princeton, N J, Princeton University Press, 1949

Lain Entralgo, P, *Doctor and Patient*, translated by Frances Partridge, London, Weidenfeld and Nicholson, 1969

Lambert, R, *Sir John Simon 1816-1904 and English Social Administration*, London, MacGibbon and Kee, 1963

Larson, M S, *The Rise of Professionalism*, Berkeley, Los Angeles and London, University of California Press, 1977

Leake, C D, 'Percival's Medical Ethics: Promise and Problems', *California Medicine, 114*, 1971, 68-70

Leake, C D, (ed), *Percival's Medical Ethics*, Baltimore, Williams and Wilkins, 1927

Lemay, E H, 'Thomas Hérier: A Country Surgeon outside Angoulême at the End of the XVIIIth century: a Contribution to Social History', in Branca, P (ed), *The Medicine Show*, New York, Science History Publications, 1977, 229-42

Little, Ernest Muirhead,*History of the British Medical Association, 1832-1932*, London, British Medical Association, nd

Lonsdale, H, *The Life of John Heysham, M.D., and his Correspondence with Mr. Joshua Milne Relative to the Carlisle Bills of Mortality*, London, Longmans, Green, 1870

Loudon, I S, 'Historical Importance of Outpatients', *British Medical Journal*, 1978, *1*, 974-77

McConaghey, R M S, 'Medical Ethics in a Changing World', *Journal of the College of General Practitioners, 10*, 1965, 3-17

McKeown, T, *Medicine in Modern Society*, London, Allen and Unwin, 1965

McKeown, T, 'A Sociological Approach to the History of Medicine', *Medical History, XIV*, 1970, 342-51

McLachlan, G, and McKeown, T (eds), *Medical History and Medical Care*, London, New York and Toronto, Oxford University Press, for the Nuffield Provincial Hospitals Trust, 1971

McMenemy, W H, *The Life and Times of Sir Charles Hastings, Founder of the British Medical Association*, Edinburgh and London, Livingstone, 1959

Marshall, D, *Eighteenth Century England*, London, Longmans, 1962

Marshall, T H, *Sociology at the Crossroads and Other Essays*, London, Heinemann, 1963

Mingay, G E, *English Landed Society in the Eighteenth Century*, London, Routledge and Kegan Paul, 1963

Musgrove, F, 'Middle-Class Education and Employment in the Nineteenth Century', *Economic History Review*, second series, *XII*, 1959-60, 99-111

Neuberger, M, 'C G Carus on the State of Medicine in Britain in 1841', in Ashworth Underwood, E (ed), *Science, Medicine and History: Essays in Honour of Charles Singer*, London, Oxford University Press, 1953, vol II, 263-73

Newman, C, *The Evolution of Medical Education in the Nineteenth Century*, London, Oxford University Press, 1957

Parry, N, and Parry, J, *The Rise of the Medical Profession*, London, Croom Helm, 1976

Parry, N, and Parry, J, 'Social Closure and Collective Social Mobility', in Scase, R (ed), *Industrial Society: Class, Cleavage and Control*, London, Allen and Unwin, 1977, 111-121

Perkin, H J, 'Middle-Class Education and Employment in the Nineteenth Century: A Critical Note', *Economic History Review*, second series, *XIV*, 1961-2, 122-130

Perkin, H J, *The Origins of Modern English Society 1770-1800*, London, Routledge and Kegan Paul, 1969

Peterson, M J, *The Medical Profession in Mid-Victorian London*, University of California Press, Berkeley, Los Angeles and London, 1978

Pickstone, J V, 'The Professionalization of Medicine in England and Europe: the State, the Market and Industrial Society', *Japanese Journal of Medical History*, 25, 1979, 1-31

Porter, R, *English Society in the Eighteenth Century*, Harmondsworth, Penguin, 1982

Poynter, F N L, 'The Centenary of the General Medical Council', *British Medical Journal, 5107*, 1958, 1245-8

Poynter, F N L (ed), *The Evolution of Medical Practice in Britain*, London, Pitman, 1961

Poynter, F N L (ed), *The Evolution of Medical Education in Britain*, London, Pitman, 1966

Poynter, F N L, *Medicine and Man*, Harmondsworth, Penguin, 1973

Reader, W J, *Professional Men: The Rise of the Professional Classes in Nineteenth Century England*, London, Weidenfeld and Nicholson, 1966

Ringoir, D J B, *Plattelandschirurgijns in De 17e en 18e Eeuw*, Bunnik, Uitgeverij Lebo, 1977

Riznik, B, 'The Professional Lives of Early Nineteenth Century New

England Doctors', *Journal of the History of Medicine and Allied Sciences, 19*, 1964, 1-16

Rook, A, 'General Practice, 1793-1803: the Transactions of a Huntingdonshire Medical Society', *Medical History, 4*, 1960, 236-52

Shryock, R H, *The Development of Modern Medicine: An Interpretation of the Social and Scientific Factors Involved*, London, Gollancz, 1948

Singer, C and Holloway, S W F, 'Early Medical Education in Relation to the Pre-history of London University', *Medical History, IV*, 1960, 1-17

Smith, B Abel-, *The Hospitals, 1800-1948: A Study in Social Administration in England and Wales*, London, Heinemann, 1964

Smith B Abel- and Stevens, R, *Lawyers and the Courts: A Sociological Study of the English Legal System 1750-1965*, London, Heinemann, 1970

Smith, F B, *The People's Health, 1830-1910*, London, Croom Helm, 1979

Sprigge, S Squire, *The Life and Times of Thomas Wakley, Founder and First Editor of the "Lancet", Member of Parliament for Finsbury and Coroner for West Middlesex*, London, Longmans, Green and Co, 1899

Starr, P, 'Medicine, Economy and Society in Nineteenth Century America', in Branca, P (ed), *The Medicine Show*, New York, Science History Publications 1977, 47-66

Starr, P, *The Social Transformation of American Medicine*, New York, Basic Books, 1982

Stevens, R, *Medical Practice in Modern England: The Impact of Specialization and State Medicine*, New Haven and London, Yale University Press, 1966

Thomson, A P, 'The Influence of the General Medical Council on Education', *British Medical Journal, 5107*, 1958, 1248-50

Toennies, F, 'Estates and Classes', in Bendix, R, and Lipset, S M (eds), *Class, Status and Power*, 2nd edition, London, Routledge and Kegan Paul, 1967, 12-21

Turner, E S, *Call the Doctor: A Social History of Medical Men*, London, Joseph, 1958

Vaughan, P, *Doctors' Commons: A Short History of the British Medical Association*, London, Heinemann, 1959

Vogel, M J, 'Patrons, Practitioners and Patients: the Voluntary Hospital in Mid-Victorian Boston', in Howe, D W (ed), *Victorian America*, Philadelphia, University of Pennsylvania Press, 1976, 121-38

Waddington, I, 'The Struggle to Reform the Royal College of Physicians, 1767-1771: A Sociological Analysis', *Medical History, XVII*, 1973, 107-26

Waddington, I, 'The Role of the Hospital in the Development of Modern Medicine: A Sociological Analysis', *Sociology, 7*, 1973, 211-24

Wardle, R M, *Oliver Goldsmith*, Lawrence, University of Kansas Press and London, Constable, 1957

Weber, M, *From Max Weber: Essays in Sociology*, trans and edited by Gerth, H H, and Mills, C W, London, Routledge and Kegan Paul, 1961

Woodward, J, *To Do the Sick No Harm*, London, Routledge and Kegan Paul, 1974

Index